AF790592

Praise for *Enabling Data*

'*Enabling Data* is a timely and important contribution to the growing conversation on data and AI transformation. Rather than adding another framework to an already crowded field, the authors offer a compelling model grounded in real-world experience, showing how trust, governance, enablement, and technology must work together to create lasting value. A thoughtful and highly practical guide for modern organizations.'
**Mark Esposito, Professor of Tech Policy, Northeastern University and Faculty Associate, Harvard Berkman Klein for Internet and Society**

'"Enabling data" has become one of those phrases the industry loves to repeat without ever stopping to define. David Castro-Gavino and Boyan Angelov do both: they cut through the buzzword to show what enabling data actually requires in practice, and more usefully, what trips organizations up along the way. From the modern data stack to data mesh to AI, they name the traps, debunk the misconceptions, and offer practical guidance rooted in first principles. A thorough read, and definitely required reading for anyone working in data.'
**Tiankai Feng, author of *Humanizing Data Strategy* and *Humanizing AI Strategy***

'Best book out there to understand what AI-ready data really is all about and how to get there. It tackles the AI revolution at exactly the messy, unglamorous point where organizations are stuck and at the same time offers a new, sharp new lens on building data foundations that moves beyond "just build a big data platform" advice. Highly recommended reading for anyone who has more AI ambition than running a few ChatGPT prompts.'
**Tobias Zwingmann, author of *The Profitable AI Advantage*, Managing Partner at RAPYD.AI**

'This book is therapeutic for any data leader who has navigated vendor and consultancy hell. David and Boyan write from the inside, you feel as if you are sitting with them, living the experience. The manifesto and enabling data model are not theoretical constructs; they are forged through real experience leading data in large, complex organisations. Required reading for anyone serious about making data work.'
**Akin Arikan, author of Multichannel Marketing Metrics and Analytics Leader**

'David Castro-Gavino and Boyan Angelov have written an exceptional book that cuts through the hype surrounding data and AI to address what truly drives organisational success. Drawing on deep practical experience, David and Boyan show that lasting impact comes not from chasing the latest technology, but from building the right foundations, culture and capabilities. Rich with real-world examples and clear insights, this is an essential read for executives and anyone determined to turn data into sustained competitive advantage.'
**Professor Ajay Bhalla, Bayes Business School, London**

'Most data leadership books present a framework. This one doesn't. Castro-Gavino and Angelov focus on the root cause of our industry's problems; that data initiatives often fail to deliver what was expected of them, not because of talent, data or technology, but because of flawed assumptions about what data leadership is and what it could be delivering. Those assumptions create structural problems that prevent good work from ever delivering value. This book frames that pattern clearly, then offers a genuinely practical way through to challenge and change those assumptions, backed by real-life examples. A must read for people trying to turn data activity into tangible business outcomes.'
**Kyle Winterbottom, Founder & CEO Orbition Group**

# Enabling Data

Every purchase of a Facet book helps to fund CILIP's advocacy, awareness and accreditation programmes for information professionals.

# Enabling Data

## A New Model for Data-Driven Success in Your Organization

David Castro-Gavino and
Boyan Angelov

facet
publishing

Published by Facet Publishing
www.facetpublishing.co.uk

Facet Publishing is wholly owned by CILIP:
the Library and Information Association.



*British Library Cataloguing in Publication Data*
A catalogue record for this book is available from the British Library.

ISBN 978-1-78330-851-4 (paperback)
ISBN 978-1-78330-852-1 (PDF)
ISBN 978-1-78330-853-8 (EPUB)

First published 2026

MIX
Paper | Supporting responsible forestry
FSC® C013604

The manufacturer's authorised representative in the EU for product safety is Logos Europe, 9 rue Nicolas Poussin, 17000 La Rochelle, France (contact@logoseurope.eu, www.logoseurope.eu).

Typeset from authors' files by Flagholme Publishing Services in 10/13 pt Palatino Linotype and Open Sans.
Printed and bound by CPI Group (UK) Ltd, Croydon, CR0 4YY.

I dedicate this work to all of my past and current clients in the world of data. As much as you learned from me, I learned from you.
Boyan Angelov

For Louisa, Thomas and Charlotte, the heart behind every chapter and every move. You have been the quiet constant through all the noise, the reminder of what truly matters. This journey has taken us across countries, time zones and late nights, but you have always been there with love, laughter and patience. And to everyone who has shared a piece of this path: colleagues, mentors and friends who believed in the idea that data could be both human and transformative. Your trust and curiosity made these pages possible.
David Castro-Gavino

# Contents

| | | |
|---|---|---|
| **About the Authors** | | **xv** |
| **Acknowledgements** | | **xvii** |
| **Foreword by Thomas C. Redman** | | **xix** |
| **Preface** | | **xxv** |
| **Abbreviations** | | **xxix** |
| **1** | **Groundhog Day** | **1** |
| | Introduction | 1 |
| | The root cause | 2 |
| | The modern data stack (MDS) | 3 |
| **2** | **The Promise of AI** | **7** |
| | Introduction | 7 |
| | Via negativa and waste | 7 |
| | Two stories of unmet expectations | 8 |
| | Current state | 12 |
| | How to fulfil the promise: understand the business | 14 |
| **3** | **The HelloFresh Data Story** | **25** |
| | Introduction | 25 |
| | New beginnings: a promise of transformation | 27 |
| | Diving deep into the challenge: uncovering a hidden iceberg | 30 |
| | The moment it hit me | 32 |
| | Turning the tide: from chaos to coherence | 34 |
| | From structure to momentum: delivering at scale | 45 |
| | Beyond the model: data as a product, leadership as legacy | 50 |
| | Looking back to move forward | 62 |
| **4** | **The Dark Side of the Role** | **65** |
| | Introduction | 65 |
| | The many-headed beast | 66 |
| | Why the seat burns so many | 67 |
| | The burden of proof | 68 |
| | The human cost | 69 |
| | A broader pattern | 70 |

| | | |
|---|---|---|
| | Building resilience | 71 |
| | Why stay? | 72 |
| **5** | **The Data Manifesto** | **75** |
| | Introduction | 75 |
| | Principle 1: Tech is never the problem, you are | 76 |
| | Principle 2: Scalability, performance and cost – choose two | 78 |
| | Principle 3: Buy, don't build (unless you can afford it) | 81 |
| | Principle 4: If your use case is not measurable, you don't have a use case | 84 |
| | Principle 5: Stop measuring everything: start measuring what matters | 86 |
| | Principle 6: Beware of pilotitis (but do experiments) | 89 |
| | Principle 7: You have no right to ask for a budget unless you know how you contribute to the value chain | 91 |
| | Principle 8: Start with the end: work backwards | 93 |
| | Principle 9: Your new framework is probably a cargo cult | 96 |
| | Principle 10: Preach data, but not to the choir | 97 |
| | Principle 11: If everyone owns the data, no one does | 99 |
| | Principle 12: If data is not an asset, it is a liability | 101 |
| | Principle 13: Data modelling is more important than anything (do it as early as possible) | 102 |
| | Principle 14: Balance offence and defence in your projects | 104 |
| **6** | **A Model in Practice** | **107** |
| | Introducing the model | 107 |
| | Why we need a model | 109 |
| | A model for friction, not just maturity | 112 |
| | A model for enablement | 114 |
| | The first pillar: People | 115 |
| | The second pillar: Governance | 118 |
| | The third pillar: Technology | 121 |
| | The fourth pillar: Enablement | 125 |
| | Making it real: diagnostic toolkit | 128 |
| | What good looks like: outcomes | 130 |
| | Bridging the gap from model to value | 131 |
| | Reflection | 132 |
| **Conclusion** | | **133** |
| **Closing reflection** | | **134** |
| **Appendix 1: Applying the Enabling Data Model** | | **135** |
| | How to use this section | 135 |
| | Listening before leading | 136 |
| | Why a diagnostic approach? | 138 |
| | Friction is not uniform | 139 |
| | Diagnostic rubric: the backbone | 141 |
| | Full enabling data diagnostic rubric by pillar | 142 |
| | Making the rubric actionable | 144 |

Toolkit in action: personas 145
Assessing platform fit: from friction to architecture 149
Narrative in practice 151
Execution playbook: 0–30–60–90 days 158
Measuring what matters 161

**Appendix 2: Model in practice: metadata as a product 165**
Diagnose: surfacing the friction 165
Design: from features to capabilities 166
Deliver: pilots, Governance and Enablement 166
Scale: from catalog to contracts 167
Lessons learned 167
Templates and artefacts 168
Pitfalls and anti-patterns 169
FAQs for sponsors and teams 170

**References 171**

**Index 181**

# Figures, Case Studies and Tables

## Figures

Figure F.1: Five elements are essential to success in data xx
Figure F.2: Four components for successful change xxii
Figure P.1: Strategic operations visualised xxvi
Figure 2.1: The investment–value curve 13
Figure 2.2: The sources of complexity have changed 14
Figure 2.3: Simplified value stream map of a pizzeria; there's data everywhere 16
Figure 2.4: Difference between narrow AI and generative AI 18
Figure 2.5: GenBI shortens the path to value tremendously 20
Figure 3.1: From listening to impact, a single curve that dips before it rises 35
Figure 5.1: Pilotitis vs enabled ways of working 89
Figure 5.2: Amazon's Building Backwards method 95
Figure 6.1: The differences between tasks, frameworks and mental models 107
Figure 6.2: Flywheel of Insight 111
Figure 6.3: The Enabling Data Model 111
Figure A1.1: Baseline vs target scores for selected dimensions 144

## Case studies

1.1 Case study 1.1: Did data mesh fail? 5
2.1 Case study 2.1: Generative business intelligence 17
5.1 Case study 5.1: Building backwards at an enterprise 95

## Tables

A1.1 The four-point scale of operational maturity 141
A1.2 People 142
A1.3 Governance 142
A1.4 Technology 143
A1.5 Enablement 143
A1.6 Model in practice: persona voices 148
A1.7 Platform Fit Canvas with example 150
A1.8 Common pitfalls 169

# About the Authors

**David Castro-Gavino** is a data and AI executive, author and advisor whose career has taken him across five continents and nearly three decades of international leadership. He has built and led data functions at some of the world's most recognised organisations, including AstraZeneca, HelloFresh, Booking.com and dunnhumby, working across some of the most complex and regulated industries in the world.

His work has consistently focused on the same problem: closing the gap between data producers and consumers. That means building not just the technical foundations, but the governance, culture and organisational conditions that allow data and AI to deliver real and lasting value. At HelloFresh, he scaled the global data function from the ground up, embedding self-service capability, governance and a data-first culture across eighteen countries and seven brands. At dunnhumby, he directed large-scale data and analytics transformations across four regions for nearly a decade, working with some of the world's leading retailers and consumer brands.

He contributes to the global data community through speaking, writing and lecturing, and advises boards and executive teams on data and AI strategy. Recognised in the DataIQ 100 as one of Europe's most influential data and analytics practitioners, he brings to this book the same conviction that has shaped every role: the challenge of data is never primarily technical. It is organisational, human and about the quality of leadership applied to it. Based in London, UK, he is guided by three enduring principles: trust, clarity and craftsmanship.

**Boyan Angelov** is a data and AI leader who after a start as an individual contributor in the machine learning space transitioned into strategy and management consulting with the sole goal of helping organisations deliver more value from data. Currently he is a principal consultant for Exxeta AG, where his objective is to scale data and AI initiatives for enterprise clients across the Germany, Austria and Switzerland region.

Before this, he held leadership positions up to the chief technical officer level, leveraging his understanding of technology beyond data, advanced analytics and AI. He has been prominent as a thought leader, most notably with his books *Python and R for the Modern Data Scientist, Elements of Data Strategy,* well-cited research in the explainable AI field and articles for reputed journals such as *Handelsblatt* and *CDO Magazine.*

He resides in Berlin, Germany and is dedicating his career to making data and AI work for all of us.

# Acknowledgements

**David Castro-Gavino**

This book was born out of three decades of learning, unlearning and building in the world of data. After working on smaller projects early in my career, it was when I joined CACI more than 20 years ago that my passion for data truly took flight. There I began to see how data could reveal patterns, tell human stories and shape decisions in ways that extended far beyond the technical. That experience set the course for everything that followed.

Since then, I have had the privilege of working with extraordinary people: colleagues, clients, mentors and teams across five continents, each leaving a mark on how I see the craft and purpose of data. Their curiosity, persistence and generosity have shaped not only the ideas within these pages but also the person I have become through them.

I owe a special debt to the professionals who joined me in the long arc of this journey, from the early days of customer science at dunnhumby, to the fast-paced experimentation of Booking.com, the incredible scale of HelloFresh and now the enterprise transformation at AstraZeneca. Every team I have led, every partnership I have shared and every challenge we faced together has taught me something lasting about trust, clarity and the quiet courage it takes to build with purpose.

A special thanks to Boyan Angelov, who encouraged me to finally write this book, something I had wanted to do for years. It has been a privilege to create it together and to share the many reflections, debates and ideas that shaped its pages.

This book is my way of passing those lessons forward. It is the guide I wish my younger self had found, something to make the journey a little clearer for those who come next. The path through data is rarely straightforward. It demands precision and empathy, rigour and imagination, and above all resilience. My hope is that these pages help others navigate that tension and see the beauty in it.

To my family, who have been the constant through every country, company and chapter. To Thomas and Charlotte, whose love, curiosity and sense of adventure have turned every move into a shared story, and who continue to meet each new challenge with the passion and energy of living without regrets. And to Louisa, whose strength, love and unwavering support have carried me through every transition and made every chapter possible. None of this would have happened without you.

**Boyan Angelov**

After finishing my previous book, the *Elements of Data Strategy,* I had the feeling that I had said everything I needed to say in the data and AI field. The years that have passed since then, however, were filled with hundreds of small and large stories of data and AI in the real world. In that time I had the privilege to work with some of the biggest organisations in the world and help them move forward productively. Slowly, new ideas started to emerge, patterns that could be teachable, that many seemed to be ignoring so far.

There is a saying that the motivation for writing the book has to be bigger than the pain of doing so. To write successfully you really must have something to say. And when I met David and we started to develop our shared ideas together, I felt there was something new to add. Writing is often a lonely endeavour, but doing it together with David I realised the most important thing for such a project is to see the world from the same angle, and this has been a wonderful journey. Thank you, David.

The list of people who have inspired me in the data field is too long to write here. And I hope that with this contribution we have made a step forward and give an opportunity to a new generation to build on our ideas next!

Finally to my wife, Eva, and my children, for all the patience and support during the long evenings when I was on the laptop hammering away on the keyboard, contributing to *Enabling Data.*

# Foreword: Setting a High Bar for Enabling Data

*Thomas C. Redman, 'The Data Doc'*

I love the title of your book, Boyan and David, particularly the *Enabling Data* part. The promises to make day-in, day-out work more productive, to make better decisions, to actually get something out of AI and to empower people intoxicate! Even better, we've seen plenty of 'points of light' over the past several years to know the promise is there for the taking.

Unfortunately, those points of light tease but do not satisfy, as the vast majority continue to struggle with data. Most data is of poor quality; source systems conflict with one another; much data is never used for anything, never mind used to its potential; and the associated costs are high! Indeed, it seems that many people and organisations actively resist! So if your book is to succeed and actually change practice, at scale, it must answer at some pretty tough questions:

1. What's changed? Role-model successes span data quality, shared vocabulary, simpler architectures, data science and AI, data-driven decisions and maybe a couple more. But none has fully taken root. What is different now that might reduce resistance and/or make these points of light more attractive?
2. Data is a second-class citizen. How do we make it first class? There is some really good news here: a generation ago, data wasn't even on the radar screen. Going from 'not on the radar screen' to 'second class' in a generation is a great accomplishment. Still, I suspect the pathways to first-class citizenship will be very different. What do we need to do?
3. *The Economist* suggests that, if AI succeeds, it could usher in an era of economic growth of 20%/year (Economist, 2025). How do you prepare to get your share? Interestingly, I find that almost all people and companies say the right things when it comes to data, but they are not doing the work. In some respects, I get it: the task is daunting, as they have underinvested in data! And, as Google researchers note, 'Everyone

wants to do the model work. No one wants to do the data work' (Sambasivan et al., 2021). But c'mon! Isn't leadership supposed to make the right investments and assign people into the right roles?

## A lot to cover

The ultimate test is practice: can companies understand how your materials apply to their specific situations, sort out how to use prescriptions, do the work and actually enable their data. The data space is incredibly broad and concerns are diverse. Some years ago I introduced a five-element 'It takes a lot to succeed with data' model to cover this breadth and diversity (Redman, 2018a; and Figure F.1: Five elements are essential to success in data.

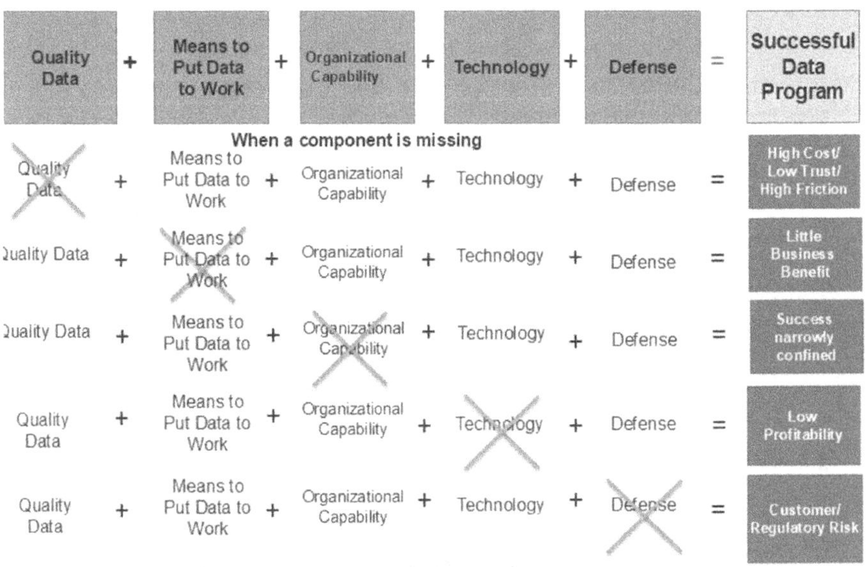


**Figure F.1** *Five elements are essential to success in data.*

Let's dive a bit more deeply into the five elements:

1 *Quality data:* Bad data adds enormous costs in 'running the store,' acquiring customers, delivering their stuff, keeping track of the money and so forth. It is a brutal killer when it comes to data-driven decision making (you can't expect people to use data they don't trust to make a decision), data science and AI.

2 *Means to put data to work:* As noted above, companies use data to run the store. Other ways to put data to work, including AI, data-driven decision making, monetisation (e.g., selling data) and informationalisation (improving products and services by building in more data), go over and above running the store.
3 *Organisation:* This includes people, structure and culture. As Arthur Jones observed, 'Organizations are perfectly designed to achieve the results they achieve.' It is no surprise that today's organisations are 'unfit for data'. After all, they were developed and perfected for industrialisation. For example, departmental silos get in the way of data sharing, which is so necessary to enable data.
4 *Technology:* By and large, technologies enable companies to increase the scale and decrease the unit cost of well-performing processes. They are bound up in productivity growth, so essential for economic well-being. Note this distinction – well-performing processes are effective in that they meet customer needs. Technology helps make effective processes efficient. But automating an ineffective process does not work. Too many fail to make this distinction. From time to time, truly *disruptive 'this changes everything'* technologies come along. Today, many predict that AI will prove to be such a technology, but I think that judgement can be made only in retrospect. Quite obviously, technology dominates most data discussions. In so doing, it distracts leaders from the hard work on other elements.
5 *Defence:* Includes things you need to do even though you can't make money from them, such as regulatory compliance and reporting, ethics, privacy and security.

In addressing the three challenges above, you must incorporate features that embrace these five elements. You are free to knit the work of others together with your own. Thus, steal liberally from my work on quality and organisation (Redman, *People and Data: Uniting to Transform Your Business*, 2023), Davenport and Miller's *Working with AI: Real Stories of Human–Machine Collaboration* (2022), Laney's on putting data to work (*Infonomics: How to Monetize, Manage, and Measure Information as an Asset for Competitive Advantage*, 2018), O'Keefe and O'Brien's on defence (*Data Ethics: Practical Strategies for Implementing Ethical Information Management and Governance*, 2023) and plenty of others!

## Getting there

The second big issue *Enabling Data* must address is large-scale transformation. I've already noted that we've seen enough great work in everything from quality, to architecture, to data science and AI to prove 'this stuff works'. So well that I sometimes find it stunning that more companies don't pick them up! Some of these have proven transformational in their own right. But we've not seen very many sustaining 'flywheels', where success in one department led to two more joining the effort, then four more, and so forth until the entire company was transformed. A big transformation in one department may save millions, while the rest of the company continues with business as usual, leaving hundreds of millions, maybe billions, on the table!

What's going on? How do we resolve this apparent paradox of the great benefits there for the taking with companies' reluctance to claim them?

The resolution, I believe, lies in the observation that 'change is hard!' At best, transformation is a messy affair; at worst, it forces organisations to challenge every assumption they've ever made, pits colleagues against one another and requires persistence through thick and thin. No wonder few in leadership positions are up to it.

I use the four-element model presented in Figure F.2: Four components for successful change.

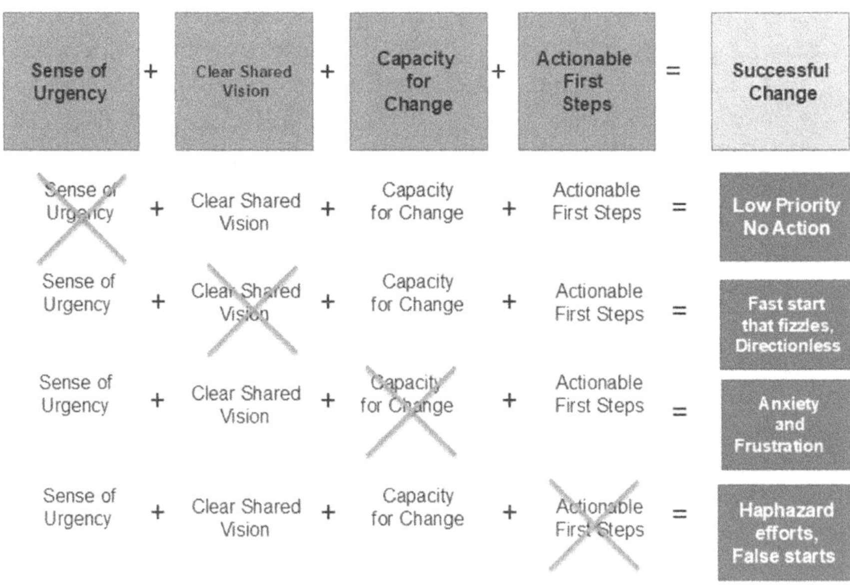


**Figure F.2** *Four components for successful change.*

Let's dive deeper into each element.

1 *Sense of urgency:* Employees have a lot on their plates, so most people work on what is most urgent most of the time. Since 'transformation' always appears to be in the distant future, it rarely meets the 'most urgent' criteria. Change leaders must find ways to put transformation high on employees' to-do lists.
2 *Clear, shared vision:* Transformation requires an 'end-in-mind', a vision of what the transformed reality will look like. 'Shared' is the most important word here – those involved have to be reasonably well aligned if a transformation is to succeed. Employees are smart to wonder 'how will I personally be affected?' Absent a solid answer, 'fear' is the certain result.
3 *Capacity to change:* It takes investment (e.g., money) and brains to transform. It also takes the emotional capacity, at both the individual and company levels, to change. I've already noted that too many leaders lack the courage to change.
4 *Actionable first steps:* Change is daunting and employees and companies can 'freeze up' without actionable first steps.

There is a lot to do and a lot can go wrong! No wonder many leaders sigh, 'People are the problem'.

Personally, I find this reaction incomplete at best, more often simply wrong, and sometimes offensive. I find employees going over and above everyday – to help customers get their stuff, to assemble a report, to resolve a problem – in the face of a lack of support, poor systems and inconsistent leadership! Yes, change is hard. But in every company I've worked with there has also been a wellspring of people who want to make things better!

Enabling data (the concept, not just the book title) runs through such people. In this tech-centric world, this observation gives me great hope!

## And that's not all!

It is easy to call out some common reasons why companies are yet to embrace data. These seven top my list:

- confusion about 'effectiveness' vs 'efficiency'
- subordinating data to technology
- lack of systemic thinking: 'control' and 'planning' and 'improvement'
- leaders staying on the sidelines, often because they don't know what to do
- people not liking their IT departments
- too many 'sacred cows' (e.g., governance) in data simply do not work
- silos making everything more difficult.

Still, to (roughly) quote Tolstoy, 'All good families are the same. All dysfunctional ones are dysfunctional in their own unique ways.' Unfortunately, this means that *Enabling Data* will have to help companies suss out and remove their own dysfunctions! A tall order indeed!

## Go for it!

I'm well aware that I've set an impossibly high bar for you, Boyan and David. There are three incredibly tough questions, nine elements across two demanding areas, seven common dysfunctions and the observation that all companies are dysfunctional in their own way! So, more realistically, shed some light on some of these; show, by way of example, what can be done; and provoke companies to think in new, different and powerful ways!

# Preface

Should we tackle the challenge posed by Tom head on? Can we explain what it truly means to be data driven, showing how data can become first class within an organisation? From the beginning of our work together, the answer has been a resounding 'yes', because the question itself defines the purpose of this book.

As alluded in the Foreword by Tom, nowadays it is impossible to take two steps in any direction without encountering either the usage of artificial intelligence (AI) or someone talking about it. It is not just a promise of riches for many organisations, but can also become a question of survival (more on this in 'Via negativa and waste' in Chapter 2). Even if your business becomes successful due to unforeseen circumstances – i.e. you are in the right place at the right time – eventually the larger context in which you are operating will invariably change, and the unique circumstances that led to your success (coupled with your performance, of course) will either diminish or cease to exist altogether. And if you don't pay attention and lay the foundations in time, your business will be left behind by your more nimble competitors who thought proactively into the future, built the right foundations and gained a competitive edge with advanced analytics and AI.

This is not the first book attempting to improve how we do data; in fact many of the best books have been foundational in informing some of our ideas, and we have cited them throughout. The goal of avoiding reinvention of the wheel is a consistent topic throughout the book, and we want to address it from the get-go. Are we just doing exactly the same thing that we complain everyone else is doing? As Tom asked in his Foreword, why will it be different this time? Are we simply doing what everyone else has done before? Let us show you what is different in our approach:

- We are not proposing a new framework, we are sharing a *mental model* based on common patterns we have seen in our careers. The main purpose of this model is not to make a nice drawing or a workshop canvas,

but to make the reader think holistically, to look at both the forest and the trees. To use a biblical reference, instead of giving you fish, or teaching you how to fish, we show how successful fishermen catch fish!
- We support the mental model with first principles in the social movement we call the *data manifesto*. The principles are concrete and understandable, and by working on them together with the data community we finally establish a single source of truth in the field of data, so we can avoid having the same conversations in the future and direct our collective energy to building the future of data and AI.
- We use *product thinking*. A constant thread throughout the book is the *enabling* nature of data; on its own, rather than an asset, it can be seen as a liability. Most of the time data does not contribute directly to the bottom line of the business (with the notable exception of when it is directly monetised [Laney, 2018]) and just supports other value-generating functions. Changing from a traditional set-up to being a product organisation is enormously beneficial, enabling organisations to harness knowledge and resources to generate more value, as is reflected in our work, where we think use case first, rather than boiling the ocean.
- We follow a *strategic operations* approach. Due to the complexity in data work, we need to adapt quickly. Long gone are the days of static data strategies developed by expensive external management consultants, well written and visually polished, but with zero impact – gathering dust in C-level drawers (more on this in 'Merchants of complexity' in Chapter 1). The environment is so complex that we need to react quickly and adjust to changes in the market accordingly. For example, if your data and AI strategy was developed in mid-2023, you would have missed out on many tremendous benefits of the newly released GPT 2. Have a look at Figure P.1: Strategic operations visualised.

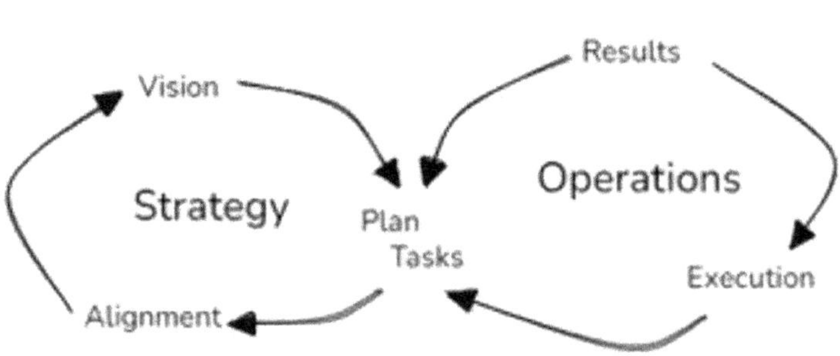


**Figure P.1** *Strategic operations visualised.*

The idea of Strategy Operations (Hanf, 2021) is that there are constant feedback loops between these two elements. Once an initial plan is available and broken down into separate tasks, it is set in motion immediately (sometimes following a building backwards approach), with the aim of gathering learnings very fast. As soon as the first results appear, the strategic team incorporates them, refines the plan and the cycle continues, creating a living rhythm of acting, learning and adapting that defines our approach throughout this book.

# Abbreviations

| | |
|---|---|
| AI | artificial intelligence |
| API | application programming interface |
| AWS | Amazon Web Services |
| BI | business intelligence |
| CCPA | California Consumer Privacy Act |
| CEO | chief executive officer |
| CTO | chief technical officer |
| CI/CD | continuous integration and deployment |
| EHR | electronic health record |
| ETL | extract, transform, load |
| GDPR | General Data Protection Regulation |
| genBI | general business intelligence |
| HIPAA | Health Insurance Portability and Accountability Act |
| KPI | key performance indicator |
| MDS | modern data stack |
| ML | machine learning |
| MLOps | machine learning operations |
| NHS | National Health Service |
| OKR | objectives and key results |
| PoC | proof of concept |
| QAR | quarterly alliance review |
| QBR | quarterly business review |
| QDR | quarterly data review |
| ROI | return on investment |
| SaaS | software as a service |
| SLA | service level agreement |
| SLO | service level objective |
| SQL | structured query language |
| StratOps | strategic operations |

CHAPTER 1

# Groundhog Day

Boyan Angelov

## Introduction

In the film *Groundhog Day*, Bill Murray's character, Phil Connors, is stuck in a time loop. He is forced to relive the same day over and over again, with no end or escape in sight. For those of us leading data functions in organisations, this film feels like our daily reality: we are running in circles, struggling to find lasting solutions to the same old challenges.

I could first express this predicament some time ago, when talking to an experienced thought leader in the data space, asking his opinion on some new topics that I was looking into, such as applying principles from lean manufacturing to data projects (we'll cover this later in the book). While he listened carefully and was very polite, I vividly remember the look he gave me, as if he already knew where this all was going even before I had even started explaining. He told me, 'Boyan, listen, we had the same problems with data in the '80s, inventing a new framework is not going to fix the fundamental issues.' These words stuck with me. I felt like an inexperienced idealist who believes that they can change everything with a new framework supported by pretty drawings. From that point onwards, I vowed to myself to always think deeper and avoid reinventing the wheel: focus on first principles.

Fast-forward several years. I was already exploring these ideas with David when, attending an event and talking to newcomers in the field, I felt the roles reversed. This time I was talking to a younger person who was explaining to me the newest framework; I looked at them and asked the basic questions: what is the value of data? The next day, we talked with David and made a pact that we didn't want to be old and *still* talking about the same issue. It was about time we did something about it. Before we go into that, let us take stock of where we are and how we got into this mess in the first place.

## The root cause

### Merchants of complexity

While there are differences between data and traditional software projects, we can take a lot of learnings from the history of that field and see what useful insights it can bring. In a keynote at the largest Ruby on Rails conference (Heinemeier Hansson, 2025), David Heinemeier-Hansson (or DHH as commonly abbreviated) gave an excellent overview (based on an essay he had written) on how we have overcomplicated things tremendously in tech. DHH is known for his opinionated hot takes (for example, he has also advocated a shift from the cloud back to on-premise servers, to save costs and maintenance, so he has a history of being sceptical of vendors and has always tried to keep his company's products simple and focused), but I think he hit the mark here.

He explained how, in the early days of the web, you could serve useful, scalable products to a huge number of users by using one PHP file and a simple database (remember, WhatsApp was built by 12 people), while nowadays you need a team of 50 engineers, everything on the cloud, different microservices, CI/CD (continuous integration and deployment) etc. Now deployments regularly take hours, while in the good old days it was a matter of a simpler transfer to the FTP file server. He also wonders why, in times of tremendous connectivity, excellent software frameworks and hardware, it feels as if the tech world is in deep trouble and struggling. His answer is the same as ours: complexity. We have lost our way, and I think we are doing a very similar thing in data: one look at the MAD (ML, AI & Data – https://mad.firstmark.com/) landscape is more than enough to see the fragmentation of the vendor ecosystem.

DHH frames the merchants of complexity as people who sell you complexity, either on purpose or by accident, because it is an easier sell – it can justify 'rent', 'quick wins' and 'dependence'. There are some historical parallels to this; for example, Walter Kiechel, in *The Lords of Strategy* (2010), criticised consultants in the same way, since they tend to generate complexity instead of eliminating it, using fancy frameworks and useless analyses, all with the goal of making clients dependent on them, generating a lot of noise and insecurity for the client and obfuscating the key first principles that any business should have. A second important element is the usage of the asymmetric distribution of knowledge. When one side (i.e. the consultant) hoards more knowledge than the client – let's say on how to set up data governance on Amazon S3 – they can lock in the client and generate a whole new job title of hyper-specialised data engineer. Basically, complexity is monetised.

How does this play out in the data world? There are so many vendors, platforms and SaaS (Software as a Service) solutions flooding the market. Data leaders get hundreds of inquiries every week from complexity merchants selling their products and services. At a time when complexity is failing us (brittle systems, a negative reinforcing loop), it can be very attractive for a data leader under pressure (more on this in Chapter 4) to succumb to these requests and purchase these products or services. But they just reinforce the problem, delegating unnecessary complexity to the future, and so the cycle goes on. In 2025, even the most experienced and careful teams, also working in a greenfield context, will struggle to contain growing complexity in the mid-term, as I observed in my own experience as a chief technology officer (CTO).

So many tools are marketed as 'holistic', notably many of the observability platforms. They often end up being heavy and hard to integrate, introducing a lot of dependency (and the vendor can use that leverage to change the price at will – here we have some of the geopolitical tensions now present in the world playing out). Many offer these abstractions of complexity, but tend to increase it, requiring deeper and deeper certifications by your technical people. Another good example are many of the Machine Learning Operations (MLOps) tools – all the model versioning, CI/CD and other bells and whistles make you think this is all you need for your Proofs of Concept (PoC) to scale and be 'enterprise ready', when a simple endpoint can serve your customers just as well, at a fraction of the cost and (most importantly) complexity.

The merchants of complexity in data can have a huge negative impact on our efforts to make our organisations data- and AI-driven. It results in lost agility, where our teams are spending time learning and maintaining bloated frameworks instead of using their time and talents to tackle real business problems. They introduce dependencies which make decision making more and more difficult, with huge pressures from large vendors at large organisations. They create a false sense of progress – very similar to what we discuss later in this book as 'pilotitis' (see Chapter 5), the disease of doing pilot projects – generating a lot of noise for little tangible impact. And finally, also perhaps most insidiously, they change the culture of the company. The Conway principle (that the software architecture tends to approximate the organisational architecture in shape and form) applies here; our technical people start to embrace the complexity and multiply it, forgetting that simplicity is what solves the problems.

## The modern data stack (MDS)

A second huge source of complexity is the MDS. We can start with the name; using the word 'modern' can be tricky (and I am guilty of doing the same, since it is in the title of my very first book); it can quickly become outdated.

You say 'modern' in 2012, but can you do the same in 2025? Probably not.

But let us start with the benefits. First, it is much easier to use the MDS tooling than what came before it; dbt and Looker are much nicer than Hadoop. This democratisation enabled smaller and mid-sized companies who didn't have the infrastructure and know-how (i.e. talent) of their larger competitors to use data productively. This democratisation also spread to other professions; suddenly not only data engineers could do the heavy lifting, but analysts became closer to the technology and could do more engineering work – dbt, for example, allows analysts to build their own transformations using structured query language (SQL). The MDS was made to be easy to integrate with many other tools, but as you'll see in the following paragraphs, this is actually a double-edged sword.

> I remember having coffee with a friend whose job was preparing business reports, so a lot of Excel and SQL (and some R). Suddenly, when he joined a new organisation he started doing a lot of data engineering and deploying his own models at work. At the time I was working as a data scientist, and got very nervous. How could he, with his background, manage to do data engineering? For me it looked tremendously difficult, since I was going into map-reduce and similar topics. It turned out that his new company was using the MDS and Google Big Query – exactly the democratisation that I have mentioned as a benefit of the MDS.

So, what are the negatives of the MDS? Well, to start, it fragmented everything exponentially. Now you had to think about different solutions for ingestion, orchestration, metrics layer, reverse ETL (extract, transform, load). We started to see companies doing meta-orchestration to manage their orchestration (truly inception-level stuff). This inflation in the stack resulted in a lot of venture capital money being piled into new solutions, bloating everything even further. Smaller companies in order to look cool (also coupled with the frequently-mentioned-in-this-book propensity of technical people to want to learn and use the shiny new technology instead of solving business problems within their specific context and constraints) started to use tools they didn't really need. Most of the use cases could be done with a simple Postgres database, a cron job and Metabase.

Additionally, the new pay-as-you-go pricing models, seeming attractive, fragmented the billing further, making the management of it that much harder to track. The culture shifted. Training by the vendors created whole teams of evangelists within the companies who flatly refused to work with rival technologies – now locked-in in their stack. At this point, thought leadership on social media (especially on LinkedIn) started to blur the lines between itself and the marketing of tech products (this is a problem that unfortunately persists to this day and is just growing). The MDS changed itself and became a victim of its own success. The early push spearheaded by it was aimed at reducing complexity, but eventually it started to do the exact opposite.

It is interesting how the data industry often works as a pendulum. Now, especially because of new economic pressures, organisations are reverting to basics. The message of DHH was heard, and some organisation are starting to focus on basics and become more pragmatic. This has greatly benefited solutions such as Databricks and Snowflake which aim to take the complexity out of the equation – but if we take the lessons of history, we can expect even these platforms to succumb to their own complexity if they are not careful (and perhaps we can see some early warning signs of this, for example, in how Snowflake now wants to integrate more generative AI tooling within its stack – which, while very useful, technically does not feel like a core part of their product).

Let's now go through an example of how not the technology but a way of thinking can also contribute to the issues in enabling data.

**Case study 1.1: Did data mesh fail?**

This is a provocative question. We have both been fans of the data mesh approach ever since the first article by Zhamak Dehghani appeared on the Thoughtworks blog (Dehghani, 2019). We would argue it did not fail, in the sense that it made a tremendous push in the right direction, shifting left (to the data producers). Unfortunately, many organisations started blindly copying it like a dogma (similar to a cargo cult), instead of adapting the framework to their specific contexts. Piethein Strengholt (2024) has made a wonderful contribution to this in many blogs, posts and talks where he shows the messy reality of implementing a data mesh in the enterprise. Some datasets can remain centralised and under almost complete control by the IT department, and that is fine. This shows the objective reality once we move from clean-looking, idealistic frameworks into the field. In Appendix 1: Applying the Enabling Data Model, we will try to avoid the fate of the data mesh.

A second reason for the failure of data mesh to live up to the hype was the conscious or unconscious misinterpretation of it by vendors; each product had to have 'data mesh' in its name and call itself 'mesh-ready'. It became more of a sales buzzword than a concrete enabling project.

Organisations were also not ready; a lot of the enabling work was not done. And, as is one of the main messages of this book, most of the complexity arises not on account of technology but due to the people who have designed it, operate it and are its customers. The domain clarity and the product mindset were missing. Organisations should have first tried their hands at more tried and tested methods for reducing complexity, such as Domain Driven Design (Evans, 2003) and Event Storming (Brandolini, 2019). There was also a significant issue in regulated industries such as pharma, where the data was siloed and all applications were subject to many more rules and regulations and closer scrutiny from management.

Similarly to the MDS, data mesh ended up worsening the problem in many cases by adding catalogs, data contracts and many more committees. It was like adding fuel to the fire, and this is a lesson for any complex system, like the ones that data leaders normally operate in: if the fundamental workings and context of a system are already dysfunctional, increasing the superficial efficiency of the machine will lead only to cascading effects and more problems. First we have to refactor the machine, and start working from first principles.

**Analogies**

Throughout the book we rely heavily on two analogies to drive home the points of *Enabling Data*. The first is the iceberg. The idea behind it is that there is a whole set of 'invisible' work that needs to be done to get value from data and AI, and if we ignore it we are bound to crash our ship. The second analogy is that of building a house on solid foundations; if we ignore them, it will fail. Here I have an interesting saying from another analytics leader, who said yes, we should build solid foundations, but if we spend too much time in the basement working on them, the people in the house will have to continue living without windows! As with many things in our book, balance is key.

These stories show the importance of learning from failed attempts and setting up feedback loops. We do need to focus on the complete data hierarchy of needs, since, if we ignore the bottom of it, there is simply no chance that the advanced analytics and AI use cases on the top will become operational and drive real value. Complexity is the root cause of all problems. We should also learn from the issues and stay away from the merchants of complexity, and learn from the lessons of lack of adoption of otherwise thoughtful frameworks such as data mesh.

If Groundhog Day has taught us anything, it is that insight without change keeps us trapped. To move forward, we need a new kind of promise. Now that we have contextualised the problem and the thinking behind our approach, let us turn to where the journey leads: the promise of AI. After all, how can we chart a course through the choppy waters of data without a North Star to guide us? This will be the topic of the next chapter.

CHAPTER 2

# The Promise of AI

Boyan Angelov

## Introduction

I was too young to feel the effects of the dotcom bubble bursting, but based on what I have heard it certainly seems that we could be heading in the same direction. At the same time, I have been fortunate to have worked on real-world AI applications that delivered value to our economy, so I can see both the current value and the future potential. Where is the truth? Before we get into that, let me establish a fundamental way of thinking that informs our approach to AI. After all, the old ways of thinking about data and AI have hit a wall, and we need new approaches in our thinking and attitude.

## Via negativa and waste

We often think of AI as an *innovation* topic, something to be developed towards, a new capability that *adds* to the current state. This thinking becomes apparent when resources are limited, due either to the environment in which the company operates or to its internal budgeting structure, incentives and maturity. In such cases, the appetite for 'innovation' or 'strategy' topics decreases, with a notable shift towards 'optimisation', 'efficiency' and 'lean' operations. This is understandable, but also often irrational, since innovation and new products are precisely what will provide competitive advantage and revolutionise business models across the board.

So why is this thinking prevalent? The reasons are that innovation topics are seen as risky, difficult to define, experimental and requiring a ton of expertise – all things that organisations in such environments normally lack. But there is some logic to this too. Let me introduce the concept of 'via negativa', or the 'negative way', as formalised by the statistician and economist Nassim Taleb in many of his books, most notably in *Antifragile: Things that Gain from Disorder* (Taleb, 2012).

In his work Taleb describes the type of advice that we get from our parents when we are children growing up; it is focused on the *positive*: get a good job, find a good partner and be a good person. Even as kids, we realised that this type of advice does not feel very actionable at all. We would ask ourselves what do you mean, a 'good person', or a 'good job'? The former can be very subjective and context/culture dependent, while the latter changes with time. Now, if you are the parent, try switching the advice to the negative. Instead of looking at what *good* needs to be done, think what *bad* can be avoided. For example, don't take drugs, don't mix with the wrong people, don't smoke. Such negative advice, probably due to the evolution of our reptilian brain, feels much easier to understand and actionable – also easier to follow. And the wisdom goes that as long as we avoid the bad stuff, we will be fine.

How does this apply to data and AI? Instead of innovation and how to do AI 'right', the best way forward, pragmatically, without hype and unrealistic expectations, is to follow the via negativa way and avoid committing the obvious mistakes. Much of this chapter will follow these principles, most notably their application from decades of lean management. These words might seem negative and depressing, but my goal is to convince you that this is the pragmatic way forward.

## Two stories of unmet expectations

In this spirit, let me illustrate some of the main issues with two stories; they together describe much of what I have seen going wrong in data and AI projects. If we avoid such scenarios we will be good to go.

### Digging the perfect hole in the wrong garden

What is the favourite thing for most technical people to do? That's right: solve cool technical problems with even cooler tools. As any manager of tech people would attest, if left to their own devices, they will do everything possible to maximise the time spent on new, cool technology. For the record, there is tremendous benefit to diving head first into new technology; it's one of the fundamental ways to drive innovation. Still, in this case I'll discuss the drawbacks of this incentive and how they manifest in data and AI projects.

In one consulting project, the client requested that we build a machine learning (ML) model that would predict the deviation of the budget of a construction project. At that time I was an inexperienced manager myself and succumbed to the same temptation to dive head first into the modelling part of the work. I led the team to train an ML model to predict the deviation. After that work, we packaged the model in a Docker container and deployed it as a service that we wanted to use for demonstrating the PoC.

Once we got to the end of the engagement, we organised a meeting to show the results. I vividly remember the client's impression while we were showing our modelling results: they were a bit overwhelmed by the technical detail, but at the same time impressed with the performance of the model. Once our presentation was over, we were unfortunately in for a rude awakening. The client asked, 'Is that it, are you done?' We were confused and said, 'Yes.' It turned out that they were not interested in having a prediction application programming interface (API) but actually wanted a graphical user interface (GUI) to explore the data and understand it. We had to build that and run over budget, at our own expense. I call this mistake 'digging the perfect hole in the wrong garden'. In other words, developing amazing technological solutions that nobody will use – one of the most frustrating things in the careers of many technical people. If we had been thinking about the user (data thinking, as discussed in the Preface) first, we wouldn't have ended up with this failure.

## A slip on the finish line

The second story is a bit different, but equally frustrating. When telling this story I use one particular image that many football fans will recognise – Liverpool FC's captain, Steven Gerrard, slipping while trying to catch a loose ball in the dying minutes of their Premier League game. His team has had a consistently successful campaign over the course of almost ten months, with the team showing their best form day in and day out. A group of 28 players, all fighting to win the much-coveted title at the end of the season. By the time the team meet rival Chelsea FC, they have been leading the pack at the top of the table. A draw in the game would suffice for the team to stay in the race, with easy final games coming up. And then disaster strikes – the captain slips while trying to intercept a ball and an opposing player scores a goal to give the opposing side the lead. Chelsea went on to win the game 2:0, and Liverpool lost their chance to win the title, prolonging their wait by another seven years.

You might ask yourself, what does this sport story have to do with data? Well, 'a slip on the finish line' is also, unfortunately, a common failure in data and AI projects. The following is a story not from my own experience but from that of a close friend who has built a successful career in data engineering. At a large German retail organisation, his task was to support the data science team in operationalising the predictive models they had trained. While this resulted in the famous 'throwing over the fence' problem, where the handover between data science and data engineering is lacking in quality, my friend managed to avoid the issues and established a gold standard for MLOps work: the models were versioned, tagged, tested and deployed following best practices. The team was proud of their good work and the time arrived to show it to their clients, the product team. The presentation was confident, showing the robust and modular pipeline and accuracy of ML predictions. But when the time came to present the integration with the product, disaster struck. The web page that should consume the prediction showed a spinning wheel for several seconds before rendering the outcome – in other words, it took several seconds for the interface to submit the data, fetch the results of the inference and show it to the end user. While for the ML engineering team this looked reasonable, the product people were appalled. In their words: 'How can we make our users wait for such a long time? When was the last time that you had to wait more than several milliseconds for a product recommendation to show up on the Amazon shopping page? What kind of user experience is this?' They requested the MLOps team to improve the performance to match the expectation and deliver inference results in milliseconds rather than seconds. From the product team's perspective, this didn't seem like a very big ask – after all, the whole MLOps set-up was complete, with all the tooling, bells and whistles.

However, my friend already knew the hard reality. While it is relatively easy to do a first version of many such systems, due to the amazing tooling (especially open source) available, improving them relies on more involved coding and optimisation – something that only the most experienced and skilled data engineers can accomplish. Getting that extra several-second latency reduction might seem possible, but there are often diminishing returns in building such systems. This was a real 'slip on the finish line', and, much like in football, it can derail the otherwise fantastic work done by large groups of people in an instant. Now let's wrap up the stories of failure by covering two final common anti-patterns.

### *Stop boiling the ocean*

Another factor contributing enormously to the complexity of our work in data is the sheer amount of it, together with the number of systems that it goes through. When coupled with the lack of agility in the organisation (often doing the opposite of StratOps [strategic operations] principles, with large and slow bureaucratic processes and centralised organisational set-ups), it leads to the doomed-from-the-get-go attempt to try to fix all data-related problems first, before proceeding with doing use cases. At a large European pharma organisation I witnessed work which took hundreds of people months to accomplish, cleaning and cataloguing data – but without any meaningful use-case-first prioritisation as to why the data should be used. And, as many technical data professionals will attest, not all data are created equal. For example, log data, or other IT-backend signals, rarely have useful analytic importance and may need to be down-prioritised when we implement the data strategy. Unfortunately, these activities can quickly generate a lot of noise, and *feel* like progress, but without any tangible benefit.

### *Don't follow a cargo cult*

Some companies are much further ahead of others in their data and AI journey – so much is clear. The question of how much of the learnings, processes and blueprints are transplantable between organisations is one that has been concerning management consultants for decades. There is widespread acceptance that while context is essential, there are *some* patterns that are common, and some topics that can be addressed between organisations even if their product portfolio, workforce, history and culture are markedly different.

But there are limits to what we can do. Many of us can be inspired from the successes of American or Asian tech giants such as Google or Alibaba, but attempts to copy their patterns often fail. This is because we fall victim to a phenomenon called 'cargo cult'.

**Cargo cults**

During the Second World War, the inhabited islands in the Pacific Ocean were in the crosshairs of both the Axis and the Allied forces battling for control and edge in the region. This led to numerous disruptions for the local populations, since supply routes were either blocked or scrapped altogether. As the war front shifted further towards Japan, the Allied forces became increasingly responsible for providing aid and supplies to the local communities. The locals observed the far superior technology and how the American soldiers were receiving supplies through the air. Once the conflict was over, they decided to attempt to replicate the 'rituals' by building airstrips, aircraft, radar stations and all other pieces of technology that had impressed them – all in the hope of getting supplies – of course, in vain.

This might seem a faraway story, but it is surprisingly common, specifically in the technology and data domains of the modern world.

Finding new ways to run our organisations as they go through digital transformation is one of the most difficult challenges that we have today. The old operating models of companies designing, building and selling products and services have truly been upended in the age of the internet, data and, now, AI. The speed of change is exponential, the technologies change all the time and the overall complexity is staggering. One of the fundamental reasons why there are difficulties in getting value from data (and this points to many of the issues that we cover in the Data Manifesto), is the suboptimal way that we put our teams together.

At the same time, there are organisations which are much further ahead on this journey than others, specifically the tech giants in the US. It is difficult for us not to be envious of their tremendous success in harnessing the new technologies and becoming some of the most valuable companies in the history of humankind. The next logical step would be to see what works for them and try to transplant learnings to our own organisations. Who said that a *Mittelstand* (SME) organisation in southern Germany cannot learn from them? While the motivation is noble and makes sense in many cases, there is a fundamental issue.

We can take the example of a framework that became popular in one of the most successful organisations of the digital era: the music streaming company Spotify. They became famous for the way they organised their teams in what was called 'matrix organisation'. They had guilds, squads and tribes dedicated to different product lines. This distributed way of working seemed poised to provide huge benefits to the digital workforce, and many companies (and yes, that *Mittelstand* company in Germany) were quick to pounce on the concept and try to adopt it for themselves.

Unfortunately the results were less than spectacular. This set-up, while providing some benefits, created even more chaos in organisations which lacked the maturity and context of Spotify. In an ironic turn of events, many organisations continued to attempt to use it, after Spotify themselves had abandoned it. This is a classic example of a cargo cult.

Now, with these cautionary tales in mind we can take a step back and take stock of where we are today. How representative are they of what is currently going on in the AI world?

## Current state

In many of her famous talks, Cassie Kozyrkov, Google's former Chief Decision Scientist, used a fantastic analogy to describe what AI is for a non-technical audience. She describes AI as being a fancy dish served to customers in a restaurant, and the data that it needs as the ingredients for the dish. We can take this analogy further and describe the 'kitchen', 'utensils' and other important elements that go into making the dish as the architecture and infrastructure behind AI. If we use this analogy, what is currently lacking in cooking the perfect dish? Why is it that so many restaurants are empty, and either the dishes don't taste good or you can't order what you see on the menu?

Tom teased some of the answers in the Foreword, but let's recap the main three reasons.

- There is a *lack of clear problem definitions*: many AI projects start because of a fear-of-missing-out situation and in a hurry, before the enabling activities and projects are established. This leads to the 'digging a perfect hole in the wrong garden' type of problem, as previously described.
- *Data quality and availability*: we'll go through this specific issue in Case study 2.1 at the end of this chapter.
- *Lack of organisational set-up*: another consistent topic throughout this book; the technology is often not the problem, but people and how they are organised is.

And the end result of these failures? Take a look at Figure 2.1.

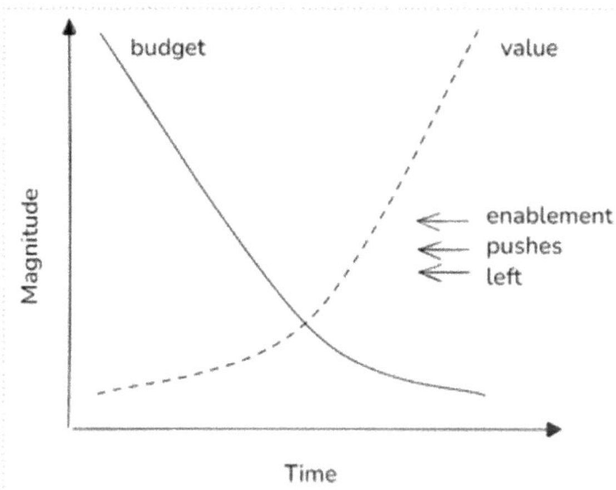


**Figure 2.1** *The investment–value curve.*

What do we see here? Unfortunately, money is rarely unlimited, and especially in a difficult macro-economic concept even investments in efficiency and value are becoming scarcer. The value of data analytics and AI normally takes a longer time to manifest, as compared to more traditional software projects and leaders of organisations need a lot of patience in waiting for them as the budgets run dry, sometimes stopping right before the impact. The whole purpose of the Enabling Data Model that we show in Chapter 6 is to push the value curve to the left.

If we look historically at the issues behind the difficulties in getting value covered, is there a pattern? I would argue that while in the early days of data (1980–2000) we were heavily constrained by technology – for example, in computing and storage availability, maturity of technical tools and technical knowledge – in the current era of advanced analytics and AI we are more constrained by the ways we organise (or don't) and prioritise our teams and work (Figure 2.2).

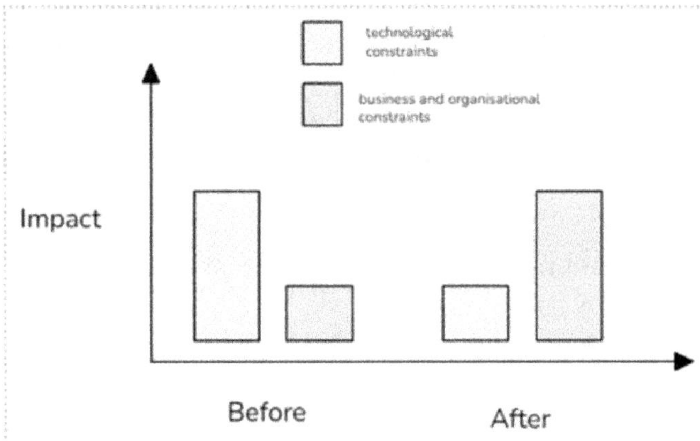


**Figure 2.2** *The sources of complexity have changed.*

These patterns are not random. They reflect a consistent failure to build data capabilities in the right order, something often described as a 'Data Pyramid of Needs', where foundational layers such as data quality, access and governance must be established before advanced analytics and AI can deliver value (Rossi, 2021).

Now that we have seen the main issues and reasons for the failure to address the foundational layers of the Data Pyramid of Needs, let me provide you with my favourite tool for reducing complexity in any data and AI project by doing what every experienced leader in data will advise you to do, *before* the very first line of code, very first dataset that you download and visualise, and *before* thinking of any ML or AI solution: understand the business.

## How to fulfil the promise: understand the business

Several years ago, in a conversation with a data leader with a Top 4 international consultancy, who was one of the first people to push for Data and AI Strategy consulting in the Germany, Austria and Switzerland region, I asked him the number one piece of advice he would have given to his younger self when starting his journey in data and analytics. His answer – and one I have heard from numerous other data leaders with a stellar track record – was: 'Make sure you understand the business.' Excellent advice, but the devil is in the detail. How are we to do that? He suggested something that felt out of the left field: read more newspapers. At first I did not understand, but he quickly explained: 'As a technical person, the more newspapers you read, the more you understand how the world works.' Ultimately, any business is in the business of making money – by providing value to its customers. We don't need to make the situation much more complicated than that.

This discussion stayed with me for some time, and was brought into focus later, when, for a client engagement, I needed to make a value stream map (you can see an example at https://en.wikipedia.org/wiki/Value-stream_mapping). I realised that this was a direct representation of what he meant by understanding how the business is making money (value). We can make such a map for the main variants of business set-up (B2B [business to business], B2C [business to customer]) and trace how products and services are designed, developed and delivered to customers. The diagram is split into three lanes, representing the flow of information, the product flow and the time flow. I will describe them in reverse order, since the very first one is of particular significance for our data context. We start by looking at the time flow, a log of how much time certain *processes* take in this stream. This is a very valuable direct indicator for any bottlenecks and waste appearing and proliferating in the organisation (Atwal, 2019). The second lane shows the product flow – how it is designed. For example, if the product that a company sells to customers is a car, the assembly and delivery process is described here. Now we can talk about the final process – the information. And guess what, here we can use 'information' interchangeably with 'data'. If we are talking about the very first car companies of Henry Ford, this information was stored on sheets of paper, documenting and coordinating customers' and organisations' requests for automobiles, and the different parts required for the eventual assembly.

With all of these pieces together, you can construct the value stream map of any business. Normally these diagrams are used to discover potential bottlenecks and optimisation potentials, but they have the additional effect of helping us to *understand the business*. By constructing them, we get a high-level understanding of what the company is selling and, perhaps even more importantly, how. This is why, in any consulting engagement I do with clients, I ask my junior colleagues to construct and understand a value stream map of the client's business (it does not need to be too detailed; a high-level view can be gained in one or two interviews with a key person).

How can we use value stream maps in data? Let's try to imagine a different business. I have picked the example of a pizza shop, mostly because all of us understand the product and there have been many pizza-related examples in works that provide advice on tech topics. Now, you might think that a pizza business is relatively simple, as compared to large automotive or tech companies. You are right, but still, if you draw a value stream for it you might be surprised at even the most basic of complexities that are required for a business to function in the modern world. While, historically, restaurants have been on the relatively simpler side of business – as opposed to, let's say, a factory producing machine parts for trains – they too have entered the digital age and are taking advantage of the amazing technology and innovation that is all around us. A picture is worth a thousand words, so let's take a look at the value stream map of our pizza restaurant in Figure 2.3.

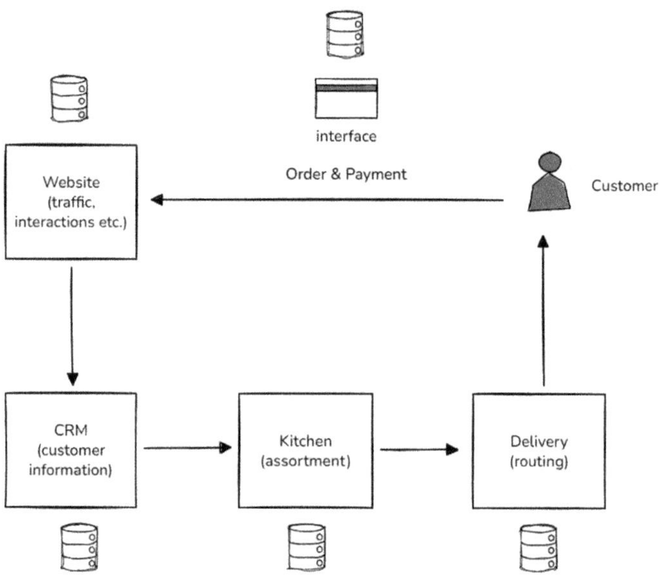


**Figure 2.3** *Simplified value stream map of a pizzeria; there's data everywhere.*

So, what is standing between you and that amazing pizza? A modern restaurant now makes a significant portion (if not the larger one) of its income from food delivery, as compared to clients ordering and eating at the establishment. This means that the customer needs to have some way to order the product. First it was by telephone, but with the advent of the internet other options became easier, most importantly, ordering through a website. Ideally, if you are a data-driven pizzeria you will track as much data as possible about the customer, so they will need to log in to their account. You can start collecting data already at this very first point, and can use various methods to analyse anonymous user behaviour in this initial funnel. For example, users from which locations, and when, click on which elements? These data can help to inform potential decisions regarding the front end of the site. A/B testing is expected of all modern data-driven organisations, where you can check if a certain new font, colours or button positioning results in better value outcomes (i.e., people ordering more pizzas). Also, here you can already do market basket analysis. Which cohorts of people (another use case: marketing segmentation) are ordering which products together? Maybe the people who love salami pizza are also more inclined to order ketchup, as opposed to mayonnaise?

> I often use value stream maps for two types of ideation workshops: one is more obvious, where we look at automation potentials, and the inefficiencies that can be alleviated with data and AI. The other looks at data-driven use cases; for example, for a large automotive client I was very surprised to learn that they did not track the user session for a leasing calculator.

Value stream mapping as described here is an essential tool for understanding the business. It is also a mental model – as is the Enabling Data Model that we'll introduce later. Its main purpose is to help us see the work in a more holistic way so we can take more directed and organised action. We'll now go through a case study from our work that combines both the promise of AI and the difficulties in bridging the gap between the current state and getting value.

## Case study 2.1: Generative business intelligence

What brings value to an organisation? Is it the data catalog? Is it the data upskilling programme? Indirectly, yes (this is the whole point of the book), but technically the value drivers are the products that a company offers. This case study uses the example of a product that I developed together with an enterprise customer, to showcase the missed potential and a potential North Star.

While many consultants love to work with clients on shiny products, such as computer vision, robotics and others, I have always been more inclined to deliver the arguably more *boring* cases, which, while not being press-release ready or compelling for your next board meeting as a chief data officer (CDO), can actually push the bottom line of the business and make it more data driven. These products are normally more centred on the lower part of the Data Pyramid of Needs. One such product is generative business intelligence, or genBI.

Preparing reports has been a fundamental operational task in business since the very early days. If we look back in history, the first reports – the systematic gathering, storing and display of quantitative information – can be traced all the way back to ancient Mesopotamia, where, around 3000 BCE, grain and taxes were tracked on cuneiform tablets. Of course, most of what we talk about now in the modern context follows closely from the Industrial Revolution and the need of businesses worldwide to start adopting various accounting practices. Now, in the digital age, the amount of data that we can collect in a business has exploded, and so has the need and desire to have an accurate picture of these datasets. Thus we can trace the origin of modern reporting systems to some of the earliest records of human civilisation. The need to quantify, measure and share information has been there all along (in his book *Quantitative Display of Visual Information*, Eduard Tufte (2001) covers this history with brilliantly illustrated examples and best practices that we can use even in today's modern context), but the way we go about it has been upended by technology. Now, products that would normally take months to develop because we needed to train our own models can be done in weeks, without the ML expertise required (Figure 2.4).

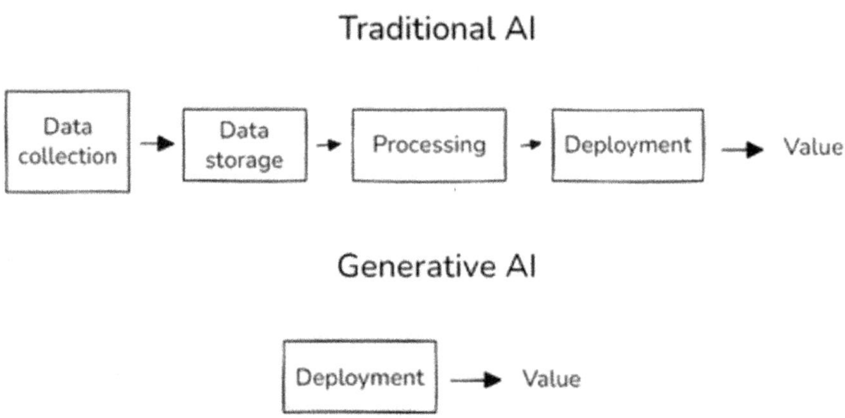


**Figure 2.4** *Difference between narrow AI and generative AI: now the time to value is exponentially shorter.*

Let's start with the basics. We can first attempt a definition of a 'report' in our context: it is the structured communication of collected information, prepared for a specific audience, to support understanding, decision making and/or accountability. These reports allow humans to make rational decisions that are not supported by feelings only, but by hard facts – data.

In the old days of technology (in this case we can consider the early 2010s old, but even at the time of writing I was talking to someone who works in the financial services sector, whose whole job is to take Excel files from different sources and run a script that does several basic calculations and adds some text semi-automatically, resulting in a PDF report that he can share with managers), if you wanted a report you first needed to know what data points you were interested in. Here I often tell the story of how some of the largest organisations in the world, once they hit a size of more than 100,000 employees, struggle to have an adequate, regularly updated record that enables them to say with certainty, at any given point in time, how many people actually work there. Other companies have even bigger problems, starting with the need to know what data is available at all, before they can request someone more technical to provide it. What happens here is that a seemingly basic question, such as 'How many products did we sell in region X in the last quarter?' immediately gets bogged down in follow-up questions and issues. Your counterpart will often ask, 'What do you mean by "product"?' because it is defined in different ways in different places. Also, 'What do you mean by "sold"? In our databases and associated applications we have around 40 different statuses for our products.' And you haven't even touched on the omnipresent data quality issues. Even worse, let's say, for some products the data quality is less than for others – perhaps because the fields are entered manually, and thus more prone to error. In such a scenario it would be even more difficult to come up with standardised data quality improvement procedures that could make a significant difference on all datasets at the same time (beyond the basic presence/absence checks). Another caveat that we'll cover later in the book, and one of David's favourite topics – 'don't do dashboarding as a sport' – is to always ensure that the dashboards and reports you spend significant resources in developing have a user in mind.

Now, even if you manage to avoid many of these issues and actually know what data you need (and also what is possible), a non-technical user will not normally be able to get the data from the different systems or even create the final report. For this they will need a technical colleague – normally a business analyst. The requester will brief the analyst with the requirements, and the analyst will then work on the report. They will need to connect to the different systems required – and in most cases these connections will exist already, since this is probably not the first time that someone in the business has asked them to pull some data for a report. But maybe, if they are new to the organisation, or the systems have not previously been used in this way or have changed in some significant way, there will be many other problems behind this seemingly easy reporting task. Then they will need to check the data quality, whether the fields that were requested in the briefing really exist and whether there are potential issues (often, here they will loop back to the requester). If the data is available and of sufficient quality, they will start writing the SQL code. Depending on the analyst's skill, the complexity of the queries (difficult joins between different systems) and the size of the queries (if they are too time consuming they can strain the resources of the system, especially if other people are using it at the same time – another important point to motivate the creation of a scalable and suitable data architecture as soon as possible, and one of the key enabling projects that you can see in the Enabling Data Model in Figure 6.3), this can take anything between an hour and several days of work. And then the report is ready and is provided to the requester.

Unfortunately, at this point other problems can arise. Let's say the business user is not happy and somehow does not trust the data (similar to the footballer's 'slip on the finish line' problem), or actually wants to have a look at other related datasets as well. In this scenario, the analyst needs to go back and redo some of the work, rinse and repeat. (Of course, this scope creep – which is very common even for successful reports – can actually be a good thing, as it shows how people can become excited when you provide them with useful data points that can make them more successful.) But, even worse, by the time the report is provided to the requester (and it can often take days), the data is already too old or the requirements have changed. This delay between the request for a report and its delivery is very detrimental to the success of any data-driven organisation.

By now, it should be clear why automating such a case can be very useful for a business. Here are some of the benefits that it can provide (visualised in Figure 2.5):

- faster access to data
- business users can get data themselves, without technical support
- more opportunities for domain experts, who understand the data well (at least better than the IT or even members of the data team), to be part of the process
- greatly reduced time to insight (more on this in Chapter 3)
- quicker iteration between query and result.

**Figure 2.5** *GenBI shortens the path to value tremendously.*

As already mentioned, this is not a new problem and many attempts have been made throughout the years to improve it. From low- or no-code solutions – including some very successful examples such as Tableau or Microsoft's Power BI – they do help tremendously, but still fall short of the holy grail of self-service analytics: the ability to *talk to your data* (in natural language). Basically, the idea is to translate from a natural language – let's say English – to SQL, and then it should work. The issue is that SQL is a deterministic language that is useful to a machine; it cannot be the least bit vague. Which is very different from normal language, where every time we write or speak, a certain error rate is acceptable for our meaning to be understood by the recipient (always another human). So the accuracy of the solutions that have been attempted until now has been lacking, and up until recently we have always written SQL code for such reports.

This all changed in the spring and summer of 2025, when OpenAI released their ChatGPT version 2. At the time, many people were impressed, but still struggled to see how it could be more than just something to talk to. But more forward-looking engineers and researchers immediately saw the use case to try to translate natural language queries into SQL that can query a database. Another essential benefit of using generative AI to overcome this problem is that it has the ability to remember and learn from examples and mistakes. Thus, if the AI gets an error message from the SQL runtime, it can use the output and log of that error message to debug itself – and do self-healing in the process. Thus started the very first experiments to do this. Around a year later, I and my team were tasked to do exactly this for a large client.

In their words, they gave us the cleanest dataset in their organisation. The dataset contained the distribution data of their product worldwide: where it was produced, where it was stored and when and how it was sold. You can understand that this dataset was one of the most important in the organisation, since it provided mission-critical information on the most important value driver: the product itself. The same data also powered a multitude of applications (we didn't have an overview of them all, but estimated in the tens to hundreds) which were used worldwide. You can imagine the importance of these data. If it was wrong, people who purchased the product wouldn't be able to track where it was and when it would be delivered; and the line-level employees directly supporting the sales process and customers wouldn't be able to do their work properly. This was also one of the oldest datasets in the organisation, dating back to the early 1990s.

This was the dataset that was given to us to build genBI. Imagine typing queries such as 'How many of product X we sold in time window Y in city Z' – essential information for any business, let alone a world market leader in the specific product category. The very first thing we did, of course, was to analyse the quality of the data – we couldn't take our client's word for it. Data which looks good to the business on first glance could be completely unsuitable for a technical use case – specifically, machine learning or AI. To our surprise (it rarely happens this way with most customers), the data actually was pretty clean and consistent. Leaving aside a major drop-off in the 1990s, when there was a big switch to different data collection and gathering systems, many fields were available and clean for decades. So, we started building. We deemed the lack of long-standing historical data not to be a significant blocker – after all, a business is mostly interested in recent data (data freshness is a fundamental metric in assessing data quality) so it can take actionable decisions. Here there is a marked difference from similar use cases in scientific work, where, ideally, we would have data dating far back so that we have enough information to find patterns.

In the process of developing the AI solution we first built a PoC, which included talking with the potential business users to see what SQL queries they often need to write for their basic reports. An important focus was on the queries being not too technically complex (avoiding big joins and pivot tables). As often happens, the PoC looked awesome and we managed to generate a lot of excitement and (unfortunately) sky-high expectations. It is difficult not to get carried away, even if you are acutely aware of all the potential upcoming stumbling blocks. If only you could have seen the excitement on the faces of the end users when they ran their first natural language queries and got good results! They already knew that this technology could save them a huge amount of time – time that they could use for other, more interesting and rewarding tasks, such as interpreting the data and coming up with good questions – tasks that are still far away from being automated by AI. We built a small user interface for them to play around with (this was one of the key learnings that I had taken away from the 'slip on the finish line').

After doing the PoC successfully and proving that the natural language translation into SQL works, we needed to move closer to production level. Now the queries that we got from the potential business users became more complex, and very rapidly so, because there's almost nothing that a human loves better to do when presented with an interface to test an AI/automated solution than to try to break it – find any potential shortcomings. (There must be something inherently psychological at play here, for all of us to want to do it, probably ever since we were small children.) Also, we needed to think about performance (What would happen if multiple users queried our product at the same time? How about hundreds or thousands of users? How about the same engine being used by one of the previously mentioned multitude of applications, which can then remain just as a front end for the natural language queries on the dataset?

As we continued the work we began to encounter issues, and two of them were game breaking. The first one was the metadata. It was only a question of time until we reached the point at which the AI could not understand some of the queries being asked. Column 'age18' could be relatively easy to infer, for both a human and AI, but how about 'customers_in_18'? Does that mean all the customers aged over 18, or all the customers in India who bought product number 18? Even for a human this would be tremendously difficult to understand. Our AI needed more context. The natural thing was to ask if there was some description of the columns available in a data catalog (metadata). The answer shocked us: we were provided with an Excel file. It was not complete, it was at least several years old and some of the columns had been changed in the meantime. This complicated matters tremendously because we then needed to go through all the columns manually, find the people who understood them and document what they were about. We already knew that even if we did our work well, the data that we were so carefully curating should technically go into a data catalog. (This is why we think that having at least some form of data catalog is probably the lowest-hanging fruit and most impactful first enabling activity you can do in your organisation.) Coupled with this were the tremendous issues with scaling the product to support many users and be performant - people expected the queries to be very fast, which is something we saw in one of the stories earlier in this chapter, highlighting the importance of gathering good requirements.

---

So, what learnings can we take from this? First, foundations are essential. This is a classic story of shiny PoCs catching attention and raising expectations. But they become literally impossible to deliver to a production-level state if the foundations for data are not there. And these foundations also take time and resources. Sometimes, for start-ups and innovative products people use the metaphor that they feel like they're building a plane and learning to fly it at the same time while falling down a cliff. For some products this might work, but not for advanced data analytics and AI; there we need the foundations from day one. A second learning is that the potential of this technology is completely real. If you are following the data and AI discussions in the LinkedIn and social media ecosystem you will face both extremes – either complete hype that AI will be a game changer *tomorrow*, or that it is all a bubble doomed to burst at any minute. The truth, as so often, lies in the middle.

There is a third significant learning that we can take from this story. In the months and years that followed the project, many other tools such as Databricks and Snowflake started integrating natural language queries to their data sources – so you would get the complete feature with the basic tools that you use. In such cases it sometimes pays to be slow, because instead of trying to build such an obvious and significant use case the organisation could have waited for a time to get it out of the box – with much improved quality, zero patching and maintenance work and bound to improve over time. It felt like trying to come up with new spreadsheet software at the same time that Excel rose to prominence. (This classic build-versus-buy dilemma is covered Chapter 5.)

Several months later, an additional interesting thing happened that data leaders should pay attention to. As I had suspected, the 'talk to your data' use case became extremely widespread. The demand for this interface is so huge that it is now integrated into many tools and platforms, most notably Databricks and Snowflake. Once again, sometimes it is beneficial to wait a bit before trying to build your own solution, and to focus on more platform-centred technologies rather than designing, patching and maintaining loose software components that need a huge amount of resources to keep operational and complete (an impossible task), requiring the resources of billion-dollar organisations. In such cases it is better to be slow, rather than fast and innovative.

This chapter, hopefully, has demonstrated how some of the most beneficial and value-producing use cases can be derailed if we do not *enable* them beforehand. If we are to reap the benefits of these tremendous technologies, spearheaded by AI, we must build solid foundations. Now, enter David and his story from HelloFresh. Let's see how a journey to value was successful.

CHAPTER 3

# The HelloFresh Data Story

David Castro-Gavino

> In every business, there is a moment when the data outgrows the system that holds it. What comes next, chaos or clarity, depends on the choices made in that moment.
>
> (Author's reflection)

## Introduction

This is a story of transformation, of complexity faced head on, of building the data organisation you wish you had while still running the one you do.

It began for me on a quiet Berlin morning in October 2020, having arrived from the UK with my family just a few days before. That morning, I stood outside the HelloFresh office for the first time, not as a visitor, not for an interview, but as someone about to lead a newly formed data function through the heart of hypergrowth.

That first day, I felt the same mix of excitement and unease I'd experienced many times in my data career: on the one hand, HelloFresh's meteoric rise (HelloFresh Group, 2021) was clear proof of a company on the cutting edge; on the other hand, the very success of that growth threatened to overwhelm our data systems. I'd seen before how well-intentioned analytics or AI projects stall when vital but 'invisible' fundamentals like quality, governance and ownership aren't addressed. It was apparent that if we couldn't tackle these underlying obstacles head on, we risked spinning our wheels, despite all our talent and resources.

What made this journey resonate deeply with me – and, I hope, with you – is that these challenges aren't unique to HelloFresh. They're the tensions that every rapidly growing organisation feels at some point, trapped between ambition and infrastructure, between creativity and chaos. The only difference lies in proportion. Some industries wrestle more with governance missing owners, unclear definitions, catalogs no one trusts, while others are hobbled by architecture, pipelines stretched beyond their limits, legacy systems creaking under new demands. Elsewhere, adoption is the sticking point: brilliant tools or frameworks built but never embedded, or platforms rolled out that quietly gather dust. The pattern is the same, only the weight shifts.

At HelloFresh, we encountered all of these symptoms, just in a particular balance. Governance gaps collided with architectural fragility, and both amplified adoption hurdles. But the pattern itself is universal. Every organisation eventually discovers that ambition runs ahead of infrastructure, and the bill for shortcuts always comes due. The solutions we discovered, then, offer not just a path for HelloFresh but a roadmap for any leader facing the complexities of scale.

What you're about to read isn't a polished playbook or a heroic success story. It's a fable of reality, equal parts vision, velocity and vulnerability. It's the unfolding of a transformation that touched every layer of an organisation: its data, its people, its language and its culture. In those early weeks, I saw everything from brilliant PoC dashboards that never made it to production, to repeated firefights over inconsistent definitions. There was a pervasive sense that we were always on the brink of something big, but also on the brink of chaos.

Beneath the technology, it was people all the way down. Imagine a Venn diagram of product managers, analysts, engineers, scientists and operators, each circle with its own incentives and dialect. Where the overlaps were strong, momentum carried us forward. Where they were thin, misunderstandings bred rework. We learned that shared language is infrastructure: definitions are not just glossary entries, they are social contracts. Without them, models mislead, metrics compete and dashboards become mirrors of disagreement rather than instruments of decision.

Yet, in those stumbling-blocks lay the seeds of an idea: a practical approach to bridging the gap between ad hoc pilots and truly scalable data practices. My notebook rapidly filled with notes on 'data producer onboarding', 'coherent governance' and 'what real trust means in analytics'. Step by step, frustration turned into models and small experiments evolved into guiding principles that helped us reorient the entire data landscape.

Through these chapters, I invite you to walk with me. To meet the challenges as they arrived, some expected, others not. To sit in the ambiguity and to celebrate the turning points. You'll see systems built, models introduced, habits reshaped and, most, importantly, trust rebuilt, one conversation, one product, one metric at a time. Bit by bit, we learned how to reinforce the invisible scaffolding of data so that each new dashboard or ML model rested on solid ground.

If you're a data leader, a transformation architect or simply someone who believes that clarity is possible even in complexity, this story is yours too. By the time we reach the end, I hope you'll recognise the subtle but profound shift that can occur when an organisation stops treating data initiatives as 'special projects' and starts weaving them into its cultural DNA.

## New beginnings: a promise of transformation

It started with a message.

On a warm May afternoon in 2020, an e-mail arrived in my inbox, quietly, without ceremony but carrying the weight of something life changing. The sender: Dominik Richter, chief executive officer (CEO) and founder of HelloFresh. The subject line: 'Data Leadership Opportunity'. It wasn't a job offer. Not yet. It was an invitation. A chance to explore an idea, to join a conversation that would soon gather momentum and pull me into something much larger than a role. There was no recruiter pitch. No templated blurb. Just a founder reaching out directly with vision, intent and clarity, something I'd rarely seen even in decades of data leadership.

Dominik's message struck a chord. He didn't treat data as just an operational tool; he saw it as a strategic engine. From our first call, he spoke of data as both *compass* and *catalyst*: a force that should inform every decision, empower every team and flow seamlessly throughout the business. It was surprising, and refreshing, to see that level of literacy and ambition coming from the very top. Dominik got it. He didn't just believe in data; he believed in what it could unlock if cultivated deeply, responsibly and at speed.

> Boyan: One of the most important ingredients for an effective data strategy delivery is having the backing of the board. We call these people 'data champions', and will cover strategies to get them on your side.

Dominik was that champion. Without him, the conversations that followed might never have gathered momentum. Having a CEO who could articulate data not just as infrastructure but as competitive advantage created a North Star for the rest of the leadership team. It meant that when I spoke of governance, trust or enablement, it didn't sound like technical housekeeping; it was understood as essential to sustaining growth. That alignment at the very top is rare, and it gave the whole endeavour a legitimacy that no tooling or methodology could have provided.

That was the first spark.

At the time, I was four months into a new role at Booking.com. I had joined in January 2020 with high hopes of shaping the next chapter at one of the world's most data-mature companies. Then, almost overnight, everything changed. COVID-19 brought the travel industry to its knees. Borders closed, flights were grounded and bookings evaporated. Suddenly, instead of focusing on innovation and optimisation, we were navigating survival. Booking.com was forced to make heartbreaking decisions, eventually announcing plans to cut a quarter of its global workforce (Valinsky, 2020). Professionally and personally, it felt like the ground had shifted under my feet. I'd barely unpacked before the world turned upside down.

Meanwhile, I was also deep into my Executive Global MBA at Hult Business School, spending weekends immersed in case studies on crisis response and sustained transformation. At the time, insights from McKinsey & Company on organisational agility and resilience felt particularly relevant, emphasising how learning and adaptability underpin performance during disruption (McKinsey & Company, 2021). HelloFresh featured in my coursework too, not just for how it rode the waves of disruption but for how it reinvented meal delivery. They weren't merely shipping recipe boxes; they were re-engineering the supply chain. Their model was direct-to-consumer, lean by design and anchored in sustainability by matching production to demand and tracking carbon in logistics (HelloFresh Group, 2024). This wasn't just resilience; it was *intentional*.

Then came that e-mail from Dominik.

While much of the world scrambled to adapt, HelloFresh accelerated. Customers poured in, new markets launched and complexity soared. At a time when people everywhere were hunkering down, HelloFresh was reaching them exactly where they lived, at their kitchen tables (Reuters, 2020). Yet the very speed of that success exposed cracks in how data was handled, posing questions of clarity, trust and visibility.

The cracks weren't unique to HelloFresh; they were the predictable shadow of hypergrowth. Conway's Law tells us that systems reflect the communication structures of the teams that build them. As HelloFresh expanded organically, every new market, every new function and every hurried data pipeline added another strand to the organisational web. The architecture mirrored the organisational chart: fragmented, locally optimised and straining under global ambition. What had worked when the company was smaller now risked becoming a constraint, a drag on the very momentum it had created.

Dominik's ask was simple: 'Help us shape how data guides our decisions. Help us turn insight into action, at every level. Help us build the data organisation we need to keep pace with our ambition.'

And that ... that was the challenge I had been waiting for.

In many ways, the timing felt poetic.

I'd spent nearly three decades in data, starting with early work in customer classification, then winding through consulting, product, analytics and strategy. I'd guided organisations in designing data operating models and scaled teams across continents. My time at dunnhumby had been especially rewarding, a near-decade of transforming raw data into genuine customer understanding for global retailers and CPGs (Consumer Packaged Goods). I travelled so frequently that my son once told his teacher I was a pilot.

But, over time, consulting left me craving not just the thrill of diagnosing problems but the satisfaction of living through the solutions. At Booking.com, I'd tried to find that deeper sense of ownership. Yet, with the pandemic's upheaval, I found myself yearning for the chance to build something fundamental, from the ground up.

As the conversations widened, touching everyone from the chief of staff and the CTO to leaders in Product and People, the outlines of the challenge began to take shape. Each perspective added a new layer: the chief of staff highlighting the pace of organisational change; the CTO underscoring the strain on infrastructure; Product leaders calling out scattered definitions that slowed experimentation; and People leaders voicing the need for consistency and trust in workforce data. Taken together, these dialogues revealed not just isolated pain points but a systemic picture of a company whose ambition was outpacing its ability to harness data with clarity and confidence.

They had poured resources into a MDS and toyed with decentralised models, convinced that data could be a decisive edge. But potential goes only so far without a stable foundation. Yes, the teams were incredibly talented, but they were stretched thin. Yes, there were plenty of metrics, but the definitions were often scattered or overlapping. Data was *available*, but rarely *discoverable*, and while pipelines did run, they were prone to brittleness and breakdown. Even the much-discussed data mesh had landed more like a catchphrase than a coherent system (Dehghani, 2019). What they lacked was not ideas or effort, but the cohesion to turn fragments into a foundation.

They didn't need a fixer. They needed a builder, someone who could bring alignment, structure and momentum, and, more than anything, a sense of trust. It felt as though everything I'd learned, from big-picture consulting to hands-on transformation, could converge here. And as the professional case for joining grew clearer, the personal calculus began to shift as well.

On a personal level, the decision carried weight. My wife and I have always lived by a simple mantra: *Live with no regrets.* We were used to relocations, risk and reinvention, so Berlin didn't feel like a reckless leap. It felt like the next step in a life of intentional adventure.

This was our kind of story. It was a company that prided itself on scaling with purpose, a leadership that truly appreciated the power of data and a role that would offer real influence, reporting directly to the CEO. More than that, it was an opportunity to create something meaningful for the business and the communities it reached.

So I said 'Yes'.

The e-mail in May became a contract in July. My first day came in October. And with it, the beginning of a new chapter, not just for me but also for HelloFresh. A chapter where data would no longer be reactive, but *intentional*. Where decisions would be guided by trust, not guesswork. Where growth, at last, might be matched by clarity.

## Diving deep into the challenge: uncovering a hidden iceberg

Every leadership transition begins with optimism. A new role, a new mandate, a new set of problems to solve. But, in my case, the first few weeks at HelloFresh felt less like onboarding and more like stepping into a boardroom post-mortem – except that the body was still breathing and the surgery had already begun.

On paper, the set-up was enviable. I reported directly to the CEO, a structure few data leaders are afforded. It meant I had unfiltered access to the business's core concerns, without the competing agendas of Finance, Tech, or Marketing clouding my view. In theory, I was perfectly positioned to drive transformation from the centre.

But reality came fast. From our first biweekly one-to-ones, it was clear that Dominik wanted truth, speed and tangible results, not abstract strategies or long-term white papers. He made no effort to sugarcoat the current state of data at HelloFresh: 'The data team is seen as a black box. It doesn't deliver. People don't trust it. They don't think it adds value.'

The metaphor fit perfectly. A black box is something you feed inputs into, hoping for useful outputs, but the process in between is hidden from view. That was exactly how much of HelloFresh experienced data. For business teams, requests went in and numbers came out, but the journey between the two was opaque. Few outside the data function understood the fragile pipelines, the shifting definitions or the firefighting it took just to keep things running. And when something went wrong, the opacity made it easy to blame the box, not the conditions around it. It was like flying on a plane where passengers could feel every patch of turbulence but never glimpse the cockpit – unsettling and hardly reassuring.

That invisibility carried a heavy cost. When outputs didn't match expectations, people assumed incompetence rather than complexity. When definitions shifted, it looked like evasion rather than iteration. And when delivery was slow, local teams stopped waiting and built their own workarounds. A black box may produce answers, but it does not inspire trust.

In one Supply Chain discussion, for example, local teams told me they had built their own shadow spreadsheets to track fulfilment because they simply didn't trust the central dashboards. They weren't trying to be difficult; they were trying to survive. But every duplicate model or manual workaround only deepened the sense that central data couldn't be relied upon.

Marketing painted a similar picture. Campaign teams admitted that they often redefined conversion metrics on their own, arguing that waiting for central approval would cost them momentum. The result was agility in the short term but inconsistency in the long term: the same campaign could be deemed a success in one report and a failure in another, depending on whose numbers were used. It wasn't just inefficiency; it eroded trust at precisely the moment data was meant to unify decisions across the business.

These weren't edge cases; they were everyday workarounds. And they showed me that rebuilding credibility would matter as much as rebuilding architecture.

Those words landed heavily, but not as a surprise. In fast-scaling companies, perception often lags behind effort, yet here the disconnect was painfully stark. Even at the top, there was doubt. The US market, responsible at the time for about 60% of HelloFresh's global revenue, painted an even sharper picture. There, the data organisation was widely seen as a blocker to innovation, with local teams working around, rather than with, the official data function. According to the notes I took in those earliest sessions with Dominik, the local sentiment was blunt: 'They're too slow,' 'They don't speak our language,' 'We can't trust their numbers.' That told me this wouldn't be a mere technical reset; it would be a reputational one.

I didn't rush in. I never do. From day one, I approached the challenge with the same methodical curiosity I had honed over decades. I listened. I met with analysts, engineers, product leads, marketers, supply chain managers and local data teams across regions. I asked where their data came from, what they trusted, what they avoided and where they got stuck. I tried to map how data moved, or didn't move, through the organisation. My goal was simple: understand the terrain before attempting to redraw it.

> Boyan: What David did here is a best practice in dealing with complex systems at the start. Instead of trying to do dramatic changes, it is better to gain information as fast as possible; to uncover useful levers and patterns before doing first experiments that can then change the system behaviour and steer it in the right direction.

This approach wasn't just instinct, it was strategy. In complex systems, rushing to impose fixes without first uncovering patterns is like adjusting a compass without checking north: you risk steering everyone further off course. By listening first, I could begin to see not only what was broken, but where the natural levers for change might lie.

That's when a clear pattern emerged. There was, in theory, a modern data strategy anchored in decentralisation and powered by cloud-native tooling, branded under the hopeful banner of 'data mesh' (Dehghani, 2019; Gavish, 2023). Yet, as many companies discover, a mesh architecture requires far more than a slogan: it demands robust governance, shared standards and careful enablement (Ellens, 2024). Paper can't ingest pipelines, and it can't referee tribal definitions or debug ETL failures at two in the morning. Beneath the polished exterior of hypergrowth lay a mosaic of unfinished migrations, outdated infrastructure and improvised workarounds, an example of how the 'wrong' application of mesh can breed chaos (Rollin, 2023). The road to hell, as the proverb reminds us, is paved with good intentions (Speake and Simpson, 2015), and here those intentions had hardened into silos rather than solutions.

## The moment it hit me

The realisation crystallised during a call with the vice-president of Platform, not long into my onboarding. We were reviewing the infrastructure landscape when he made a casual remark: 'We've been trying to move away from Cloudera by using HDFS into S3, but we ended up with two poorly implemented systems.'

That sentence felt like a jolt. Two systems, neither fit for purpose: one out of warranty, the other half built, with no roadmap to completion. Between them was a maze of fragile dependencies, outdated tooling and undocumented hacks. I paused, thinking, 'How is a €3.5 billion business running on this?'

Internally, I felt an unsettling mix of frustration and determination. I knew in that instant that this wouldn't be just a technical clean-up, it was a leadership crucible that would test everything I knew about navigating complexity and motivating teams. It wasn't that I'd never seen technical debt. But HelloFresh's surface was so polished: robust growth, expanding teams, a culture celebrating innovation. Yet underneath lay a legacy stitched together by necessity, not by design. And now it was mine to understand, fix and rebuild.

### What I found beneath the surface

As I dug deeper, the iceberg kept revealing new depths. Beyond the mismatched systems and half-baked migrations, I discovered a landscape where documentation was nearly non-existent and each pipeline seemed to live or die by tribal knowledge. One ingestion job relied on 4,000 lines of SQL, another was triggered only if someone remembered to poke it at midnight. The 'modern' data push to the cloud had collided with leftover on-premise systems that no one dared fully decommission. Incremental processing was the exception, full table reloads were the norm and overhead costs, both human and financial, kept climbing with every ad hoc patch.

I vividly recall an engineer confessing quietly, 'Honestly, nobody knows how this works anymore.' That candour, though troubling, became invaluable. It told me we weren't just missing documentation; we were missing collective confidence in the very systems meant to sustain the business.

I had seen technical debt before, at dunnhumby, where legacy ETL scripts stubbornly clung onto life, and at Booking.com, where rapid scaling often left a trail of half-finished migrations. But this felt different. The scale of HelloFresh's growth meant that fragility wasn't confined to a single system or region; it was embedded across the stack. The very things that made HelloFresh successful – speed, expansion, relentless experimentation – had compounded into a lattice of dependencies that no single person, or even single team, could fully explain. This wasn't just debt to be repaid; it was an iceberg to be mapped.

Meanwhile, the idea of data mesh had arrived with the best of intentions but no real structure behind it. Teams wanted autonomy and local ownership, but with no standard guardrails or shared definitions, decentralisation drifted towards chaos, not empowerment (Dehghani, 2019). Some teams layered on more tools and homegrown scripts, yet the result felt like spaghetti code: complicated, repetitive and easily broken.

## When culture and architecture collide

All of this was underpinned by a deeper paradox. HelloFresh prided itself on being data driven. Leaders championed experimentation, real-time dashboards and key performance indicator (KPI) trees for nearly every domain. But love for data goes only so far without the underlying trust. People wanted to rely on data but found it too fragile or inconsistent to trust wholeheartedly. The cultural drive to 'move fast' clashed with an architectural foundation still trapped by legacy constraints and misaligned processes.

In my earliest one-to-one notes with the CEO, he flagged that the US teams were so frustrated they'd begun creating their own mini 'data squads', forging direct pipelines that bypassed the central infrastructure. Speed overcame standards. I saw the same patterns in Europe on a smaller scale: pockets of local heroics leading to shadow systems, each with its own logic and definitions. The data was scattered, and so was trust.

I remember a conversation with a frustrated marketing manager: 'We love data,' she said. 'But we can't build our strategies on hope alone.' Her words captured the core of our challenge: turning passion into genuine confidence.

### Listening before leading

Those first 90 days were a crucible, a trial by fire – or, in this case, by data. It was a time of listening, mapping and holding back from bold declarations. I had seen enough transformations fail because someone had tried to fix problems too quickly without truly understanding them. So I shielded the existing teams from blame, catalogued our mess and started designing a path forward.

It became clear to me: how can you get somewhere if you don't know where you are? Before you can change an organisation, you have to *understand* it. Before you rebuild, you have to *unearth what's beneath*. And beneath the dashboards, quick wins and impressive growth trajectory, HelloFresh had a fractured data ecosystem – but also the will to fix it.

In my first days, I was told point blank: 'Expose the truths we're scared to face. Then we'll handle them.' That was enough to begin.

Privately, I grappled with self-doubt during this mapping phase, constantly questioning whether I was moving too slowly or too cautiously. But that early clarity anchored me: we had permission to surface difficult truths before offering solutions.

## Turning the tide: from chaos to coherence

There's a moment in every transformation when the weight becomes too much to carry silently. When every workaround, every metric dispute, every failed pipeline, accumulates – not as tickets, but as a quiet organisational fatigue. You feel it in the clipped tone of Slack threads, in the way meetings open with caveats and in the hush that follows the question, 'Which number is right?'

It is the moment where early confidence gives way to a harder truth. As illustrated in Figure 3.1 opposite, the journey from listening to impact is rarely linear. It dips before it rises. What begins with optimism and quick wins often leads into a reality check, where shared language, governance and enablement must be rebuilt before meaningful progress can resume.

And for us, that dip wasn't theoretical. It was very real. For me, the weight announced itself during a question-and-answer session with one of our regional analytics teams. We were reviewing churn across three markets. One analyst said, 'Our number looks off, but we pulled it from the churn dashboard.' Another replied, 'We used a different funnel logic because we

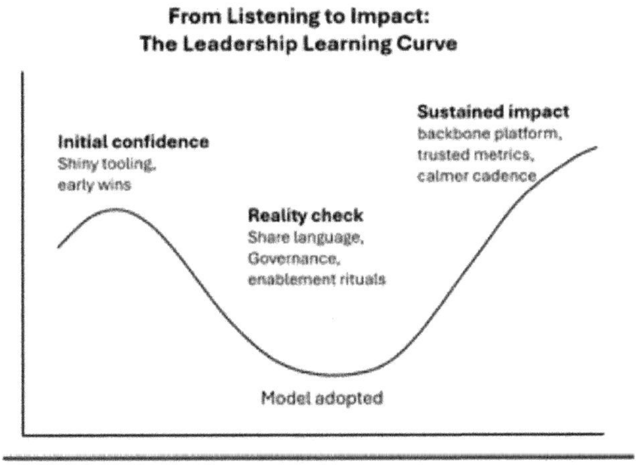


**Figure 3.1** *From listening to impact, a single curve that dips before it rises.*

didn't trust the central version.' And then the quietest voice added, 'I wasn't sure where to get it from, so I recreated it from scratch.'

Three churn rates. Three teams. One broken system.

No one was wrong. But no one was aligned either.

It wasn't about bad intentions. It was about a system that had lost its shape, a lattice of definitions and pipelines so fractured that it no longer delivered coherence. Environments like this, where semantics sprawl and trust erodes, point to a deeper breakdown in how governance, technology and culture intersect.

In that moment, I knew we couldn't keep patching. We had to rebuild. Strategically. Structurally. Culturally.

We were no longer in the phase of early wins. We had reached the dip, the point where the system reveals itself for what it is. It wasn't failure. It was clarity. And from there, we could finally begin to rise.

## The case for a model

That moment made something clear. HelloFresh didn't need another strategy slide. We didn't need more intention. What we needed was something grounded, practical, flexible, real. A working model that could absorb complexity without creating chaos. Something that could help teams move forward *together*.

A mindset shift was essential. Too many of our frameworks until then had lived only in slides, quarterly OKRs (objectives and key results), modernisation roadmaps, data governance charters. They all spoke of ambition: 'migrate platforms', 'stabilise ingestion', 'certify assets'. But without a shared way of thinking, the strategies splintered. Teams interpreted goals differently, progress felt abstract and the connective tissue was missing. In retrospect it seems obvious: people needed not just instructions but a model that explained *how the pieces connected*, one that made complexity legible and gave them confidence to act.

**What are OKRs?**

OKRs (objectives and key results) are a goal-setting framework used by many organisations to align teams around measurable outcomes.

- Objectives define *what* you want to achieve; ambitious, qualitative statements of intent.
- Key results define *how* you will measure success; specific, time-bound metrics that track progress towards the objective.

At HelloFresh, OKRs set the quarterly rhythm for teams, but without a unifying model they often became fragmented, interpreted differently across functions.

It was like the frame of a house: until you see the beams and structure, adding new rooms feels precarious. Once the frame is clear, everyone knows where to build, how to connect and what will hold. The model became that frame.

I presented my early thoughts on this model to the data leadership team one afternoon. Their reactions ranged from hopeful enthusiasm to sceptical silence, and I knew that gaining buy-in would require patience, proof and persistence.

So I designed what would become the Enabling Data Model.

It wasn't imported from a conference or plucked from a white paper. It was born from necessity, a response to years of fragmented ownership, technical debt and eroded trust. It wasn't a model to describe an ideal future state. It was a way to structure progress, make change visible and rebuild belief.

At its core were four pillars: Technology. People. Governance. Enablement.

Each addressed a root cause. And together, they became the scaffolding for something more coherent than we had ever had before. We wanted to break the cycle of 'band-aid solutions', focusing instead on building a genuinely composable, modular data architecture that could absorb change without rewiring everything (McKinsey & Company, 2020a).

## Technology: from bottleneck to backbone

When I joined, the data stack resembled a patchwork museum. We had Cloudera clusters running versions out of warranty. Impala queries nested within scripts barely understood. ETLs sprawled across Airflow, Bash and dashboard layers, all held together by institutional memory and silent prayers.

But it wasn't the stack that failed us. It was our accumulated urgency, the culture of fixing over building, of just getting things live. A 'quick fix' approach can plague organisations that aim to implement modern paradigms, like data mesh, without first stabilising a reliable platform (Dehghani, 2019).

So we paused. And asked a different question: 'What would good look like if we started today?'

That became our orientation point.

We began with the painful but necessary work: untangling ingestion pipelines, deprecating unused views, mapping lineage across critical assets. Documentation wasn't an afterthought; it became a shield for scalability. We didn't promise a brand-new data warehouse in a month. We promised clarity.

The idea for a unified platform, what would later become Tardis, was seeded during this time. Tardis was not conceived as 'yet another warehouse'. It was designed as a unifying backbone: a single environment where ingestion, storage, transformation and access could be orchestrated transparently. It introduced modular pipelines with embedded quality checks, observability and lineage by design. The goal was simple but radical: no more haunted houses of undocumented SQL, no more firefighting every Friday night. Like its fictional namesake, Tardis would be 'bigger on the inside', able to accommodate the full sprawl of HelloFresh's global data while feeling intuitive and simple to its users. At this stage, it was only a vision, a North Star. But it gave us something to move towards rather than away from.

As one engineer said to me, a few weeks into our first delivery sprint: 'For the first time, I can see where my work fits. And it feels like I'm building something that might actually last.'

When the *boxes_shipped* pipeline repeatedly broke down, stakeholders looked directly to me for answers, testing my ability to manage expectations and pressure, a balancing act that became integral to my leadership style.

That was the shift. From bottleneck to backbone.

### *When systems fail, so do offsites*

I often say that HelloFresh years feel like dog years; what we packed into a quarter would take other companies a year to process. And yet, amid the planning cycles, modernisation blueprints and framework discussions, nothing reminded us of our fragility quite like *boxes_shipped*.

It had become something of an ironic ritual.

On 30 August 2021, we kicked off our first in-person data leadership team offsite at the Michelberger Hotel in Berlin. We arrived full of energy, finally together in the same space, to talk about everything from mesh boundaries and reorganisation strategy to how we could ground our data vision in business outcomes. It was meant to be a turning point.

Then the phone rang.

One of the team called to let us know: *boxes_shipped* had failed again.

> When I gave this chapter to my wife, Louisa, to read, she paused about halfway through and said, 'It sounds too easy.'
>
> I asked what she meant, and she replied: 'Where are the 80-hour weeks? The 11 p.m. Slack calls? The times when you'd sneak out of dinner to take yet another escalation, or the weekends when we tried to plan something as a family and you were buried in your laptop because *boxes_shipped* had gone down again?'
>
> She was right. In telling the story, I had smoothed the edges. Louisa reminded me that the transformation wasn't just measured in frameworks or new platforms; it was measured in effort, exhaustion and sacrifice. The team went far beyond normal limits to hold things together, nights lost to firefighting, mornings spent writing post-mortems, afternoons pivoting priorities yet again.
>
> And *boxes_shipped* was only one of them. There were countless other fragile pipelines, brittle integrations and silent errors that demanded the same relentless attention. Each one carried its own story of pressure and recovery, each one stretching the team in ways that rarely make it into glossy strategy slides.
>
> At home, that strain was felt too. Our kids learned to recognise the glow of Slack on my phone. Conversations at the dinner table were sometimes cut short by another outage. Louisa carried more than her share so I could carry mine.
>
> Her words brought me back to the reality that transformation isn't clean. It's messy, relentless and human. And those long nights and hard conversations, both with colleagues and at home, were as much a part of the journey as any technical breakthrough. They were leadership crucibles in the truest sense.

The air changed instantly. That single asset had become infamous, a legacy pipeline holding together a critical view of our operational performance across markets. Nearly every dashboard depended on it. And yet, it was one of the most brittle, opaque and heavily patched parts of our infrastructure. At this point, it wasn't just a pipeline. It was a ticking time bomb.

And of course, it blew up just as we sat down to build the future.

We cancelled breakout sessions, opened laptops and got to work. Coordination calls started. Slack exploded. Engineers began pulling logs while our product leads braced for stakeholder escalations. The conversation shifted from 'what could we become?' to 'how do we recover, again?'

It wasn't the first time. Earlier that summer, we'd already had a string of outages: partitions failing, Amazon Web Services (AWS) S3 paths missing, data volume spikes crashing daily jobs. On one occasion, half the shipments in a major market disappeared from dashboards. The post-mortems piled up, and still the structure held by a thread.

Later that night, over a beer at the hotel bar, one of my team joked, 'Maybe we shouldn't do offsites anymore.' We laughed, but it was gallows humour. Because, deep down, we knew this wasn't bad luck. It was a signal.

We were trying to lead a transformation on top of something that wasn't designed to last. It was a lesson I wouldn't forget.

They taught us that transformation is never clean. It's bumpy, emotional, full of interruptions and unexpected resets, especially if an organisation attempts to run advanced frameworks like data contracts or continuous data quality checks (Gavish, 2023) on top of an unstable environment.

*Boxes_shipped* wasn't just a failed DAG (directed acyclic graph). It was a wake-up call.

In time, we did retire it. The fragile job was migrated into Tardis, rebuilt with proper lineage, monitoring and explicit ownership. What had once symbolised fragility became one of the first proofs that we could build differently. The day we finally decommissioned the old pipeline, the team held an impromptu toast – a small but powerful reminder that even the most painful legacy can be turned into a milestone.

But it's important to acknowledge that this was only the beginning of a longer journey. Stabilisation came first, modernisation followed, and only through 2023–25 did the order domain fully evolve and the dependency on *boxes_shipped* disappear entirely. What we celebrated that night in Berlin was not the final chapter, but a symbolic turning point: proof that the cycle of fragility could, at last, be broken.

## People: rebuilding confidence, not just capability

Technology may give you scale. But people give you trust.

When I arrived, our people were tired. Brilliant, but tired. Analysts were rewriting SQL definitions weekly, trying to make metrics match. Engineers were firefighting pipeline errors. Product managers (PMs) were building their own workarounds because asking the data team often felt slower than doing it themselves.

It wasn't a skills gap. It was a confidence gap, the same cultural rift many organisations encounter when data efforts become disconnected from business realities. Confidence erodes silently: when people aren't sure whether to trust a number, they hesitate. When they hesitate, decisions stall. Over time, that hesitation becomes cultural, a low-grade fatigue that seeps into every project.

We introduced two foundational rituals to counter this drift.

The first was HelloData YOUniversity, our internal enablement programme. It wasn't just 'training'. It was a shared language. We designed paths for analysts, engineers, PMs, marketers, anyone who worked with data. Every module made the world just a little bit more understandable. It wasn't about producing 'experts' but about giving everyone the confidence to ask, challenge and engage.

After the first YOUniversity session, one analyst wrote to me privately: 'This feels different. Like we're finally speaking the same language.' It was a small but significant sign of shifting mindsets.

Another session ended with a product lead saying, 'That's the first time someone's explained lineage in a way I could use.' That stayed with me. It showed that trust isn't only built in platforms; it's built in conversations.

The second was the quarterly data review (QDR). This became our operating cadence, a way to align on priorities, surface dependencies and keep everyone honest. QDRs moved us from reactive panic to proactive flow. They weren't glamorous, but they were grounding.

> **Quarterly data reviews**
> QDRs were structured sessions where data producers and consumers came together to review priorities, dependencies and delivery progress. They created rhythm and accountability, replacing ad hoc firefighting with a predictable operating cadence.

In 2022, as HelloFresh matured its global planning rhythm, our QDRs evolved into quarterly alliance reviews (QARs), part of a broader shift to formal yearly planning cycles across the business. The change wasn't just in the name; it reflected a deeper alignment with the company's long-term orientation. While the core intent remained, aligning across data producers and consumers, resolving tension, surfacing priorities, the QAR format brought our reviews closer to the strategic heartbeat of the business. We retained the same rituals, cadence and ownership, but now participated in a shared language used by every alliance across HelloFresh. That 'A' mattered. It meant data wasn't an exception; it was part of the operating system of the company.

As our work scaled, so did the team. But we didn't just throw headcount at the problem. We created a hybrid delivery model, a mix of internal core teams and trusted external partners embedded into our rituals. This allowed us to flex capacity while protecting consistency. It wasn't about speed for speed's sake. It was about sustainability, building a system that could last longer than the adrenaline of hypergrowth.

And slowly, the perception began to shift. We weren't the black box anymore. We were the enablers.

## Governance: from friction to confidence

When I arrived, governance at HelloFresh was mostly seen as bureaucratic overhead. It implied heavy forms, complex compliance steps and mandatory

GDPR (General Data Protection Regulation) training sessions. Most teams approached governance reluctantly, seeing it as friction rather than an enabler. I still remember a colleague joking after one compliance session, 'If governance makes us any slower, the business will start sending pigeons instead of data.' It captured the mood: governance was something endured, not embraced.

Yet, beneath that perception lay deeper structural and cultural challenges. Teams created data without clear standards or ownership, leading to isolated definitions, fragile pipelines and uncertainty around quality. As a recent industry publication noted, to effectively solve data quality issues, HelloFresh needed to address the organisational context in which data was produced, governed and consumed (McKinsey & Company, 2022a). Specifically, teams like the Marketing Data Products Tribe initially faced significant challenges ensuring data quality and consistency across diverse international markets, highlighting a disconnect between local initiatives and global governance principles.

These insights closely aligned with our internal assessments. Initial data surveys revealed widespread frustration, uncertainty about ownership, inconsistent definitions and an absence of lineage, severely limiting trust in data products. Our foundational data strategy documents echoed this sentiment, highlighting the urgent need for:

> clear governance, ownership and organisational structure to ensure HelloFresh manages valuable data assets effectively to contribute to sustainable growth.

To address these gaps, our Data Governance Function shifted focus from mere compliance to actively enabling data-driven decision making. We introduced a federated operating model, assigning named business and technical ownership to each critical domain and its data assets, an approach consistent with best practices recommended by industry leaders advocating domain-driven design and ownership as fundamental components of successful governance strategies (McKinsey & Company, 2020b).

Additionally, introducing data contracts between producers and consumers significantly altered our governance landscape. These contracts defined clear service level objectives (SLOs), outlined data quality expectations, freshness guarantees and schema stability, all enforced through observability and automated monitoring. This formalisation directly addressed pitfalls commonly identified by external experts, such as reconciling different versions of the truth, poor interoperability and frequent data changes requiring costly rework (Gavish, 2023).

**Data contracts**

Data contracts are explicit agreements between data producers and data consumers. They define what a dataset should contain, how fresh and reliable it must be and how changes will be communicated. Much like an API contract in software, they set clear expectations and reduce the risk of silent breaks, ensuring that data can be trusted and reused with confidence.

Alongside contracts, we also invested heavily in the data catalog, which became the visible face of governance. What started in 2021 as a metadata registry with scattered adoption grew into a trusted catalog of certified assets, definitions and lineage. By 2023, certifications in the catalog – gold, silver, bronze – became shorthand for reliability, and by 2024 the Atlan rollout embedded catalog use directly into daily workflows. For the first time, analysts could discover and trust assets without hunting through tribal knowledge, and leaders could point to a single, certified source of truth. The catalog was where governance stopped feeling like theory and started feeling like practice.

At this stage the catalog was still embryonic, more registry than reality. But it would later become one of the cornerstones of our governance practice, the visible front door to data, where certification, ownership and trust could be reinforced at scale.

Industry sources validated our approach, highlighting that successful data governance transformations, particularly in organisations operating a decentralised data mesh, depend on enabling domain autonomy within clearly defined governance guardrails. According to Gartner, companies successfully balancing centralised governance with decentralised autonomy achieve not just compliance but genuine trust and operational efficiency at scale (Thoughtworks, 2022).

This trust was reinforced through a clearly defined Data Product Management discipline. Our approach ensured that every data product, whether pipeline, dashboard or analytical model, had explicit product ownership, clear roadmaps and backlogs prioritised collaboratively between technical teams and end users. This structure proved vital in addressing challenges like unclear assignment of roles and lack of cross-functional alignment on business priorities.

We established structured quarterly forums (QARs, which evolved from our earlier QDR format), not just to review metrics but to reinforce accountability, governance standards and cross-domain alignment. By the end of 2024, these rituals had become deeply embedded in our governance culture, frequently cited internally as transformative in ensuring that data governance was synonymous with operational confidence, clarity and trust.

**Certification tiers and SLOs**

**What did the certification tiers mean?**

*Bronze*: Assets documented in the catalog with clear ownership, making them visible and discoverable.

*Silver*: Assets with applied monitoring, data quality checks and lineage tracking, showing they could be trusted beyond one team.

*Gold*: Business-critical assets with full governance, certified definitions and enforced SLOs.

**What are SLOs?**

SLOs (service-level objectives) are measurable targets that define how reliable and trustworthy a data asset should be. For example:

*Freshness*: Data should update every 24 hours.

*Completeness*: 99% of records must pass quality checks.

*Schema stability*: No breaking changes without notice.

By 2024, these certification tiers had become part of daily language. Asking whether an asset was Gold certified was shorthand for 'Can I bet the business on this number?'

In practice, the impacts were profound. A senior business executive, previously a vocal governance sceptic, succinctly summarised this shift: 'I always thought governance would slow us down. Now I see it gives us the confidence to move faster.'

Early meetings with initially sceptical stakeholders often ended in tension. But consistent, patient dialogue gradually transformed suspicion into trust – something I found deeply rewarding. And it wasn't just executives who noticed. Engineers reported fewer break–fix cycles, analysts said they could finally trust certified metrics and product teams told us they were spending less time arguing over definitions and more time discussing outcomes.

Governance was no longer perceived as friction. It had become fundamental. It evolved beyond compliance to become the cornerstone of our data culture, enabling teams to rapidly innovate without compromising clarity or trust.

## Enablement: the operating system of change

Among the four pillars, Enablement was always the quiet one, yet it held all the others aloft. It was never a stand-alone function but, rather, the connective tissue that turned ambition into action. Like ligaments in a body, you rarely notice it until it's missing, but when it works, everything else holds together.

Enablement translated our frameworks into something people could use: sprint rituals, metric reviews, onboarding playbooks and shared language. Beyond that, it created habits and confidence that would outlast any single initiative. It was the difference between asking people to walk a tightrope with no net and giving them a bridge with handrails. As we learned from broader studies on building a data-driven culture, true transformation requires embedding new behaviours and trust mechanisms throughout the organisation.

**Enablement**
The discipline of embedding tools, standards and behaviours into daily workflows so teams can work with clarity, trust and consistency, turning strategic goals into repeatable, scalable actions.

We learned early that teams wouldn't trust metrics unless trust was deliberately designed in. Too many definitions lived in hidden spreadsheets or in the memory of 'that one analyst who remembers how this was calculated'. People weren't duplicating work because they wanted to, but because they simply had no alternative. So we introduced Metric Standardisation, not merely as a technical clean-up but as a cultural reset. Rather than tackle every KPI at once, we started with the ones that sparked the loudest arguments. We assembled business leads and reporting owners, and together they documented assumptions, aligned definitions and created certified catalog entries. In doing so, we followed a principle often stressed in data mesh implementations: start small, deliver clarity and let the organisation build confidence step by step (Dehghani, 2019).

Almost overnight, the language changed. PMs no longer asked, 'Where did this number come from?' They asked, 'Is it certified yet?' A minor shift, perhaps, but one that carried enormous power. At one QAR, I watched a product team reference the standard churn metric across multiple regions: same logic, same documentation, no debate. That was the moment I realised this wasn't just process. It was culture beginning to shift.

The catalog became another quiet enabler. What began as a metadata registry slowly evolved into the trusted front door to data. By the time the Atlan catalog rolled out, people no longer had to chase colleagues for definitions. They could search, click and trust. I remember a marketer telling me, 'I found what I needed without having to ask anyone. That's new.' That sentence carried more weight than any governance policy.

Support mattered just as much as access. YOUniversity gave structure, but it was the day-to-day rituals, glossary links, showcase days, office hours, that made the system feel alive. Friction eased not because people became experts overnight, but because help was always close by. Slowly, the questions shifted: from 'Who do I ask?' to 'Where do I look?'

There were days when I questioned if the enablement investments would genuinely take hold. But then I'd see a new joiner find their footing in days rather than months, or watch a product team align on a shared metric without argument, and I knew the connective tissue was starting to hold. Once strong, it wouldn't just prevent things from falling apart, it would allow movement.

Meanwhile, we launched a Data Asset Modernisation stream, an initiative to transform fragile, undocumented pipelines into modular, observable products. We didn't just fix pipelines; we redesigned them with purpose, embedding data quality checks, lineage and standardised definitions from the start (Gavish, 2023). One engineer jokingly said, 'I used to feel like I'd inherited a haunted house. Now I know where the rooms are, and I have the keys.' That captured the essence of enablement better than any definition: it wasn't just about training or playbooks, it was about constructing the architecture of confidence, the subtle yet powerful force that helps an organisation begin to adopt new models and operate at scale without falling back into chaos (Dehghani, 2019).

Step by step, enablement became less about extra effort and more about how we worked. It hadn't yet transformed the culture fully; that would take time, but the shift was underway and the scaffolding was beginning to hold.

### A company learning to breathe again

By the end of that year, you could feel the change. That churn dashboard? Now it told a single story and everyone trusted it. Analysts weren't chasing fixes. PMs were aligning early. Engineers were building with less fear. People stopped asking, 'Is this the right number?' and started asking, 'What does this tell us?'

The model didn't make things easy. But it made them clear. And in complexity, clarity is everything.

At one QAR, the palpable change in morale struck me: teams weren't bracing for blame; they were prepared to celebrate their collective progress. For the first time in months, the atmosphere felt less like holding our breath and more like exhaling. This was the breathing space we'd fought to create, and the truest measure that the culture around data was beginning to shift.

It was the moment the scaffolding stopped creaking and started holding.

With the scaffolding finally holding, the question became not *if* we could move, but *how fast and how far*.

## From structure to momentum: delivering at scale

Momentum doesn't announce itself.

There's no ribbon cutting, no fanfare, just a quiet moment, often missed, when people stop asking, 'Can I trust this?' and start asking, 'What else can we do with it?' That's how I knew the Enabling Data Model was working.

In chemistry, reactions don't begin until you cross a threshold called activation energy. For us, trust was that missing ingredient. Once it appeared, the reaction was unstoppable. Trust lowered the barrier, unlocked motion and turned potential energy into momentum.

One morning, deep into 2023, I joined a QAR with our product analytics leads. What used to be a tense checkpoint full of firefighting had become something else: alignment, clarity and, dare I say it, optimism. An analyst presented a new retention dashboard. 'The metric's certified,' she said, 'built on the new standardised asset.' No one questioned it. No one hedged with their own version. That small, almost mundane moment felt like everything. It meant we'd turned a corner.

The Enabling Data Model, once a response to fragmentation, had become the organisation's internal rhythm. Not just used, but trusted. And with trust came motion.

## Technology: from survival mode to scalable motion

Before we built a modern platform, we had to survive the one we'd inherited. Our data infrastructure in 2020 was a tangle of ageing tools, patchwork scripts and clusters teetering on the edge of support, an ecosystem not just outdated, but also invisible to most of the business. Cloudera was out of warranty. Impala, our main compute engine, was stuck on a version tied to Python 2.7, which had reached end-of-life. Every deployment felt like threading a needle with boxing gloves on. Every dashboard was a potential landmine.

The problem wasn't performance, it was belief. We couldn't scale on doubt. So we paused and asked a simple but profound question: 'What would good look like if we started today?' That became our orientation point.

### *Step 1: The cost of legacy*

In early 2021, the engineering team drew a diagram capturing the entire data stack: Cloudera, Impala, legacy Hadoop jobs, Hive, ZooKeeper, half a dozen Airflow DAG clusters. Someone stepped back and said, 'This isn't a platform. It's archaeology.' They weren't wrong. The result was a labyrinth no one truly owned, one that silently failed across multiple domains.

Momentum in an environment like this is fragile. Research shows that advanced frameworks such as data mesh can falter when they're forced onto outdated systems, undermining trust in the very architecture that's meant to deliver value (Dehghani, 2019). It wasn't speed we lacked; it was stability. And stability required belief.

### *Step 2: The migration that wasn't meant to be easy*

Sunsetting Cloudera and Impala went beyond the technical; it was political, emotional and behavioural. Analysts clung to legacy logic in Tableau, stakeholders dreaded pipeline downtime and entire markets built their own private sprawl of data definitions. Small details added up: Python version mismatches blocked upgrades; essential domain dashboards had no documentation.

Pain was inevitable. To keep the migration from stalling, we introduced formal deprecation frameworks with asset audits, dependency maps and stakeholder playbooks. We tracked progress with a dashboard that showed each domain's reliance on Impala. By the end of 2023, we'd retired every Impala asset, reduced platform incidents by 67% and seen a meaningful jump in analyst net promoter score.

But the numbers tell only part of the story. What mattered most was the sense of pride that returned. Engineers who had once apologised for outages now pointed to dashboards with confidence. Analysts stopped hoarding their own extracts 'just in case'. The migration wasn't painless, but it gave people a reason to believe again.

### *Step 3: The turning point*

I knew we'd turned the corner when a new engineer, just weeks in, said, 'This actually feels like a product, not someone else's mess.' People understood how things connected. Data contracts were active, lineage was visible, observability was embedded. Metrics didn't just load faster, they were trusted.

By 2024, the platform wasn't just stable, it was something people wanted to use. We'd built a resilient stack, one that could carry the weight of the next chapter of scale (Strengholt, 2024).

## People: scaling without losing soul

By 2024, the Data Alliance had grown past 180 people, including engineering, analytics, governance and enablement. Nearly half were analysts working close to product teams. Growth at this pace is messy, but it doesn't have to be soul crushing. We believed in building a shared identity before scaling headcount, an idea often highlighted in data-driven culture research.

That's where HelloData YOUniversity came in. What began as a couple of Loom videos in 2021 had, by 2024, matured into a fully fledged global programme. It spanned technical deep dives, metric stewardship, domain literacy and detailed onboarding. We ran international cohorts, and domain-specific tracks meant a new analyst in Toronto and a PM in Berlin could both start speaking the same data language within weeks.

One of my earliest recordings opened with, 'Welcome to the mess. Scaling this rapidly wasn't without personal stress. The delicate balance of hiring and culture building felt at times like walking a tightrope, but seeing new joiners embrace our shared identity reinforced our path. We'll make sense of it together.' Over time, that phrase became something of a motto, repeated back to me by people I'd never met – proof that our shared identity was spreading.

We also introduced a hybrid delivery model, blending internal core teams and strategic external partners. 'It's the first place I've worked where external squads deliver like they're part of us,' one tribe lead said, 'because they are.' That was the essence of scaling without losing soul: growing capacity without outsourcing identity.

## Governance: from bureaucracy to belief

Governance terrified people at first. It sounded like more meetings and more gates. We did the opposite. We began with business process mapping, tracing how data actually moved across finance, supply chain and marketing. Asking 'Where does this number come from?' 'Who owns it?' and 'What happens when it breaks?' forced us to confront painful truths. One financial forecasting stream revealed four different revenue projections, none of which reconciled.

Then came the HelloFresh Data Catalog, rebuilt, relaunched and reimagined. Earlier, the catalog had been a hopeful idea. By late 2024, it was embedded practice. We had certified over 400 assets, with 100% of P1 metrics documented and discoverable. Analysts reported saving four hours a week on searching for data. Leaders began opening QARs by pulling a certified dataset straight from the catalog without hesitation.

We enforced data contracts and introduced role-based access, aligning with emerging best practices for data quality and producer–consumer agreements (Gavish, 2023). Observability caught schema drift at the source. Ownership was clear.

An analyst put it best: 'For the first time, I don't need to ask ten people if I can use a number. I just look it up, and I trust it.' Governance wasn't about friction anymore; it was about confidence at speed. Watching that shift unfold, from suspicion to reliance, was deeply satisfying. Governance was no longer our enemy. It was our ally.

## Enablement: the operating system behind it all

Although often overshadowed by technology or governance, enablement remained the quiet force that made everything *work*. Earlier, initiatives like Metric Standardisation and Data Asset Modernisation had reset expectations. By 2023–24, those same practices had become second nature.

At QARs, the debates weren't about which definition to use, but about what the results meant. Silence around definitions became its own signal, the noise of mistrust had faded. What once required ceremonies now felt obvious: of course you checked whether a metric was certified.

The catalog reinforced this shift. Certified assets weren't just listed; they were lived with. Teams bookmarked them, executives asked for them by name and analysts built on them without fear of contradiction.

Meanwhile, Data Asset Modernisation scaled into something much larger. The haunted house had been rewired. Pipelines were modular, observable and reusable. Backfills that once took days now ran in hours. For engineers, this wasn't just technical hygiene, it was liberation.

Enablement showed up in small ways too: playbooks embedded into sprint rituals, templates adapted without permission, glossary links tucked into dashboards. It was the quiet connective tissue that made the right way the easy way. And when that happens at scale, culture doesn't shift by decree. It shifts by design (Dehghani, 2019).

## The business begins to believe

It wasn't metrics or tools alone that changed everything, it was posture. In a leadership offsite, a senior executive saw a new dashboard and asked not 'Where did this come from?' but 'Is this one of the standardised ones?' That single question showed how far we'd come: no longer a black box, we were now a strategic asset.

A distinct turning point came when our chief financial officer (CFO) casually referenced a standardised dashboard without questioning its reliability. It was subtle but powerful validation. The data function wasn't a bottleneck anymore; it was something the business leaned on.

The results spoke for themselves. Our time to insight shrank from weeks to days. Data privacy requests were down from four days to under 12 hours. Analysts spent more time on strategic tasks than firefighting. And, crucially, teams used data together, not reluctantly but confidently.

Yet momentum creates pressure. With delivery came dependency. With trust came demand. Suddenly, the very success we had built exposed a new tension: 'How do we scale excellence without becoming the bottleneck again?'

Privately, I felt the weight of increasing organisational reliance. It was a testament to success, but it carried with it deep responsibility, and sometimes anxiety, about maintaining standards at scale. The answer wouldn't lie in more standardisation. It would require a new mindset.

### Looking ahead: product thinking begins

With structure in place, we saw the next evolution for HelloFresh's data landscape: a pivot from pipeline thinking to product thinking. Rather than focusing on what we could standardise further, we started asking what we should genuinely *productise*. It was no longer about speed or definition alone; it was about generating true business value by pairing robust governance with a flexible, user-centric architecture (McKinsey & Company, 2022b). That shift would be our next frontier, and our newly resilient framework was ready for it. Personally, I anticipated needing new approaches to leadership, shifting my own mindset to fully embrace and champion product thinking as the core of our next chapter.

## Beyond the model: data as a product, leadership as legacy

It starts quietly. Always. There's no fanfare, no dramatic announcement, just a subtle shift. It's that moment when the relentless push you once had to provide yields to a momentum all of its own.

For me, that transformation crystallised in mid-2024 as I attended a review session for a new churn metric in one of our key product verticals. This time, I wasn't leading the discussion; I was only observing. Analysts arrived prepared, metric lineage meticulously mapped out, experiment contexts made explicit and upstream–downstream dependencies thoroughly documented. The domain PM stood confidently alongside the data PM. The exchange was simple: 'We've tagged it for certification, aligned it with two critical experiments and it's scheduled for QBR [quarterly business review] sign-off.'

No escalation, no hesitation, no firefighting. The machinery of transformation had transcended completion, it had reached operational autonomy.

It was a profound realisation: my role had fundamentally shifted. The team no longer required constant protection or oversight; what they needed, and now had, was the autonomy and space to scale.

### The rhythm behind the rush

Time moved differently at HelloFresh. The pace was relentless; what other organisations might tackle in a year, we often delivered in a matter of weeks. But what looked like acceleration from the outside was, in truth, the product of something more composed: a carefully built rhythm of structure, intent and operational clarity.

By Q4 2023, we had launched our first broadly adopted version of the Global Data Catalog, giving teams granular insights and dramatically improving data visibility across Human Resources (HR), Finance and Marketing. Around the same time, our Presto clusters had replaced fragile, manual workflows with scalable infrastructure. But these weren't just technical upgrades. They were signals of a deeper shift, one rooted in trust, reinforced through habits and guided by the steady cadence of the Enabling Data Model.

Speed was never the goal for its own sake. It was a by-product of clarity, a result of architecture, rituals and mindset coming into sync. The Model, which had begun as a response to fragmentation, became our internal tempo. Sprint reviews, QARs, documentation standards and enablement sessions all became part of a shared pulse that made excellence repeatable.

It wasn't always visible to the outside. But internally, it felt like the business was learning to breathe again.

And that's what made the difference. Not the fireworks of delivery, but the rhythm that sustained it. A rhythm built on design, discipline and the belief that true scale doesn't just require motion, it requires music. Reflecting on this relentless pace, I acknowledged the importance of sustaining my own well-being and that of my team; balancing relentless ambition with compassion became essential.

## From asset to product

By early 2024, our focus shifted. We were no longer just repairing pipelines or modernising legacy systems; those battles had been fought. Now, it was about elevating our output from raw data 'assets' to genuine data products, a transition that resonates with the industry's push towards product thinking in analytics (McKinsey & Company, 2022b). Dashboards, metrics and analytical models evolved into curated, user-centric products, each with clear documentation and lifecycles.

Our data catalog, once an internal documentation portal, became a dynamic gateway. It actively tracked usage, gathered feedback, measured satisfaction and even flagged potential anomalies. Metrics like Pause Rate, once a notorious source of confusion, turned into exemplars of product thinking: they had dedicated owners, well-defined documentation and a lifecycle managed through formal reviews. What used to be a burdensome chore became a natural part of the continuous delivery process, grounded in the models we'd built.

As one analyst put it: I used to spend hours explaining the same definitions. Now I just share a catalog link.'

But behind this maturity was another pivotal shift, the emergence of the data product manager (DPM) role.

We were deliberate in separating responsibilities: product owners brought analytics and domain fluency, while DPMs focused on platform integration, governance and data engineering enablement. This 'two-in-a-box' structure reflected our belief that data products are both technical systems and user-facing experiences and must be treated as such (Dehghani, 2022). This transition wasn't easy for me initially; I had missteps and learned to adjust my own understanding, gaining humility about product management in data.

The impact of the DPM role was particularly visible in complex domains like Marketing and Supply Chain Management, where aligning fragmented stakeholders, establishing ownership and defining lifecycle accountability made a real difference. These early wins validated the potential of the model and offered blueprints for broader scale.

Yet, the journey was far from uniform.

While DPMs helped lay the groundwork, their influence often encountered friction, especially in navigating the boundary between the central data teams and the broader Product Organisation, which remained primarily oriented towards digital feature delivery. As a result, operationalising the full vision of 'data as a product' remained an aspiration more than a widespread reality.

Even so, the role marked a pivotal step in evolving our thinking. It introduced a new way to manage data work, not as discrete deliveries but as coherent, lifecycle-managed products. That mindset, even if not fully embedded everywhere, was a foundational part of how HelloFresh's data maturity continued to evolve.

It wasn't achieved by grand proclamations. It emerged naturally from a disciplined structure that let us scale ownership without chaos, aligning with modern best practices for data mesh and domain-oriented data management (Thoughtworks, 2022).

## Industrialising capability without losing soul

This evolution was never just about standardisation. It was about deliberately industrialising capabilities in a way that retained the spirit of the teams who built them. The groundwork laid by DPMs gave us the scaffolding to treat assets as products, and the Asset Modernisation programme became the vehicle to scale this thinking across domains. Similar to the principles of software industrialisation described by Cusumano and Yoffie (1999), our aim was repeatability without losing craft.

We introduced a simple delivery rhythm that everyone could recognise: Discovery, Planning, Execution and Closure. It gave our work a heartbeat and a common language.

- Discovery was about surfacing fragile pipelines and hidden dependencies. I remember a supply chain sprint where an analyst admitted to maintaining ten separate cost models in parallel, none fully trusted but all somehow needed. It was a quiet confession that revealed how brittle the foundations had become.
- Planning translated those discoveries into modular designs with clear ownership. These sessions often felt like therapy. People laid bare years of frustration about inconsistent naming, duplication and shadow data. Only then could we agree on simpler schemas, aligned KPIs and shared definitions.
- Execution was where engineering discipline met business pragmatism. Assets were rebuilt with schema validation, automated tests and reference checks. We often argued about whether to optimise for speed or for governance, but the framework forced us to find balance.
- Closure was the real test. It was never just a tick-box exercise. Success was measured by whether analysts reused the new definitions, whether redundant scripts were retired and whether stakeholders trusted the outputs enough to shut down their spreadsheets.

This cycle gave us repeatability without becoming mechanical. It drew on agile patterns of sprint-based capability building (Rigby, Sutherland and Takeuchi, 2016), but we applied those ideas at the level of data pipelines rather than software features. It let us scale while still listening to the people who used the data.

**Industrialisation ≠ automation**

In data, industrialisation does not mean replacing people with machines. It means codifying best practices so they can be repeated reliably across teams and domains. Automation may be an outcome, but industrialisation is about embedding consistency, from schema validation to metric reviews, without stripping away the human judgement that gives data its meaning (Davenport and Westerman, 2018).

The results spoke for themselves. In supply chain analytics, brittle cost prediction pipelines were rebuilt into modular forecasting products that could serve multiple regions with shared assumptions. In customer experience, static dashboards gave way to real-time sentiment analytics, cutting response times and improving satisfaction. In marketing, pipeline refactoring alone delivered a 33% uplift in Display ROI (return on investment).

Yet the deeper breakthrough was cultural. One engineer put it simply: 'For the first time, I don't feel like I'm firefighting. I feel like I'm building something designed to last.' That captured why industrialisation mattered. It gave us clarity and consistency, but it never asked people to surrender their craft.

I often thought of Toyota's principle of *jidoka*, which is quality built into the process with human judgement still intact (Ohno, 1988). Industrialisation, done right, was not soulless efficiency. It was a way of making trust scalable. People stopped asking whether the data could be trusted and started asking what it could teach them.

With those foundations secure, we could finally look upwards. Industrialisation gave us the scaffolding. The next challenge was reach: how to put insights into everyone's hands, not just of the few with the patience to wrestle with dashboards.

### *Delivering on the promise of AI*

Industrialisation gave us scaffolding, but scaffolding is only useful if it helps you reach higher. For us, that meant facing into the question everyone was asking by 2022: what about AI?

The promise of AI was never about shiny prototypes or vanity pilots. At HelloFresh it was about embedding intelligence into everyday decision making. That meant reimagining how insights reached people: faster, more transparent and more trusted.

We articulated this as a Self-Service Analytics Platform: a layered approach where self-service reporting formed the base, diagnostic insights the middle and conversational interfaces the peak. AI sat at the very top of this pyramid. It was never the starting point, but the outcome of solid foundations. And so we asked ourselves the boldest question yet: could we make data feel as natural as conversation?

In practice, this vision meant three things. First, reducing dependency on over-stretched analysts, so front-line teams could answer their own questions. Second, building transparency into every insight, so people understood not only the numbers but also the methods behind them. And third, instilling confidence that the insights were accurate, timely and actionable. This was not about removing people from the loop, but about giving them the tools to work with more speed and trust.

**Conversational BI**

Conversational BI refers to business intelligence tools that use natural language processing and AI assistance to let users query, explore and act on data as easily as asking a question, blending automation, explainability and accessibility.

The ambition was clear, but in practice our first steps came through targeted pilots. We began by applying natural language processing to areas where unstructured text was already abundant.

Recipe feedback was one of the richest sources. Each week, customers left thousands of free-text comments, far too many to read manually. By layering language models on top of this data, we could detect themes: recipes labelled 'too spicy' in one region, 'too bland' in another, or repeated complaints about portion size. This gave our menu planners and product developers a real-time pulse of customer sentiment that had never been visible before.

In parallel, customer service was experimenting with Conversational AI. A virtual assistant, later known as 'Brie', used natural language understanding to handle queries about delivery issues, address changes or damaged goods. It was a small but concrete example of AI bridging the gap between people and data.

Elsewhere, personalised recommendations were being enhanced with machine learning. By building embeddings of recipes and customer preferences, HelloFresh could suggest meals that felt increasingly intuitive, almost conversational in the way they reflected past behaviour.

These were early steps, not the destination. Conversational BI remained the ambition – the peak of the self-service pyramid we were steadily climbing towards. The pilots showed that natural language could unlock new ways of interacting with data, but they also underscored how fragile trust could be. Queries sometimes misfired, classifications weren't always right and people needed transparency to believe the answers. As Ransbotham et al. (2020) highlight, trust in AI systems depends on transparency and understanding of how outputs are generated.

For me, the promise of AI at HelloFresh was never about replacing human judgement. It was about giving the machinery we had built a voice, and giving people confidence that that voice could be trusted. We hadn't yet reached full conversational analytics, but the foundations were firmly in place and the direction of travel was clear.

### *The Bento Box: first steps in self-service analytics*

If Conversational BI was the ultimate ambition, our first practical step was to deliver curated self-service analytics. We knew we could not leap directly into open-ended natural language querying. The technology was still immature, trust was fragile and the variety of questions people asked was far too broad. Instead, we began with something simpler but powerful: a carefully structured set of insights, presented in a way that was accessible to different user groups but anchored in a single source of truth.

The starting point was clear. Our North American Marketing stakeholders were frustrated. The centralised analytics team faced an endless queue of requests, and the bottleneck pushed teams into extracting data into Excel or

Google Sheets. The result was misalignment, irreproducible results and isolated workflows. Every market and channel ended up using slightly different definitions of the same KPIs, leading to inconsistent strategies and noisy debates about whose number was 'right'.

This first step in self-service was designed to break that cycle. Its objective was to reduce time-to-insight, empower marketers to make faster decisions and begin building a genuine culture of data-driven decision making.

We curated the initial solution around the questions that mattered most:

- How is Customer Acquisition Cost trending week-over-week and year-over-year?
- What revenue are we generating from campaigns on Facebook and other digital platforms?
- Where are conversions stagnating, and how can we reallocate spend to improve them?
- Which channel partners are performing well, and which need intervention?

To make this work, we had to design for different personas. Some users, the spreadsheet-focused 'pivot table heroes', wanted data they could slice and drill without code. Others preferred flexible dashboards that could be tailored to their questions. A smaller group demanded direct SQL access so they could manipulate data themselves. The challenge was to cater to all three, while keeping everyone aligned on the same certified definitions.

The tooling decision was critical. We used Tableau as the backbone, pairing curated datasets with dashboard licences for most users, SQL Workbench access for advanced explorers and, importantly, Tableau's Ask Data feature as a PoC for natural language interaction. Users could type questions in plain English and, with curated synonyms and certification tags, receive answers without needing to know the underlying schema. It was not yet Conversational BI, but it moved us closer.

Governance and education underpinned the whole effort. Every dataset was documented and certified, complete with lineage, definitions and update schedules. Training programmes walked users through not only the tools but also the meaning of the metrics themselves, building data fluency alongside technical skill. As DAMA-DMBOK highlights, clear definitions and certified lineage are essential to prevent self-service from devolving into chaos and to ensure trust in the outputs (DAMA International, 2017).

Looking back, this first step was never about scale. It was about proving that self-service could be designed with intent rather than left to chance. It showed that with curation, certification and thoughtful packaging, teams could trust what they were seeing and act on it. Gartner (2018) observed that augmented analytics would be the dominant driver of business intelligence by 2025. McKinsey & Company (2022a) emphasised that scaling analytics requires as much investment in culture as in technology. And as we saw firsthand, explainability is essential if AI and analytics are to be trusted. Our early experiments reflected all three lessons.

This step was modest, but it changed expectations. For the first time, data felt designed for the user rather than for the system. And it gave us the confidence that one day, the scaffolding could reach all the way to making data as natural as conversation.

### *Augmenting decision making*

The ultimate measure of success was never how many dashboards we built or pilots we ran. It was whether decisions themselves began to change. Data mattered only if it altered the conversation in the room.

I remember one leadership review in particular. The numbers came up on the screen, and for the first time no one challenged them. No one asked whose query was used, or whether Finance had a different figure. Instead, the debate went straight to action: *what should we do next?* It was a subtle shift, almost easy to miss, but for me it was a moment of inflection. It was the first time I saw data truly augmenting decision making rather than distracting from it.

What followed was a new rhythm. Analysts no longer spent their days firefighting inconsistent queries. They had the space to question assumptions, to dig deeper into the patterns behind the numbers. Managers grew confident enough to make adjustments between reviews, acting in real time rather than waiting for the next quarterly checkpoint.

This was the essence of augmentation. It was never about replacing human judgement. It was about reinforcing it. Intuition and creativity still shaped our decisions, but now they were strengthened by a layer of evidence people trusted.

Industry research echoed what we were experiencing. Tableau defines *augmented analytics* as technology that extends rather than replaces human judgement, using automation to surface insights that people can interpret and act on (Tableau, 2025). McKinsey observed that organisations achieving the greatest impact were those that embedded analytics directly into their decision cycles, treating data as an operational capability rather than a one-off project (McKinsey & Company, 2022a). DAMA International reminded us that without clear governance and accountability, even the best analytics lose their integrity and erode decision quality (DAMA International, 2017). And *MIT Sloan Management Review* emphasised that explainability is essential for trust in AI-supported decision making; people must understand the reasoning behind algorithmic recommendations to use them responsibly (Renieris et al., 2025).

Looking back, this stage was not about flash or speed. It was cultural, cumulative and, at times, invisible. But it was the stage where data stopped being a bystander and became a genuine partner in decision making.

### *From hype to habit*

Every transformation carries a risk of stalling at the hype stage. The launch of a new tool, the buzz of a pilot, the excitement of a dashboard demo, all of these can generate noise without ever changing the way people work. What mattered at HelloFresh was whether those experiments turned into habits.

The ambition of Conversational BI was never a silver bullet. It was another layer in our Enabling Data Model, dependent on contracts, catalogs and cultural trust. Its value, we believed, would lie in habit formation. Once teams could see that AI might provide consistent, certified answers, they would begin to explore more: churn rates, forecast accuracy, cost per meal.

The turning point was not a single event but an accumulation of small changes. Analysts began to log less time on repetitive requests, because those answers were now available in certified self-service reports. Managers came to reviews armed with insights they had pulled themselves, confident enough to make recommendations without waiting for validation. And front-line teams stopped asking *if* they could trust the data, and instead asked *what the data suggested they should do next*.

One moment stays with me. I walked into a quarterly review expecting the usual cycle of queries and clarifications. Instead, I watched as a regional manager quoted a certified metric straight from a self-service dashboard. No one challenged it, no one cross-checked it and the conversation moved directly to strategy. It was a quiet but powerful sign that the hype was fading and the habit was forming.

And yet, we resisted the temptation to oversell. AI in data too often arrives with fireworks and exits in disillusionment. We remembered the lesson from our early self-service work: start contained, build trust, scale slowly. As Forrester has argued, governance is the foundation of trust in augmented analytics (Forrester, 2023). Without that, the ambition of Conversational BI would be little more than a parlour trick. With it, however, it could one day become a natural extension of decision making.

In hindsight, the ambition was never just about technology. It was about confidence at speed, the same principle that underpinned every pillar of the Enabling Data Model. For me, Conversational BI was less a product launch and more a glimpse of the future: a future where data would no longer need protecting by a central priesthood, but would speak for itself, fluently, at every level of the business.

## Decentralised doesn't mean disconnected

By 2025, embedding data roles within business domains was second nature. Analysts, engineers and PMs sat inside the functions they served, close to decisions and accountable for outcomes. But our approach to decentralisation was never laissez-faire. It was deliberately federated.

The risk of pure decentralisation is well documented. Every team defines its own KPIs, builds its own pipelines and launches its own dashboards. The result is duplication, misalignment and noisy debates over whose number is 'right'. At HelloFresh, we felt those risks early. I remember one review where a regional operations team proudly presented a cost-per-meal dashboard, only for Finance to present a different figure later in the same meeting. The clash was not about intent, but about definition. It was a glimpse of what fragmentation could look like if left unchecked.

**Federated vs decentralised governance**

In data, decentralisation pushes accountability outwards. Domains or business units define and manage their own data locally, which brings speed and ownership, but if left unchecked it risks silos, duplication and inconsistent definitions (TDAN, 2021). Federated governance provides the balance. It introduces a unifying layer of policies, taxonomies and councils that keep domains aligned while allowing them the freedom to execute within their context. This balance of autonomy and oversight is what makes large-scale analytics sustainable (Alation, 2023; Atlan, 2022).

As Zhamak Dehghani describes in *Data Mesh*, the principle of 'federated computational governance' ensures that distributed teams can innovate independently while staying connected through standards for quality, security and interoperability (Dehghani, 2019). The lesson is clear: decentralised does not have to mean disconnected. With federated governance, autonomy and alignment reinforce one another.

Federation was our answer. Quarterly analytics reviews brought domains together to challenge and align their metrics. Shared taxonomies created a common language across markets. Experimentation standards ensured that when teams tested ideas, they did so in comparable ways. Metric councils provided the final guardrail, debating definitions until they reached consensus, then embedding those definitions into contracts and catalogs.

One People tech analyst described it best: 'We no longer treat data as something we just consume. We see it as something we own.' That sense of ownership was the cultural shift we had been striving for.

I often thought of it as *a constellation with gravity*. Teams orbited independently, but the pull of common standards and rituals kept them aligned. It was not a tidy hierarchy, but it was sustainable.

Industry research reflected what we were experiencing. Databricks (2023) defines federated governance as the balance between central standards and local ownership that enables large organisations to scale analytics responsibly and consistently. McKinsey & Company (2022a) observed that decentralisation without coordination often creates isolated excellence that fails to generate enterprise-wide value. DAMA International (2017) emphasised that shared vocabulary and stewardship are what turn distributed data into a genuine enterprise asset. Thoughtworks' (2022) review of data mesh implementations confirmed the same lesson in practice: autonomy works only when paired with shared standards and rituals.

Looking back, this principle was one of the quiet strengths of our journey. Decentralisation gave us speed. Federation gave us trust. Together, they allowed scale without silos, and created an ecosystem where data was no longer guarded at the centre but owned at the edge.

## Legacy isn't a platform

Earlier in my journey, I believed our 'legacy' would be the code we wrote, the SQL that stuck around or the architecture diagrams that endured. These were the visible artefacts of our work, the things most likely to be remembered once we had moved on. But legacy turned out to be something else entirely.

It revealed itself in quieter ways. I remember scanning a Jira board one afternoon and noticing that my name was no longer attached to any tickets. The work was still being done, pipelines monitored, metrics certified, definitions updated, but the processes were carrying on without me. It was both bittersweet and liberating. The system was no longer dependent on my presence. It was working because of the frameworks we had put in place, not because of any single individual.

The same realisation struck me when a new PM confidently certified a metric without ever knowing who had built the framework that enabled it. What mattered was not attribution, but the continuity of trust. That was the legacy: a culture and an ecosystem where good practice outlived its architects.

Nassim Nicholas Taleb (2012) describes systems that do not merely survive shocks but actually benefit from them as *antifragile*. In practice, that was what I saw emerging. Each outage survived, each metric contested, each pipeline rebuilt made the organisation more capable, not less. The data culture learned and adapted, building resilience not in spite of disruption but because of it.

**Antifragility**

Antifragility, a concept coined by Nassim Nicholas Taleb, describes systems that improve when stressed, as opposed to fragile systems which break and robust systems which merely resist. In a data context, antifragility means every failure or dispute becomes fuel for building stronger, more reliable practices. Outages expose weaknesses that are corrected; contested metrics lead to clearer definitions; and each rebuild strengthens the ecosystem.

Netflix's approach to Chaos Engineering is a vivid industry example. Their Chaos Monkey tool deliberately disrupts live systems to expose vulnerabilities, ensuring that services grow stronger through stress, rather than weaker (Basiri et al., 2016). In the same spirit, data organisations that embed learning into every failure build not just robustness but true antifragility.

Industry research reinforced this insight. *Harvard Business Review* has observed that the most resilient organisations are those where routines evolve under pressure rather than collapse, using disruption as a catalyst for learning and renewal (Davenport and Westerman, 2018). Reeves and Whitaker have likewise shown that resilience depends on principles such as adaptability, diversity and embedded learning, qualities that allow systems to strengthen through uncertainty rather than simply withstand it (Reeves and Whitaker, 2020). And resilience theory, first articulated by C. S. Holling (1973), reminds us that systems are defined not only by their stability but by their capacity to absorb disturbance and reorganise.

Looking back, the true legacy was never the platform itself. It was the confidence, trust and independence that endured beyond individual leadership. It was the knowledge that each failure, each dispute, each debate over a metric left the organisation stronger than before. That was the deeper ambition: not to leave something delicate that required protection, but to build something resilient enough to thrive under pressure.

## What I hope endures

As I reflect on my tenure, I do not expect that specific metrics or even stable architectures will remain. Technologies shift, markets evolve and new challenges inevitably emerge. Rather, I hope the principle of enablement persists as a way of working, not just as a one-off initiative. I want governance to remain synonymous with confidence rather than compliance, and I hope that data continues to be seen not as a necessary evil but as a force for creativity and clarity.

Above all, I hope that in the future, perhaps years from now, some analyst I have never met will open the data catalog, check a certified metric and know, without hesitation: 'This was built with care, and it still works.'

Steve Jobs was famous for insisting that even the unseen parts of a product, the inside of a cabinet or the back of a circuit board, should be crafted with the same care as the visible parts. Not because customers would notice, but because builders would know. I recognise the same instinct in data: the lineage scripts, the schema contracts, the governance reviews. Invisible to most, they are deeply felt in the trust they create.

Industry research suggests this instinct matters. Perucci and Swanson (2024) show that trust in data systems depends as much on the invisible scaffolding that supports them as on the visible outputs, emphasising that transparency, accountability and collaboration are critical to sustaining confidence in data. Databricks (2023) describes enduring organisations as those that embed governance into culture through federated standards and continuous stewardship, rather than treating it as a compliance project (Databricks, 2023). McKinsey & Company (2022a) has observed that the companies that thrive through disruption are those that invest in data as a long-term capability and enabler of resilience, not a short-term deliverable.

That, for me, is the real legacy: not the architecture we leave behind, but the confidence, trust and autonomy we instilled in the people who inherit our efforts. My personal hope, and sometimes quiet fear, is whether this trust, carefully cultivated, will endure as the organisation inevitably changes and faces new challenges.

## Looking back to move forward

It began on a crisp Berlin morning, 15 October 2020. We had just arrived from the UK, our car packed with more than belongings; it carried a quiet mix of anticipation, purpose and the weight of a new beginning.

I've already told the story of that first day. But standing outside the HelloFresh office, taking a breath before stepping into a role that would reshape how data lived inside a hypergrowth company, is a moment that deserves revisiting. Not because it was grand, but because everything that followed still traces back to that simple step through the front door.

Looking back, the people I worked alongside profoundly shaped my leadership journey, leaving insights I carry forward even now. What surprised me most about myself during these years was the resilience I discovered and how deeply I came to appreciate that leadership is ultimately an act of stewardship.

What unfolded over the next four and a half years was one of the most intense, creative and rewarding chapters of my professional life. HelloFresh didn't operate in quarters; it operated in pulses. Weeks contained more decisions, more delivery, more transformation than most organisations manage in a year.

We rebuilt the foundation of the data function: from tangled pipelines to certified metrics, from firefighting to structure, from the black-box perception to being seen as a strategic partner. We moved quickly, but not recklessly, creating systems that would do more than deliver. They would endure. Even *boxes_shipped*, that old symbol of chaos, became a certified asset, no longer feared but trusted. A fitting reminder that even the most fragile systems could evolve when invested in with care.

And we did it together. This was never my story alone. Some colleagues followed me from previous companies, many I met there for the first time. All of them brought creativity, clarity and grit to a transformation that demanded our absolute best. They absorbed the weight. They held firm when others might have compromised. They made the rituals stick, wrote the language that became our framework, challenged the status quo and taught others to do the same. They kept showing up not because they had to, but because they believed in the work.

As April came to a close, I stepped back, gently at first, observing the model we'd built operating on its own. QARs (once QDRs) ran without me in the room. Metrics were certified with no requirement for my final sign-off. New data products emerged using the templates we'd established. The rhythm held. The belief stayed strong.

The model wasn't just a tool. It became a mindset. One that proved you don't need perfect conditions to create something lasting. Just shared belief, structured action and the will to keep showing up.

One colleague once told me: 'We stopped asking if we could trust the data, and started asking what it could teach us.' That shift was everything. It was the true marker that scaffolding had turned into culture, and that culture into habit.

Now, as I begin a new chapter, I take with me more than models and wins. I take the memory of a team who chose structure when chaos would have been easier. I take the rituals, the QARs, the catalog reviews, the enablement sessions that made belief scalable. I take the trust we rebuilt, not in one grand moment, but across hundreds of small, deliberate acts. And I carry a deeper understanding of leadership not as control, but as design; not as ownership, but as stewardship; not presence, but purpose.

If the systems we built keep serving others, if the culture we nurtured holds strong, if new ideas spring from the seeds we planted, then I'll know that our work wasn't just valuable, it was enduring.

This was never just about dashboards. It was about people and the systems we built so they could thrive. This was never just a job. It was a journey.

If there's one thing I'll always carry, it is this: in times of uncertainty, choose structure. That is where belief is built.

And as my story continues down a different road, with new challenges and new possibilities, I move forward with the same core belief: that clarity matters, that structure enables and that transformation, done right, always begins and ends with trust.

Yet, for all that endured, not everything was effortless. Every transformation, no matter how principled, carries a shadow. The same clarity that empowers can also expose. The same structure that creates order can create strain. And the same belief that unites a team can, at times, isolate its leaders.

That is where the next part of this story begins.

CHAPTER 4

# The Dark Side of the Role

David Castro-Gavino

## Introduction

Every bright promise casts a shadow.

When I first stepped into a senior data role, it felt like arriving after a long ascent, where years of persistence and belief finally met opportunity. The years of building, persuading, and proving that data could serve as a strategic engine had finally converged into a single moment of possibility. The opportunity seemed luminous, a direct line to the executive table, a mandate to build something enduring, the sense that data was at last recognised as more than a supporting function.

After years of working to earn a seat where decisions were made, I felt I had arrived at the moment the discipline itself had been striving towards. Yet light, by its nature, creates contrast. What begins as visibility can quickly become exposure. The same proximity to influence that empowers can also unsettle. Across industries, the story repeats itself: data leaders are invited to the table, only to find that the table keeps shifting.

In my own journey, I watched this shift unfold at close range. As the organisation grew, new layers of technical oversight were introduced, a CTO here, a transformation office there, and the dynamics changed overnight. What had once been a direct line of communication with decision makers became a conversation filtered through competing priorities. What had felt like partnership began to feel like translation.

At first, the change seemed procedural: more structure, more process, more operating discipline. In theory, these were signs of maturity. But in practice, the tone changed. A culture once driven by curiosity, collaboration and discovery became increasingly dominated by control, documentation and cost. Conversations that had once centred on value began to revolve around efficiency. Data, once seen as an enabler of insight, was recast as an expense to be managed.

I later came to understand that this was not a unique experience. Through conversations with other data professionals across industries, I began to recognise the same patterns repeating in different contexts. Whether in retail, finance or healthcare, the stories echoed one another: early optimism, structural friction and eventual recalibration. It was through those exchanges that I realised the challenge was not personal but systemic.

Research has since confirmed what those conversations revealed. Chief data officers have the shortest tenure of any C-suite role. The average lasts between two and two and a half years, compared with four to five for a CFO and five to seven for a CEO (Eastwood, 2022). The role that symbolises modernity often conceals a deep structural fragility.

Organisations champion the idea of data-driven leadership, but they still struggle to integrate it meaningfully into their operating models. When a new technology or transformation leader arrives, the data function is often the first to be repositioned. What starts as empowerment becomes absorption: the mandate narrows, the focus shifts and the strategic ambition begins to fade behind delivery targets.

This pattern, I realised, was not about individuals. It was about the architecture of modern organisations themselves. The way power, trust and accountability are distributed in the digital age is still evolving. And within that evolution, data occupies an ambiguous place, both everywhere and nowhere, owned by everyone and no one.

## The many-headed beast

Every data leader, sooner or later, encounters the same adversary: a many-headed beast born of structural ambiguity. One head is Blame, quick to appear whenever a number does not align. Another is Politics, whispering through decision-making corridors, shaping perception faster than truth can travel. A third is Fragility, the delicate bridge between expectations and the technical reality beneath them. And above them all towers Expectation, a giant that feeds on promises of precision, speed and transformation.

It is a creature that cannot be defeated, only managed. Cut down one head and another emerges. The shape it takes depends on the industry, but the presence is always familiar. In retail, when a promotion faltered, the first instinct was to question the algorithm rather than the merchandising strategy. In digital marketplaces, when growth slowed, it was the data pipelines that took the blame long before the product–market fit was challenged. In high-growth start-ups, ambition often outpaced infrastructure, leaving teams chasing clarity in systems that were still being imagined. In financial institutions, the beast simply wore a different mask: compliance, audit or regulation. The expectations were the same, only the language changed.

Over time, I came to understand that the beast is not a flaw in the system but a feature of it. The closer an organisation moves towards using data to inform decisions, the more it exposes the inconsistencies that already exist within its structure. Data does not create friction; it reveals it. And once revealed, it demands attention. The beast, in truth, is not the enemy. It is the mirror, reflecting the unspoken tensions between precision and perception, ambition and capability, promise and delivery.

## Why the seat burns so many

The statistics confirm what experience already teaches. The role of the CDO, or its equivalents, remains one of the shortest lived in modern corporations. According to DataIQ's *2025 AI and Data Leadership: Executive Benchmark Survey*, 84% of organisations now have a CDO or CDAO (chief data and analytics officer) in place, yet only 47.6% describe the role as very successful and well established. Just over half view it as nascent, evolving or in flux (DataIQ, 2025). The title has become commonplace, but its authority remains fragile.

This contradiction captures the enduring paradox of modern data leadership. Companies continue to invest heavily in the idea of data transformation, but few grant their data leaders the structural autonomy required to deliver it. The CDO role is elevated in ambition but constrained in execution, simultaneously tasked with delivering innovation and absorbing inherited complexity. The result is a mandate that begins with enthusiasm and too often ends in attrition. As Boyan described through the investment–value curve in Chapter 2, organisations often accelerate investment faster than they build the foundations to sustain it. What begins as promise soon collides with structural reality. The same pattern plays out in leadership, where initial optimism and funding surge ahead of readiness for change. The same DataIQ study revealed that 24% of data leaders leave their post within two years, and more than half within three, a pattern consistent across industries (DataIQ, 2025).

Reporting structures tell a related story. Deloitte's CIO Pulse Survey (Deloitte Insights, 2024) found that 63% of US technology leaders now report directly to the CEO, a marked improvement from less than half a decade ago. Yet the same proximity has not translated into stability for data leadership. For many organisations, the data function remains nested under Technology or Finance, functions that prioritise cost, control and operational efficiency over strategic enablement. Within these hierarchies, the data mandate is filtered before it begins, its strategic potential constrained by its reporting line.

The symbolism matters. Reporting to the CEO signals that insight is seen as a driver of competitive advantage. Reporting elsewhere implies that data is a utility to be managed rather than a capability to be cultivated. These organisational choices, though rarely discussed openly, quietly define the boundaries of ambition.

And so, the pattern persists. The role that promised transformation often becomes consumed by translation, reduced to explaining, defending and justifying rather than shaping strategy. Across industries, many data leaders recognise the same uneasy truth: the seat burns bright, but it rarely burns long.

## The burden of proof

If structural fragility defines the role, perpetual justification sustains it. Few executives spend as much energy proving their existence as data leaders do. In most organisations, the data function is still required to justify its purpose before it can demonstrate its value.

The paradox is striking. Nobody demands that backend engineers prove the ROI of an API, or that Marketing quantify the brand equity of every campaign. Yet for data, the burden of proof is constant and uniquely exhaustive. Every initiative must be translated into a business case, every platform renewal defended and every governance enhancement justified. The result is a form of organisational gravity that pulls the discipline away from creativity and towards defensiveness.

I have sat through reviews that were meant to be strategic but became rituals of validation. Instead of discussing outcomes, we debated foundations. Why do pipelines take so long? Why does governance matter? Why should we invest in data quality when the reports already exist? Each question is reasonable in isolation but, taken together, they become a chorus of disbelief. The technical challenges were complex enough; the additional effort of continually defending first principles was draining.

What makes this dynamic particularly corrosive is that it reinforces a cycle of mistrust. When leadership questions the value of data work, teams become cautious. They prioritise deliverables that are visible and easy to quantify rather than those that are foundational but unseen. Short-term optics win over long-term integrity. The consequence is a culture of compliance rather than curiosity, where building trust in the data takes precedence over using it.

This pattern mirrors what we explored in Chapter 2. The gulf between investment and realised value remains wide, not because of technology but because of belief. As long as organisations treat data as an experiment rather than an instrument, its practitioners will continue to stand trial for outcomes they do not control.

In my own experience, the turning point came when I reframed the question. Instead of asking how to prove the value of data, I began asking how to make its value self-evident. That meant shifting the conversation from justification to trust. When stakeholders could see consistency, reliability and clear lineage in the data itself, they no longer needed persuasion. Transparency became the proof.

This lesson, I would later realise, sits at the heart of mature data cultures. The most effective data organisations are those that stop trying to win arguments and start building systems that speak for themselves. Proof, in the end, is not a presentation. It is a lived experience.

## The human cost

Behind every dataset, dashboard and pipeline are people. Engineers fighting to stabilise fragile systems that pre-date them. Analysts answering the same questions about metric definitions for the hundredth time. PMs trying to reconcile ambition with dependency. For all the talk of platforms and frameworks, it is the people who absorb the friction.

The leader carries their frustration as well as their own. Shielding teams from organisational turbulence while keeping them motivated becomes an act of stewardship. Leadership in data is as much emotional as it is technical. You are not only building systems but protecting the people who build them.

Over time, the weight of that responsibility accumulates. The long hours spent firefighting issues that are not of your making. The quiet stress of defending your team's work in rooms where the value of data is still questioned. The tension between perfection and pragmatism, knowing that what is 'good enough' for others still feels like a compromise to you. These pressures are not isolated incidents; they are the daily rhythm of data leadership.

Burnout, in this context, is not a metaphor. It is measurable. Industry research confirms what many in the profession already feel. The 2024 Wavestone (formerly NewVantage Partners) *Data and AI Leadership Executive Survey* reported that while investment in data and AI remains high, turnover and short tenures among senior data leaders continue to be a major concern (Wavestone, 2024). Likewise, Gartner's analyses highlight that many CDAOs cite role overload, stakeholder conflict and alignment issues as leading causes of professional stress (Gartner, 2025).

The result is a revolving door at the top of data functions, where each new leader inherits both the progress and the fatigue of those before them.

For me, the recognition came slowly. It was not one moment of collapse but a gradual awareness that the job was unsustainable without a shift in mindset. Coaching and professional supervision became essential. They helped me separate ownership from control, care from burden. I learned to focus on what could be shaped rather than what could be saved.

That change did not make the pressures disappear, but it made them manageable. I began to see leadership less as the pursuit of constant strength and more as the stewardship of energy – my own and my team's. In a field obsessed with optimisation, the most valuable lesson was that resilience is not efficiency. It is endurance with purpose.

## A broader pattern

Over time, I began to recognise that my experience was not an anomaly but part of a much wider pattern. Across industries and continents, the same story unfolds with minor variations in detail but remarkable consistency in structure. Organisations want the benefits of data-driven decision making, yet many struggle to make the organisational shifts required to sustain it.

The result is a tension between ambition and capability. Data leaders are hired to transform, but often constrained by the very systems they are asked to modernise. The structural design of the organisation dictates how much impact they can have, regardless of talent or vision. In many cases, data leadership operates as a change function without the authority to change anything fundamental.

This paradox plays out repeatedly. The initial phase is one of enthusiasm and sponsorship. A data leader is brought in with a clear brief to modernise, integrate and elevate the role of data. Resources are allocated, momentum builds and the first wave of success stories emerges. But as the function matures, the excitement fades. Governance replaces innovation and the conversation shifts from opportunity to cost. The leader who was once seen as a visionary becomes a cost centre manager.

Academic research supports this recurring cycle. Michael Wade at IMD describes the lifecycle of digital and data leaders as one of ascent, acceleration, constraint and exit (Wade, 2019). The arc is consistent: early empowerment gives way to structural limits once the transformation effort challenges existing power dynamics. What feels personal in the moment is, in truth, systemic.

The same studies also suggest that this pattern is not unique to data. It mirrors what happens in other emerging disciplines that straddle the boundaries of technology and strategy. The early pioneers face the highest friction because they are redefining what the organisation is willing to accept. The very act of introducing clarity, standards and accountability inevitably disrupts established comfort zones.

The lesson, for me, was to view this not as failure but as evidence of progress. Resistance is a sign that something is changing. Friction is not the opposite of momentum; it is the cost of it. Understanding that distinction was liberating. It helped me to see that what felt like struggle was often a necessary phase in the system's own evolution.

Over time, I came to recognise that every data leader reaches this crossroads in their own way. Some walk away, others find a rhythm that allows them to stay. What separates them is rarely skill or circumstance, but perspective. Those who endure understand that the work is never about finishing the journey but about moving it forward. Data leadership is not a sprint to completion; it is a cycle of influence, renewal and reinvention.

## Building resilience

To last in this role, I had to learn that resilience is not an innate trait but a deliberate practice. The pressures do not lessen over time; you simply become better at carrying them. Technical excellence and strategic clarity may earn a seat at the table, but endurance is what allows you to stay there.

For me, resilience emerged through three lessons.

First, I reframed the purpose of the role. I stopped interpreting setbacks as personal shortcomings and began to view them as part of a broader organisational learning process. Data leadership, I came to realise, is not a static discipline but an evolving one. Expectation gaps, shifting sponsorship and fluctuating influence are not signs of failure but evidence of a discipline still defining its boundaries. Once I understood that, I could begin to accept it. The turbulence no longer felt personal but part of the landscape itself. Acceptance did not mean resignation; it meant recognising that clarity often emerges only after uncertainty has done its work.

Second, I built networks of support. Coaching, mentoring and peer groups became essential. They provided the perspective that is often missing inside the organisation. Conversations with other data leaders revealed the same struggles: the burden of proof, the friction between ambition and delivery, the fatigue of being simultaneously strategic and operational. Knowing that others were navigating similar terrain transformed isolation into solidarity. Those discussions helped me to find balance, humour and even perspective in what once felt overwhelming.

This principle aligns with the work of Richard Y. Wang (1998), one of the early advocates of the CDO role. He argued that information must be treated as an organisational asset rather than an individual burden. When accountability for data becomes collective, leaders gain the emotional space to focus on purpose rather than protection. It echoes the promise of data mesh, introduced in Chapter 1, where decentralised ownership was not just a technical model but a cultural aspiration. That understanding helped me to see that resilience is not about absorbing pressure alone but about redistributing it through shared ownership and clarity of roles.

Third, I focused on protecting the spirit of the team. Leadership is not just about setting direction; it is about absorbing shock. If the leader fractures, the team follows. I learned to act as a buffer between the noise of the organisation and the people doing the work. That meant creating space for them to think, to learn and to experiment without fear of blame. Celebrating small wins and making their contributions visible became essential acts of stewardship. Over time, I realised that resilience could be collective, not just individual.

Marc Roman Franke and his colleagues at Boston Consulting Group describe resilient data organisations as those that empower their people, invest in quality and maintain trust across the business (Franke et al., 2023). That framing resonated deeply with my own experience. A resilient data team is not one that avoids challenges but one that can recover quickly from them, because the people inside it feel seen, valued and trusted.

This human dimension of resilience is echoed in research by Vera et al. (2020), who describe resilience as 'thriving under adversity', a process that combines emotional awareness, shared purpose and the capacity to adapt. Their work confirmed what I had learned intuitively: that endurance in leadership is not about resistance to change but about the ability to transform through it.

Tom Redman (2023) also captures this truth. He argues that resilience in data leadership is built not on technical superiority but on trust. Trust begins with quality and transparency. When data is reliable, relationships strengthen; when relationships strengthen, the organisation itself becomes more resilient. The tools may change, but the human foundations remain constant.

Resilience, I found, is not about stoicism. It is not about pretending the challenges do not exist, or absorbing them without effect. It is about developing the capacity to bend without breaking, to keep moving without losing purpose. In a world obsessed with optimisation, the most valuable quality may not be speed or precision but the quiet endurance to stay the course.

## Why stay?

So, why stay in a role that tests patience, politics and persistence? The answer, for me, lies in the moments when light breaks through the pressure.

There is the moment when a new data product finally runs cleanly at scale, transforming chaos into clarity. The moment when a unified definition resolves months of debate and the boardroom, for once, speaks a shared language. The moment when an analyst, once buried in manual reporting, delivers an insight that changes a strategic decision. These moments may be rare, but they are real. They remind you that progress is possible, even if perfection is not.

Over time, I came to understand that the value of this role is not defined by the absence of struggle but by the presence of meaning. Leadership in data is not only about building technology or frameworks; it is about building confidence in truth. The challenges that make the role difficult are the same ones that make it significant. Every conversation about quality, governance or trust is, in essence, a conversation about integrity.

Resilience and purpose are inseparable. As Tom Redman (2023) writes, the most effective data leaders are those who see themselves not as custodians of systems but as stewards of truth. That stewardship carries weight, but it also carries privilege. Few roles offer such proximity to how decisions are made, how organisations learn and how people see the world through information.

Ron Carucci (2025) expands this idea in his work on emotional strength in leadership. He argues that endurance comes not from detachment but from emotional clarity, knowing why you are there and what you are prepared to fight for. For me, that understanding arrived late, shaped by experience rather than ambition. It was never about being the loudest voice in the room but about being the one that spoke for data when silence would have been easier.

The truth is that leadership in data will always live in tension: between ambition and constraint, innovation and governance, vision and pragmatism. That tension can never be removed, only reduced and made manageable. It is a sign not of failure but of relevance. To lead in this space is to stand in that intersection, balancing contradiction with conviction.

In the end, I learned that data leadership is not about survival but about legacy. The role may be temporary, the structures imperfect and the battles recurring, but every conversation that builds trust leaves a mark that lasts beyond tenure. The goal is not to escape the shadow but to ensure that the light keeps reaching further. That is what staying truly means.

What follows in Chapter 5 is an attempt to distil those lessons into something more enduring. The Data Manifesto is not a theory but a reflection of this lived experience, a way of giving form to the principles that have quietly guided the work all along.

CHAPTER 5

# The Data Manifesto

David Castro-Gavino and Boyan Angelov

## Introduction

I vividly remember the first feeling when David and I drew the model. Both of us, at the same time, thought: *this is it, we've nailed it.* It felt like we had captured the objective reality of what an ideal data-driven organisation could look like. For a moment we were giddy with excitement, wanting to rush forward and share it with everyone we knew.

But, as the initial enthusiasm subsided, a realisation set in. Models, no matter how elegant, are still academic in nature. They are accessible to some: those who enjoy abstraction, visual thinking or the intellectual exercise of frameworks. Yet they inevitably exclude many others. In our experience, most of the people we wanted to reach were not craving another diagram. They were looking for something more human: stories, narratives, lived experiences that connected to their reality. We asked ourselves: *what can bridge this gap?* The model alone was not enough. The HelloFresh story was powerful because it grounded the framework in practice. But even that was not sufficient. We needed something simpler, more memorable, more transportable.

That is when we realised we did not need to reinvent the wheel. There was precedent. Software had faced a similar crisis at the turn of the century. Teams were drowning in heavyweight processes, endless documentation and rigid delivery cycles. The breakthrough came not in another methodology, but in a shift of philosophy: the Agile Manifesto, seven principles and a language that reframed how software work was done. Agile did not just change practices; it changed mindsets. Let's have a look at the Agile Manifesto (Beck et al., 2001), in its raw form.

**Manifesto for Agile Software Development**

- We are uncovering better ways of developing software by doing it and helping others do it.
- Through this work we have come to value:
  - individuals and interactions over processes and tools
  - working software over comprehensive documentation
  - customer collaboration over contract negotiation
  - responding to change over following a plan.
- That is, while there is value in the items on the right, we value the items on the left more.

We thought: *why can't data have the same?* Yes, it is ironic. Data people are often sceptical of Agile. And for good reason: the rituals of sprints, story points and stand-ups often chafe against the exploratory, experimental and enabling nature of data work. Frameworks such as CRISP-DM or Microsoft's Team Data Science Process have long tried to adapt Agile to the quirks of analytics. Yet the deeper inspiration is undeniable. Agile showed that a field could be redefined not by tools or structures, but by a shared philosophy and guiding principles.

That is the opportunity we saw for data. Not another operating model. Not another set of best practices. But a manifesto: a philosophy that educates, guides and inspires. A set of principles that are easily remembered, teachable and immediately applicable. Principles that help teams make sense of the daily dilemmas of data work: Should we build or buy? Should we measure everything or focus on what matters? Should we chase the new tool or fix the system we already have?

Here, then, is our attempt to do for data what Agile did for software: to move beyond frameworks and into first principles (Rigby, Sutherland and Takeuchi, 2016).

## Principle 1: Tech is never the problem, you are

Modern data teams have developed a reflex: when something breaks, underdelivers or spirals into complexity, the blame is pinned squarely on the technology. 'The tool doesn't scale.' 'If only we had a better platform.' These responses are comforting fictions. They absolve us from self-examination.

The uncomfortable truth is that technology is rarely the problem. It is a mirror, faithfully reflecting the maturity or dysfunction of the organisation that wields it. A platform underused often signals a failure in enablement. A tool misconfigured reflects a gap in governance. A product that never finds adoption usually reveals a lack of user empathy in its design or delivery.

This principle sits at the very heart of the Data Manifesto: until organisations take responsibility for how they frame, govern and deliver data work, no technology will ever be enough. Remember: we are dealing with socio-technical complex systems.

## Lessons from industry

The urge to innovate can be relentless. I have seen teams build ingestion frameworks that were technically dazzling: batch and streaming support, schema evolution, multiformat orchestration. On paper, the systems looked bulletproof. Yet adoption often faltered. Analysts defaulted to manual, ad hoc scripts and local teams stuck with CSV uploads. The problem was not the tool but the absence of enablement, documentation and ownership.

In these cases, technology did not fail; the system around it did. Adoption followed only when companies shifted focus from engineering elegance to human enablement; when personas were mapped, interfaces simplified and onboarding embedded into training. The platform itself did not change, but the story around it did. The lesson is consistent: without investment in enablement and ownership, even the most advanced platforms remain shelfware.

Netflix faced a similar lesson when it introduced Chaos Monkey, a tool designed to randomly disable services. The technology was disruptive, but it succeeded because engineers embraced accountability and resilience. Without cultural readiness, Chaos Monkey would have been intolerable. Instead, it became a symbol of system strength (Basiri et al., 2016).

In the UK National Health Service (NHS), electronic health record systems were technically robust, yet failed to gain traction in many hospitals. Clinicians reverted to paper or shadow spreadsheets, not because the tools were broken, but because enablement and stewardship were missing. Adoption improved only when NHS trusts invested in training and clear ownership (Greenhalgh et al., 2010).

These examples show the same truth: technology can only amplify the current state – whether it is good, or bad. Without ownership, enablement and empathy, even the most advanced platforms fail.

## Why technology isn't the root cause

This pattern is not unique. Studies consistently show that failed digital transformations are more about people and process than about platforms. McKinsey & Company's (2018, 2019b) research has long shown that fewer than 30% of digital transformation efforts succeed, and in some studies only

16% sustain their gains. Similarly, Davenport and Miller (2022) argue that the success of AI initiatives depends less on algorithms and more on human–machine collaboration, trust and design for adoption.

Classic organisational thinkers knew this long before the era of cloud and data mesh. Conway (1968) showed how systems inevitably mirror the communication structures of the organisations that build them. Ohno (1988), the father of the Toyota Production System, emphasised that tools are useless without a culture of continuous improvement. As explored in Chapter 3, through Taleb's idea of antifragility, the systems that endure are those that grow stronger under stress. True resilience is socio-technical, not merely technical.

### From blame to ownership

Blaming technology is the easy way out. Taking ownership of the human system is harder. It requires humility: admitting that lack of clarity, governance or enablement, not the platform, is the real blocker. It demands empathy: understanding what users actually need, not what the roadmap says. And it calls for leadership: treating tools as products, embedding enablement and making adoption itself a measure of success.

When teams internalise this principle, the reflex to chase the 'next shiny tool' weakens. They focus instead on extracting value from what they already have. They stop treating platforms as silver bullets and start treating them as living systems that thrive only when culture, process and accountability align.

In the end, technology is never the problem. We are. Which, paradoxically, is good news, because it means we can also be the solution.

*Maxim:* Fix the system, not the tool.

## Principle 2: Scalability, performance and cost – choose two

In theory, modern data systems promise everything: infinite scale, lightning speed and minimal cost. Vendors (or, remember, potential merchants of complexity) speak of platforms that are limitless, elastic and effortless. Reality is less forgiving. Every architectural decision involves trade-offs. Trying to optimise for all three leads to brittle systems and unmet expectations.

If you want scalability and performance, you will pay for it. If you want performance and cost-efficiency, you will likely compromise on growth. If you want scale and cost control, you should expect slower response times. The question is not 'how do we have it all?' but 'what matters most right now?'

This principle calls for architectural humility. It challenges us to define priorities based on use case, not ideology. It demands that we revisit decisions regularly. And it urges us to make constraints visible, so we can navigate them wisely rather than blindly. Mature data teams do not chase the mythical perfect set-up. They make transparent, context-driven trade-offs.

## Lessons from industry

The promise of scale in cloud data platforms is intoxicating. Migration often delivers early wins: queries that once took hours now run in minutes, and teams celebrate the speed. Yet it does not take long for Finance to sound the alarm. Costs begin to spike, and elasticity, the very feature that unlocked performance, becomes a liability.

I have seen this moment crystallised in a CEO's blunt question: 'Am I going to be another CEO pulling out of Snowflake?' It captured the unease perfectly. The issue was not the platform itself, but how it was governed.

Workloads had not been optimised. Lineage was unclear. Consumption was unchecked. Elasticity had been treated as if it were free, when in fact every cycle carried cost. The turning point comes when a company introduces discipline:

- governance on environment sizing so workloads are right-sized
- cost visibility by domain so teams understand the balance between performance and spend
- best-practice playbooks so engineers can optimise queries, caching and materialisations.

Only when trade-offs were made explicit: speed for Marketing, cost control for Finance, scale for Supply Chain, did balance return. The lesson is not that Snowflake is flawed, but that no platform can deliver all three dimensions without governance and human judgement.

Capital One went through a similar reckoning after aggressively migrating workloads to the public cloud. The bank saw early wins: faster product launches, more flexible experimentation and significant reductions in on-premise infrastructure. But then the honeymoon ended quickly. Consumption-based pricing models meant that poorly optimised workloads drove exponential cost growth. Internal reports showed that what was celebrated as agility on the engineering side was being felt as budget overruns in Finance.

The company's response was to pioneer FinOps (financial operations) practices, embedding financial accountability into engineering teams. Instead of cloud being seen as a central IT bill, individual teams were made accountable for their consumption. Dashboards exposed costs by workload;

budgets were delegated to product teams; and engineers were trained to treat performance tuning as both a technical and a financial discipline. In this way, the trade-off between scalability, performance and cost became transparent. Capital One's journey was a cautionary tale, but also a model of how financial discipline can transform cloud chaos into sustainable value (Conway, Saleme and Tyrman, 2023).

Spotify confronted the triangle of constraints differently when scaling its experimentation platform. As the company grew, the need for thousands of concurrent A/B tests became central to its product-development culture. To support this scale, the platform prioritised performance and throughput, ensuring that tests could be run reliably and quickly across massive user bases. The trade-off was clear: less critical analytics queries outside the experimentation pipeline often experienced slower response times.

What distinguished Spotify was not that trade-offs existed, but that they were explicit and framed as design choices. In their engineering blog, Spotify described how performance guarantees were ring-fenced for experimentation workloads, while cost efficiency and speed were deliberately compromised for less time-sensitive jobs. This honesty allowed stakeholders to align expectations with reality. Instead of chasing perfection, Spotify demonstrated that aligning architecture with strategic priorities, in this case, experimentation as the heartbeat of product development, was the path to sustainable scale (Spotify Engineering, 2020).

These cases show the same truth: no platform can deliver all three dimensions. Only deliberate choices can.

## Why trade-offs matter

This triangle of constraints is not unique to data. It echoes the 'iron triangle' of project management: scope, time and cost, where improving two almost always comes at the expense of the third. Holling (1973) showed that ecological systems also balance competing priorities: resilience, efficiency and adaptability. In each case, the art lies not in escaping trade-offs but in managing them deliberately.

Organisations seduced by vendor promises of limitless scale often overlook the hidden costs of consumption-based pricing. McKinsey & Company (2022c) note that the fastest-growing firms are not those that build for perfection, but those that align architectural choices with strategic priorities and revisit them frequently.

### From ideology to context

The most dangerous phrase in data architecture is 'best practice'. What is best in one context may be disastrous in another. Mature data teams resist ideology. They accept that choices have costs, and that these costs shift as conditions change. They document constraints, revisit them and make trade-offs visible to stakeholders.

This principle asks leaders to replace illusions with honesty. You cannot optimise for everything. You can only optimise for what matters now. The mark of a mature data culture is not the absence of compromise, but the ability to compromise transparently, wisely and in the service of value.

*Maxim:* Balance beats perfection.

## Principle 3: Buy, don't build (unless you can afford it)

The urge to build is seductive. It promises control, precision and differentiation. For some, it even becomes a badge of honour. But in most cases, building your own data tools is a costly detour from delivering value.

Off-the-shelf solutions offer speed to impact. They carry the benefit of shared learning curves, security updates and robust documentation. They free teams to focus not on infrastructure but on insight. That is not to say never build. But the bar should be high. Custom solutions make sense only when your needs are truly unique, and when you have the budget, patience and skill to own the result end to end. Build only when the problem is core to your business advantage. Otherwise, buy, adapt and move.

### Lessons from industry

Teams are often tempted to build their own data catalogs, convinced that their needs are unique. Engineers sketch out lightweight discovery layers, confident that they can add features as needed. But what starts simple, with lineage, tagging and search, quickly balloons into months of work. Role-based access, glossary integration and usage tracking are not optional extras; they are baseline expectations.

In practice, the conversation itself often proves decisive. Building means pulling engineers away from enabling analysts and into maintaining a fragile internal tool. Buying a SaaS catalog, by contrast, typically delivers 80% of what is needed within weeks. More importantly, it frees the team to focus on what matters: driving adoption, clarifying ownership and curating high-value datasets. The value lies not in the catalog's codebase but in how people are enabled to trust and use the data it exposes.

Airbnb followed a similar path. In the early 2010s, it invested heavily in developing Dataportal, a bespoke internal data discovery platform. While it shaped a strong culture of data democratisation, the engineering costs of maintaining it at scale grew steeply. Over time, Airbnb leaned more heavily on commercial solutions and open-source components, recognising that sustaining proprietary infrastructure distracted from product innovation. The lesson was clear: building had value at first, but buying freed engineers to focus on Airbnb's true differentiator, delivering world-class user experiences (Williams et al., 2017).

Uber took the opposite route with Michelangelo, its machine learning platform. Here, building was essential because no off-the-shelf solution could handle Uber's global scale and real-time demands. Michelangelo provided competitive advantage in areas like fraud detection, dynamic pricing and personalised recommendations. Yet even Uber acknowledged the cost: Michelangelo required continuous reinvestment and deep in-house expertise to sustain. The build decision worked only because the use case was mission critical and justified by scale (Uber, 2017).

Together, these stories highlight the same principle: building is not inherently wrong, but it is costly. The question is not whether you can build, but whether you should.

## The temptation of reinvention

There is an old saying in software: 'The second system you build is the one you should have built first.' Frederick Brooks (1995), in *The Mythical Man-month,* described this as the 'second system effect': the tendency of engineers, having learned from the limitations of their first design, to overcompensate in the second by adding unnecessary complexity. The temptation of reinvention is powerful. Building allows us to imagine control, to design for every edge case, to tailor tools exactly as we like. It flatters our engineering instincts, suggesting that if only we start from scratch, we can design something purer, more elegant and more suited to our needs.

History, however, shows the hidden costs. Cusumano and Yoffie (1999) described how industries repeatedly suffer when firms overinvest in custom tooling rather than leveraging shared infrastructure. Industry analysis shows that organisations can spend 60–80% of their IT budget just maintaining legacy or bespoke systems, while innovation budgets shrink accordingly (Roberts and Eisert, 2024). What begins as a symbol of craftsmanship can quietly become a burden, draining resources for years.

Examples abound. Financial institutions built custom risk engines in the 1990s, only to abandon them two decades later in favour of vendor systems with better support and compliance. Media companies invested in bespoke content management systems, only to migrate to WordPress and Drupal once they realised that building infrastructure was not their differentiator. Even technology leaders fall into this trap: Facebook rebuilt its internal configuration management system three times before conceding that off-the-shelf and open-source solutions could do the job with far less pain.

Taleb (2012) might call this fragility by design: tools that appear strong because they are custom fitted, but collapse under stress because they lack the resilience of battle-tested alternatives. Systems that thrive in production are those hardened by diversity of use cases and supported by broad ecosystems, not those maintained in isolation by a single team.

## When to build

There are times when building makes sense. If you are Google developing Borg, or Netflix creating Chaos Monkey, the case is clear. The problem is central to your strategy, your scale is unique and the investment is justified by competitive advantage. In these rare cases, the solution itself is part of the company's moat.

Netflix's Chaos Monkey, for example, was not a vanity project but a cultural artefact. It embedded resilience testing into the DNA of the organisation and gave Netflix a reliability advantage in cloud-native streaming that competitors could not easily replicate (Basiri et al., 2016). Google's Borg, which eventually inspired Kubernetes, emerged because no commercial solution at the time could manage container orchestration at Google's unprecedented scale (Burns et al., 2016).

But these examples are the exceptions, not the rule. For most organisations, the opportunity cost of building outweighs the benefits. Every engineer maintaining bespoke infrastructure is an engineer not focused on enabling customers or improving business outcomes. Building is justified only when the use case is mission critical, non-substitutable and worth sustaining as a long-term investment.

Mature teams treat building as a conscious strategic choice, not as a reflex.

## The carpenter's toolbox

Think of your data stack like a carpenter's workshop. No craftsperson builds their own saws, hammers and chisels. They buy them, sharpen them and learn to use them well. What they build is the furniture, the house, the product that gives them distinction. The same applies to data.

If you are a retailer, your value lies in customer insights, not in maintaining a bespoke query engine. If you are a pharmaceutical company, your advantage lies in accelerating clinical trials, not in building your own data catalog. Tools are enablers, not the end product.

Building tools makes sense only if those tools themselves are your craft. For Google, container orchestration was part of its craft. For Uber, Michelangelo was integral to pricing and fraud detection. For most others, the discipline lies in focusing on the craft of using tools to create value.

*Maxim:* Buy when you can, build when you must.

## Principle 4: If your use case is not measurable, you don't have a use case

What gets measured gets managed. That maxim, popularised by Drucker, has become almost a cliché. Yet, in data it is astonishing how often we forget to apply it to ourselves. Software is already difficult for non-technical leaders to evaluate, often perceived as a black box. Data, with its layers of pipelines, platforms and models, is even harder to assess. Many initiatives are enabling in nature: data engineering teams building tooling for data scientists, or analysts preparing dashboards for business stakeholders. The temptation is to say, 'Our impact cannot be measured.'

That excuse is dangerous. If we, as data leaders, cannot provide evidence that our products move the needle, who should? If our discipline is to demand data-driven decision making from others, we must apply it to ourselves. Measurement is not optional. It is the foundation of credibility.

One of the most effective tools is the KPI value tree. It provides a structured way to link strategic objectives to measurable outcomes, outputs and supporting metrics. KPI value trees help to align engineering, analytics and business teams around a shared line of sight and reduce complexity by showing how work at every level connects to organisational value. A study by Kiron et al. (2023) shows that companies that succeed with data and AI initiatives attach smart KPIs to their strategic goals and refine them regularly to maintain alignment.

### Lessons from industry

I have repeatedly seen companies invest heavily in building impressive suites of dashboards for operational efficiency. They are often clean, fast and technically elegant. Yet months later, usage metrics tell a different story: almost no one opens them. A handful of analysts may bookmark the pages, but front-line managers ignore them. The impact is effectively zero.

The problem is rarely the dashboards themselves. It is the absence of measurable goals. Success is never defined. Is the aim to reduce decision-making time, to improve forecast accuracy or to lower costs? Without targets, adoption cannot be judged and the dashboards become decorative.

The turning point comes when a company introduces usage tracking and ties each dashboard to a business outcome. Forecasting dashboards are evaluated by error reduction. Marketing dashboards are judged by their role in campaign optimisation. Operations dashboards are tracked by improvements in fulfilment efficiency. The numbers tell the story: some dashboards are abandoned, others are refocused and a few become critical assets.

The lesson is clear: a use case without measurable impact is not a use case. It is a distraction.

Microsoft encountered the same challenge in its Azure AI initiatives. Early pilots showcased technical prowess but lacked business anchors. For example, chatbots could parse queries elegantly, yet no one could say whether they reduced customer-service costs or improved satisfaction scores. Adoption improved only when Microsoft reframed projects around measurable business outcomes, such as reducing churn by a percentage point or cutting average call centre handle time by two minutes. By making the metric the product, the teams ensured that value was visible to both engineers and executives (Davenport and Miller, 2022).

Research by Kiron et al. (2023) has shown this pattern across industries. Companies described as genuinely data driven were not those with the most dashboards or largest data lakes, but those that attached measurement discipline to their initiatives. One retail bank abandoned more than half of its machine learning pilots when it became clear they were not shifting loan approval times or reducing default rates. By contrast, firms that tied metrics to customer experience or revenue growth saw adoption soar. The difference was not in the sophistication of the models but in the discipline of measurement.

Healthcare has provided some of the starkest reminders. A 2019 UK National Audit Office review found that several UK NHS trusts invested millions in AI diagnostic pilots, but without clearly defined metrics for accuracy improvements or patient outcomes. As a result, projects struggled to scale, and trust in the systems eroded. In contrast, a smaller initiative, focused narrowly on reducing missed appointments by texting reminders, was widely adopted because its outcome was measurable, cheap to track and meaningful to staff and patients (National Audit Office, 2019).

### Why measurement matters

This principle reflects a universal truth. Drucker's maxim has been critiqued for oversimplification, but its essence holds: what cannot be measured risks being ignored. Davenport and Miller (2022) stress that the success of AI projects hinges on clear, measurable outcomes that align with business objectives. Research from *MIT Sloan Management Review* reinforces that data-driven cultures are distinguished not by access to data but by disciplined measurement of value (Kiron et al., 2023).

Measurement is not just about proving worth to finance teams or executives. It is about creating feedback loops. Without metrics, teams cannot know whether to double down, pivot or stop. Holling (1973) described resilience as a system's ability to absorb disturbance and still function. Feedback signals are what allow systems to adapt. Without them, organisations keep investing energy into dead ends.

### The illusion of enabling work

Perhaps the hardest challenge is for teams whose work is enabling in nature. Data engineering, governance and platform roles often resist measurement, hiding behind complexity. Yet even here, proxies can be found. Time-to-insight, percentage of self-serve queries, reduction in duplicate pipelines or decreased downtime are all measurable. They may not capture everything, but they capture enough.

The point is not perfect precision. It is visibility. A measurable proxy is infinitely better than a claim of immeasurability.

### The compass, not the map

Think of measurement as a compass, not a map. A map tells you exactly where to go. A compass does not. But a compass tells you whether you are moving north or drifting south. Metrics do not need to explain everything. They need only to indicate whether the direction of travel is aligned with the destination.

Mature data teams do not obsess over finding the perfect metric. They insist on having one that matters.

*Maxim:* If you cannot measure it, you cannot manage it.

## Principle 5: Stop measuring everything: start measuring what matters

As with many things, the truth lies in the middle. Data teams often swing between extremes: either ignoring measurement altogether or drowning themselves and their stakeholders in an ocean of metrics. Once the habit of data-driven decision making takes hold, the temptation is to overindulge. More dashboards, more KPIs, more reports. But complexity rises, signal gets lost in noise and energy is wasted on chasing numbers that mean little.

Here, Pareto's principle offers clarity. Roughly 20% of the metrics we track usually capture 80% of the value. The rest is clutter. If we fail to prioritise, we end up practising what I once called 'dashboarding as a sport'. Data becomes performance art: colourful, busy, but devoid of impact.

## Lessons from industry

One common pitfall in hypergrowth businesses is the unchecked proliferation of metrics. Different teams define KPIs in their own way, leading to dashboards that overlap, contradict or confuse. Terms as basic as 'active customer' or 'churn' end up with multiple competing definitions. The result is predictable: trust erodes, energy is wasted in reconciling numbers and leaders spend meetings debating interpretation rather than deciding action.

This is not unique to any one sector. In many scaling organisations, the push for speed leads to metric inflation. Supply Chain, Marketing, Operations and Finance teams all create dashboards with their own logic. Without ruthless prioritisation, measurement becomes an end in itself, dashboards proliferate, but decision quality declines.

The turnaround comes when a company begins to standardise metrics and impose scarcity. Instead of tracking hundreds of indicators, teams are required to define a small number of 'North Star' metrics directly tied to business outcomes. Everything else is treated as supporting context. By making ownership explicit and surfacing certified metrics through catalogs, an organisation creates both trust and accountability. Analysts no longer have to reconcile definitions across domains. Executives regain confidence in a single version of the truth.

The lesson is clear: less is more. Standardisation and prioritisation are not constraints but enablers. They cut through noise, reduce duplication and create the foundation for scale. With fewer, trusted measures, a company moves faster, builds alignment and avoids drowning in its own dashboards.

Google went through a similar reset with its OKRs. In the early years, teams often overloaded themselves with dozens of key results. The outcome was predictable: no one knew which objectives mattered most, and progress was diffused across too many directions. As John Doerr (2018) recounts, Google institutionalised a discipline of focus: three to five measurable objectives per team, reviewed quarterly. Crucially, OKRs were designed to be transparent and visible across the company, forcing teams to prioritise only those measures that aligned with broader strategy. This sharpened accountability and made it easier to distinguish between vanity measures and true progress.

Research from *MIT Sloan Management Review* illustrates this same dynamic across industries. Organisations that track too many KPIs often end up ignoring most of them. One study found that when a company reduced its KPI set dramatically, decision making became faster and clearer. By focusing on a concise set of measures tied directly to strategic outcomes, the business aligned behaviour, improved trust in its data and restored clarity of purpose (Morgenshtern, Rosenstein and Allen, 2022).

The phenomenon has been described as metric overload. LogRocket (2024) warns that excessive metrics create analysis paralysis, where valuable insights are buried in noise. Enlighten Services (2023) similarly highlight how 'metric clutter' undermines clarity and slows action. In practice, organisations that present hundreds of indicators to executives end up with debates over interpretation rather than progress. The breakthrough comes when leaders enforce ruthless prioritisation, retaining only those measures that guide real decisions.

## Why less is more

The danger of over-measurement is well known. When teams are flooded with metrics, trust in data erodes and attention fragments. The solution is rarely to collect more data, but to focus on fewer signals that carry meaning. Reducing the number of measures is not simplification for its own sake; it is how clarity, confidence and accountability return to the organisation. Pareto's law reminds us that most value comes from a critical few indicators. The challenge is not to measure everything, but to identify and champion the measures that truly matter.

## The gardener's lesson

Think of metrics like plants in a garden. Plant too few, and the soil lies barren. Plant too many, and they choke each other out. A wise gardener knows which plants will bear fruit, and tends to those. The rest are thinned or pruned. So it is with metrics: we must cultivate only those that feed decision making, and prune away the rest.

## From vanity to value

Mature data teams know that every metric is a choice, and that choice must be justified by the value it delivers. They resist the pressure to measure for measurement's sake. They do not confuse activity with impact. They design metrics to drive behaviour, not to decorate dashboards.

The question to ask is always the same: does this measure guide a decision, or is it vanity?

*Maxim:* Fewer metrics, greater impact.

## Principle 6: Beware of pilotitis (but do experiments)

Pilot projects are everywhere. They are exciting. They offer the thrill of a clean slate: a fresh idea, a greenfield codebase, no legacy integration headaches. Pilots are also seductive for another reason. They deliver quick results. They impress investors, delight executives and convince partners that we are 'on trend'.

But there is a reason why so few data and AI pilots ever reach production. Pilotitis is a syndrome: the habit of starting many pilots without the intention, resources or discipline to take them into full-scale delivery (Figure 5.1). Pilots become shiny distractions. They promise transformation but deliver only temporary excitement. And when expectations are sky high, budgets are empty and the software never scales, trust in data erodes.

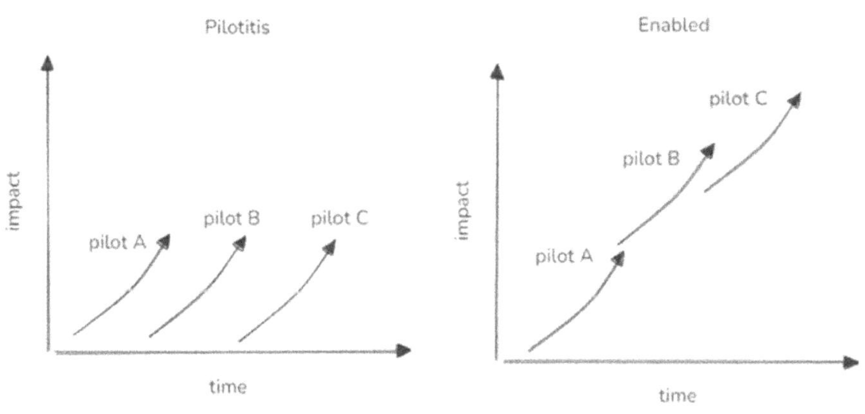


**Figure 5.1** *Pilotitis vs enabled ways of working.*

### Lessons from industry

I have repeatedly seen AI forecasting pilots dazzle in the lab. Accuracy improves, prototypes look elegant and executives are intrigued. But beneath the surface lurk thorny questions: How will the model integrate with ERP (enterprise resource planning) systems? Who will maintain it? What governance is in place for retraining? Too often, none of these are addressed. When the time comes to scale, engineers scramble to retrofit the pilot into production pipelines, business users complain about unexplained predictions and trust quickly evaporates.

Healthcare offers a vivid illustration. The UK NHS launched a wave of AI pilots for diagnostics and patient triage. Early prototypes showed promise, from radiology image recognition to cancer screening. Yet many were abandoned when thorny issues of governance, integration into clinical workflows and accountability for errors went unresolved (Heaven, 2020). What dazzled in trials faltered at scale.

Financial services have faced the same trap with AI fraud detection. Banks have repeatedly piloted models that outperformed existing systems in accuracy tests. But, when scaled, the pilots collapsed under the weight of high false-positive rates, opaque decision logic and integration gaps with legacy transaction systems. The result was not greater trust but increased operational burden and customer frustration.

These examples show the same pattern: prototypes impress in isolation, but without integration, ownership and governance, they fail to scale.

## Why pilotitis persists

The phenomenon of pilotitis is becoming widely recognised. Industry commentary indicates that a significant majority of AI pilot programmes stall before production, largely because integration and operational ownership were not addressed. McKinsey & Company's more recent research suggests that organisations running numerous isolated pilots often expend resources without generating measurable value (Sawaya et al., 2025). Davenport and Miller (2022) stress that experiments create value only when they are embedded into workflows where humans and machines collaborate effectively.

Executives want quick wins. Vendors want case studies. Teams want to try new technologies without the burden of ownership. These incentives explain why pilotitis thrives, but they also reveal how it can be overcome.

## The firework and the furnace

Think of pilots like fireworks. They light up the sky, attract attention and dazzle in the moment. But fireworks do not keep you warm. What warms the house is the furnace, designed for endurance, built to run safely day after day. Pilots are fireworks. Production systems are furnaces. The wise leader enjoys the fireworks but invests in the furnace.

### From experiments to scale

Mature data teams still run pilots, but they do so with discipline. Each pilot is framed as an experiment: What hypothesis are we testing? What metrics will prove or disprove it? How will it integrate into existing systems if successful? And who will own it in production?

Pilotitis thrives when these questions are ignored. It withers when they are made explicit.

*Maxim:* A pilot without a path to scale is just theatre.

## Principle 7: You have no right to ask for a budget unless you know how you contribute to the value chain

Budgets are the truest test of value. Every product, every service, every pipeline or API is part of a larger value chain. Yet, too often, data teams treat their work as self-contained. They describe it in technical jargon that excites their peers but leaves executives cold. 'Serverless ELT' and 'streaming architecture' mean little to a CFO in an elevator. What matters is the contribution to outcomes: faster fulfilment, lower churn, better customer experience, higher margins.

If you cannot articulate how your work advances the organisation's value chain, you have no right to ask for funding.

### Lessons from industry

I have seen data teams pitch ML models with dazzling technical detail from algorithms, ingestion pipelines and streaming performance, only to watch budget committees hesitate. Executives want to know what this means for the business: will it reduce cost per acquisition, improve return on spend or accelerate fulfilment? When the link to outcomes is absent, funding stalls. When the same work is reframed in terms of clear contribution to business levers, budgets are released. The technology does not change; the articulation of value does.

The experience of Procter & Gamble shows this clearly. The company experimented with increasingly sophisticated marketing attribution models. At first, pitches focused on the technical architecture and the variety of data sources involved. Yet funding flowed only when the models were tied directly to business impact, demonstrating how much incremental sales could be achieved for each marketing dollar spent. Executives did not approve a model; they approved a measurable path to higher return on media investment.

In financial services, JP Morgan faced similar dynamics when building AI-driven risk models. The underlying architecture was complex, involving high-frequency data feeds and advanced credit risk modelling. But budget was not secured on the strength of the technology. It was justified because the models reduced capital requirements, improved compliance efficiency and helped the bank avoid regulatory penalties. The case for funding was not 'streaming pipelines' but 'reduced risk and freed-up capital'.

**How to get budgets approved for invisible (enabling) data work (Boyan)**

For an article for the *CDO Magazine* in 2024 (Angelov, 2024), I did a series of interviews asking data leaders about their personal methods for convincing their C-level partners to provide financial support for otherwise invisible – and hard to explain – data work. An essential element in approaching this is to understand the incentives of both your organisation and the individuals responsible for making such decisions. I found that negative incentives (that is, being motivated by pain rather than gain) were the prevalent lever, rather than focusing on 'innovation'. For example, in the compliance context for a pharma company, the fear of having incorrect numbers in reports is often enough to justify significant investments in data quality initiatives.

Across sectors, the pattern is the same. Executives fund contribution to the value chain, not technical sophistication.

## Why value chains matter

Michael Porter's (1985) value chain model remains relevant decades later. It shows that every organisational activity either creates value or erodes it. McKinsey & Company note that data leaders who successfully secure investment tie their initiatives directly to strategic levers such as growth, productivity and resilience, rather than to technical features. Their research shows that high-performing organisations treat data and analytics as integral parts of the value chain, not as standalone enablers (McKinsey & Company, 2019a).

When data teams fail to connect their work to value chains, they are seen as cost centres. When they succeed, they become multipliers of business value. We looked at this issue in Chapter 2 (section 'How to fulfil the promise: understand the business'), because only by tracing how data flows into real decisions can leaders shift the perception of data from overhead to advantage.

## The bridge builder

Think of data initiatives as bridges. Engineers may admire the materials, the curvature, the technical feats. But the mayor approving the budget cares about only one question: does this bridge connect communities and drive commerce? A bridge that looks impressive but connects nothing is a monument, not infrastructure. Data projects are the same. Unless they connect to business value, they remain monuments.

### From jargon to outcomes

Mature teams learn to translate. They explain APIs in terms of faster service delivery. They describe pipelines in terms of reduced time-to-insight. They pitch models in terms of lower risk, higher conversion or more efficient operations. They meet stakeholders where they are, using the language of value, not the dialect of engineering.

Budget is not a right. It is earned by showing where and how data contributes to the chain of value creation.

*Maxim:* No value, no budget.

## Principle 8: Start with the end: work backwards

Data and AI products are complex by nature. So many moving parts, tools and even languages can be integrated into the same codebase. Requirements shift, edge cases appear in production and what began as a simple solution can become an unmanageable system. The danger is that teams focus on building features rather than outcomes.

An essential mindset to adopt is to think backwards. Conceptualise the end result even before a single line of code is written. Imagine the value created, the problem solved, the decision enabled. Write a press release for the future product and ask your stakeholders and users if they would buy it. If the answer is 'No', the product may not be worth building.

### Lessons from industry

Amazon institutionalised this mindset through its 'Working Backwards' approach. Product teams begin by drafting a hypothetical press release and FAQ for a product that does not yet exist. The press release forces clarity: what problem is being solved, who the customer is and why they should care. If the story is not compelling, the product is not built. This discipline has shaped everything from Kindle to Amazon Web Services, ensuring that products are anchored in customer value rather than technical ambition (Bryar and Carr, 2021).

The UK Government Digital Service (GDS) adopted a similar approach when building GOV.UK, a single portal for government services. Early prototypes risked becoming patchworks of agency-specific features. By working backwards from a clear vision, 'one site, one experience,' the team resisted fragmentation and forced every feature to pass a simple test: does this make services simpler and clearer for citizens? The result was an award-winning platform used by millions.

In financial services, some banks learned this lesson the hard way. AI pilots for customer service chatbots were launched to showcase cutting-edge technology. But without starting from the end – reduced call centre wait times, improved resolution rates and better customer satisfaction – the bots created frustration rather than value. Only when teams reframed success in terms of measurable outcomes did adoption improve.

## Why building backwards matters

Working backwards creates alignment between technology and value. Michael Cusumano and David Yoffie (1999) noted that software projects often fail because they optimise for technical features rather than business outcomes. McKinsey & Company (2024) note that data leaders who secure investment tie their initiatives explicitly to strategic value, not architectural features.

Amazon's method shows that working backwards is not simply a planning tool but a cultural shift. It demands clarity, storytelling and empathy for the user. It avoids the trap of 'feature creep' by forcing teams to define why the product exists before asking how to build it.

## The architect's sketch

Think of a data product like a building. An architect does not begin by ordering bricks or pipes. They begin with a sketch of the finished structure, imagining how it will be used, where people will walk, how light will flow. Only once the end is clear do they design the details of construction. In the same way, data teams must sketch the end state before writing code.

## From vision to delivery

Mature data teams adopt working-backwards rituals. They define the problem in business terms. They write the 'press release' that describes the impact. They test the narrative with users and executives before investing in engineering. And they revisit the vision regularly to ensure that delivery remains aligned with outcomes.

Products built this way are not only technically robust but also deeply relevant. They begin with the end in mind and work backwards to make it real.

*Maxim:* If you cannot tell the story of the end, do not start the beginning.

## Case study 5.1: Building backwards at an enterprise (Boyan)

In many different parts of the book we discuss the challenges of 'boiling the ocean' that we face in data. There is a saying in German, 'Erst schauen, dann bauen', which translates as 'look first, then build'. There is a similar saying in Bulgarian. I have so many stories about enabling activities in data that are bottlenecked because of an analysis paralysis: 'we have so much data, we don't know even where to start', and have been working on different methods of reducing scope for data and even software projects. This is an active focus of the whole product/data thinking, use-case-first approach that has been adopted in start-ups and tech-first organisations in recent years. But how do we do it for data and AI?

Normally in consulting, I am the one who brings innovative methods to clients, but in this particular case the client's Product Owner had an interesting idea. My work with this enterprise client was focused on ensuring that the team built successful products to serve other data- and AI-related teams in the larger organisation. But the scope was so big, and there were so many things we could do. The client proposed: 'You know what, I read about this cool product-first process at Amazon, called Building Backward, maybe we should try it?' The basic premise of the process is shown in Figure 5.2.

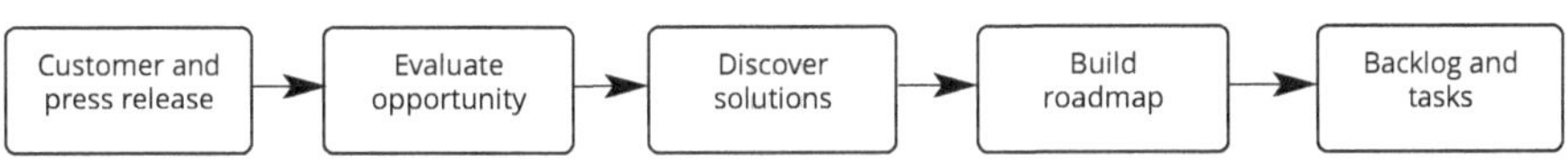


**Figure 5.2** *Amazon's Building Backwards method.*

The idea is that even before a single line of code is written, the team has to sit down and write the press release that should accompany the product. It should be as realistic as possible – for example, including testimonials from happy customers, a cool-sounding name and, of course, the specific benefit that this product will offer to users (generative AI is an excellent tool for generating such press releases). We wrote several press releases for several different products that we thought could be interesting (the ideas were generated in a standard use case ideation canvas). We then took the press releases to meetings with potential customers and teams in the wider enterprise and conducted interviews. We showed the press release as if the product was already existing and asked the question, 'If we build this solution would you be willing to pay a certain price for it?' Based on their feedback, we could prioritise and select two products to build.

You can see that this is somewhat different from a simple requirements gathering and scoping session. We could really focus on the end user, and absolutely no technical work was done (excepting some very minor feasibility work).

The product selected eventually proved successful, and we saved a great deal of time and money in building something that people really would use. Sometimes you just have to start at the end – build backwards.

## Principle 9: Your new framework is probably a cargo cult

The history of technology is littered with frameworks that promised transformation but delivered confusion. The danger is not in frameworks themselves, but in how they are adopted. Too often, leaders copy the outer form of success without understanding the inner logic. They mistake rituals for principles, ceremonies for culture. The result is what anthropologists have labelled as a cargo cult: the imitation of surface behaviours in the hope that results will follow (see Chapter 2).

Agile ceremonies without agile mindsets. Data meshes without governance or product thinking. Frameworks transplanted wholesale from Silicon Valley into contexts that have little in common. The risk is always the same: a borrowed framework becomes a burden rather than a guide.

### Lessons from industry

Spotify's team model is the most famous example of a cargo cult in tech. The language of squads, tribes, chapters and guilds spread rapidly across the tech industry. Start-ups, consultancies and even government agencies adopted it. The authors themselves cautioned that it was still evolving and not a finished blueprint (Kniberg and Ivarsson, 2012). What companies copied was not Spotify's adaptive culture, but its branding. The ritual survived, but the principle was lost.

Scaled Agile Framework (SAFe) tells a similar story. Promoted as a way to bring agile practices to large organisations, it has been widely adopted, particularly in corporate IT. Yet many implementations have been criticised for becoming bureaucratic exercises, focused on templates and ceremonies rather than adaptability (Leffingwell, 2021). Teams complain that they spend more time maintaining the framework than delivering value.

The hype around data mesh illustrates the same risk discussed in Case study 1.1. Zhamak Dehghani (2019) described it as a socio-technical shift built on decentralised ownership and domain-driven design, but many firms still treat it as a technology procurement exercise. They rename their data lakes as meshes, install new platforms and declare victory. As shown in Case study 1.1, without organisational change the mesh remains a relabelled monolith.

### Why cargo cults persist

Cargo cult adoption is tempting because it reduces uncertainty. Leaders want recipes, not riddles. They want to believe that importing the 'Spotify model' or the 'mesh architecture' will solve their challenges. Consultants and vendors amplify the effect, marketing frameworks as plug-and-play solutions. The truth is more demanding. Every framework is contextual. What worked for Spotify, Amazon or Netflix worked because of their culture, scale and timing. McKinsey & Company (2025) found that high-performing organisations treat operating models and frameworks as unique to their context, designing a 'fingerprint' rather than copying templates. Davenport and Miller (2022) likewise stress that process design works only when it aligns with the actual workflows and incentives of people using it.

### The mirror, not the mask

Frameworks should be mirrors, helping organisations to reflect on their own principles and gaps. When treated as masks, adopted for appearances, they conceal rather than clarify. Cargo cults collapse not because the frameworks are inherently flawed, but because they are applied without understanding.

### The lesson

Mature data leaders approach frameworks with scepticism. They study the principles behind them, adapt selectively and discard what does not fit. They resist the pressure to imitate and instead ask: how does this framework help us create value, in our context, with our people?

A framework is a tool, not a talisman.

*Maxim:* Adopt principles, not rituals.

## Principle 10: Preach data, but not to the choir

Data leaders often fall into a familiar trap. Surrounded by peers who understand their language and frustrations, they spend much of their time speaking to each other. The conversations feel productive, even therapeutic. But alignment within the data tribe is not the real challenge. The harder, more important task is to educate, influence and partner with colleagues outside the tribe: Marketing, Operations, Finance, Supply Chain, or Product.

Preaching to the choir may build harmony, but it does not change the congregation.

The responsibility of data leaders is not only to advance technical maturity but to expand organisational understanding. This means learning to frame insights in the language of outcomes, not schemas; stories, not pipelines. It means treating every conversation with non-data colleagues as an opportunity to bridge worlds, not reinforce silos.

## Lessons from industry

Airbnb discovered this when it realised that dashboards and models, however sophisticated, were not being widely used outside the data team. To address the gap, it launched Data University, later expanded into Data U Intensive, a training programme designed specifically for non-specialists. PMs, marketers and operations staff were taught to query, interpret and apply data in their daily roles (Feng, Coffman and Grewal, 2017). By equipping business teams with basic literacy, Airbnb created a culture where decisions were informed by data across the company, not just within the data function.

The UK NHS offers a cautionary tale. Efforts to improve data quality and reporting often remained confined to the information governance and IT functions. Clinical staff, who needed the insights most, were rarely engaged in design or education. The result was predictable: technically sound systems that were mistrusted or underused by doctors and nurses. Only when data initiatives began to include clinicians in design, training and communication did adoption improve (Greenhalgh et al., 2010).

Research from *MIT Sloan Management Review* highlights that successful data-driven organisations invest heavily in literacy and culture, ensuring that business functions, not just data teams, understand and apply insights effectively (Kesari, 2025). Díaz, Rowshankish and Saleh argue that creating a data culture is one of the key determinants of analytics success. Successful organisations build a culture where people make decisions on the basis of data and where analytics is embedded in workflows, not simply a tool boxed in technology (Díaz, Rowshankish and Saleh, 2018).

## The translator's role

Think of data leaders as translators. A translator does not simply repeat words; they convert meaning into a language that the audience can understand and act upon. Preaching data to peers may feel natural, but translating it for colleagues across the organisation is where real progress happens.

## From choir to chorus

Mature data teams resist the comfort of the choir. They see the bigger opportunity: to turn the whole organisation into a chorus, aligned around a shared language of data-informed decision making. This requires patience, empathy and humility, but the rewards are exponential.

The irony is that by teaching others, data leaders also expand their own understanding. They discover how marketing frames success, how operations measure efficiency, how finance evaluates risk. Each dialogue sharpens the relevance of data and deepens its integration into value creation.

*Maxim:* Preach data beyond the tribe, or risk irrelevance.

## Principle 11: If everyone owns the data, no one does

You have probably sat through one of those meetings at some point in your career. A project is failing or a deadline is missed, and responsibility is assigned not to an individual but to a team or, worse, to a committee. Even before the meeting ends, everyone knows the truth: nothing will be delivered. Diffusion of responsibility kills momentum.

Data is no different. Its shared nature makes it dangerously easy to duck accountability. Pipelines cross functions. Metrics travel across departments. Dashboards blend sources. With each handover, responsibility blurs. In the vacuum, ownership is claimed by everyone in theory and by no one in practice.

Personal accountability is essential. For data, that means clear stewardship. Who owns the metric definition? Who is responsible for data quality? Who has the mandate to decide when a dataset is deprecated? These questions must have answers, and those answers must connect to KPIs, incentives and performance reviews.

### Lessons from industry

One global retailer learned this lesson the hard way when reporting 'active customer' figures to the board. Marketing, Finance and Operations each had their own definition. Marketing included free trial users, Finance excluded them and Operations adjusted the figure by churn rate. Each dashboard told a different story. In one board meeting, three different numbers were presented. Trust evaporated. It was only when stewardship was formally assigned, with Finance owning the canonical definition and publishing it through a certified pipeline, that alignment returned. The number did not become perfect, but it became trusted because it was owned.

Healthcare systems show the same pattern. Van Belle and Mayhew (2016), studying a rural health district in Ghana, found that fragmented governance between multiple agencies, with unclear roles and accountability, led to duplication, mistrust and weak decision making. Their conclusion translates directly to the data context: formal structures alone do not solve ownership problems unless responsibilities are enforced and visible.

Loufek et al. (2024) describe how Mayo Clinic tackled similar challenges by embedding stewardship roles into its data governance. Clear accountability for data quality, explicit ownership of definitions and transparent reporting mechanisms helped overcome fragmentation in care data and restored trust in analytics pipelines. By pinning ownership to individuals, Mayo created the conditions for reliable, shared data across its health system.

## Why ownership matters

Research in organisational theory makes the risks of collective ownership clear. Ostrom (1990), in her work on the 'tragedy of the commons', showed how shared resources degrade when individual accountability is absent. Redman (2023) argues that data quality failures are rarely technology problems but almost always responsibility problems. Without clear ownership, no amount of governance tooling will fix the trust deficit.

This is why federated governance models, such as those described by Atlan (2022) and Alation (2023), emphasise stewardship roles. They accept that while data flows across the organisation, ownership of definitions, pipelines and quality must be pinned to individuals. Stewardship is the antidote to diffusion.

## The lighthouse keeper

Think of data stewardship like tending a lighthouse. The beacon serves every ship in the harbour, but the responsibility to keep it lit rests with one keeper. If that role is left to 'the community', the light goes dark. Ownership ensures that the signal remains strong for all who depend on it.

## From excuse to action

The complexity of data's shared nature is real, but it cannot be an excuse. It is a call to action. Organisations that take ownership seriously design stewardship into their operating models. They make accountability visible. And they connect responsibility to incentives, so ownership is not an honorary title but a real job with measurable consequences.

In data, as in life, clarity of ownership is the first step towards trust.

*Maxim:* Data without an owner is data without trust.

### Principle 12: If data is not an asset, it is a liability

We speak often of data assets. They are the gold nuggets, polished by domain experts, packaged as products and trusted by consumers. Yet for every polished nugget, there are piles of unrefined ore. Data that sits unused, unloved and ungoverned. These are not neutral. They are liabilities.

Unused data clutters our systems. It inflates storage costs. More insidiously, it clutters the mental space of analysts, engineers and business users who must sift through noise to find signal. In an age where cloud storage feels cheap, the real costs are hidden: the burden of complexity, the drag on productivity and the risks of non-compliance. GDPR, HIPAA (US Health Insurance Portability and Accountability Act) and CCPA (California Consumer Privacy Act) all remind us that forgotten data can quickly become toxic.

#### Lessons from industry

More than once, I have seen companies mistake volume for value. The assumption is simple: if storing some data is good, storing all of it must be better. But when data has no purpose, it quickly becomes a liability.

In financial services, the Basel Committee on Banking Supervision (2018) reported that global banks were holding petabytes of redundant or duplicate data. Instead of enabling insight, excess data inflated costs and created compliance risk. Inconsistent 'golden sources' of risk data led to regulatory fines, forcing banks to adopt strict retention and stewardship policies.

Healthcare has experienced the same issue. Investigations by the US Department of Health and Human Services (2020) revealed that many data breaches stemmed not from active systems but from neglected archives of patient records. Without lifecycle management, forgotten datasets became liabilities that carried both legal and reputational consequences. Hospitals that introduced stewardship roles and retention discipline significantly reduced their exposure.

Cloud-era organisations face the same challenge. Grande et al. (2020) show that while many firms pursue data growth as a strategic goal, they often underestimate the indirect costs of complexity and upkeep. Inefficient data usage, redundant storage and fragmented governance can erode value instead of enhancing it. Without oversight and lifecycle discipline, data hoarding undermines trust, slows adoption and increases operational risk.

Across industries, the story is the same. Without ownership, use cases and lifecycle discipline, data stops being an asset. It becomes clutter, debt and risk.

### Why liability matters

Redman (2023) makes the case bluntly: poor-quality and unused data do not just fail to create value, they destroy it. DAMA-DMBOK (DAMA International, 2017) stresses that unmanaged data carries legal and operational risks, particularly where retention policies are unclear. The reality is simple: unowned, unused and unmanaged data accumulates interest like debt.

### The attic full of junk

Think of an old house where every broken chair, every cracked vase and every box of unused clothes is kept in the attic. At first it seems harmless, but over time the clutter grows. You cannot find what matters. The weight strains the beams. Some items even attract pests. Only when you clear the attic, keeping what is useful and discarding what is not, does the house feel whole again. So it is with data. Cluttered systems carry risks, while curated ones create value.

### From hoarding to stewardship

The hardest shift is cultural. Many teams cling to the idea that more data is always better. But mature organisations learn that more data is often more liability. Value comes from stewardship, curation and clarity of purpose. Every dataset should either serve a use case or exit the stage.

*Maxim:* Unused data is not free, it is debt.

## Principle 13: Data modelling is more important than anything (do it as early as possible)

First-principles thinking has many fans in the tech community. The idea is to strip a problem down to its essentials and rebuild from the ground up. Few areas in data demand this mindset more urgently than modelling.

Without clear models, no amount of tooling can save you. How can you take advantage of foundation models or generative AI if seven different terms exist for the same customer, product or transaction? How can analytics drive action if metrics are defined differently in every dashboard? Data modelling may feel abstract, slow and disconnected from immediate business value, but it is the bedrock on which every use case rests.

## The temptation to postpone

Data teams often push modelling to the back of the queue. It looks less glamorous than ML pilots or flashy dashboards. It feels like 'boiling the ocean', because defining entities, hierarchies and relationships touches every part of the business. And it is hard. It demands deep domain knowledge, negotiation across stakeholders and uncomfortable trade-offs.

Yet postponing it is far more costly. Every inconsistency postponed multiplies downstream. Different names for the same thing mean duplicate pipelines, conflicting metrics and endless reconciliation exercises. Early gaps in modelling customer lifecycle data have caused entire projects to stall in many organisations as teams argue over definitions of 'active', 'churned' or 'paused'. When companies invest in clarifying the model, disputes diminish and productivity rises.

## Lessons from industry

Financial services offer a clear example. In the wake of the 2008 financial crisis, regulators identified inconsistent data definitions as a key factor behind poor risk reporting. Banks were forced under Basel Committee principles (Basel Committee on Banking Supervision, 2018) to adopt common data taxonomies for risk categories, counterparties and exposures. Without modelling discipline, risk systems could not reconcile figures, creating billions in regulatory fines. With consistent models, reporting became more reliable and compliance became achievable.

In healthcare, the adoption of electronic health records (EHRs) highlighted the same truth. Greenhalgh et al. (2010) found that inconsistent definitions for basic entities, such as 'patient encounter', created chaos across hospitals. Doctors and nurses mistrusted dashboards because the underlying models were not standardised. Only when health systems harmonised models across providers did analytics start to deliver meaningful clinical insights.

McKinsey & Company (2022d) observed the same pattern across sectors, noting that organisations that achieve meaningful scale in data and analytics are not those with the most advanced technology stacks, but those that build disciplined taxonomies, hierarchies and models underpinning data maturity.

## Why modelling first matters

Good models ripple upwards. They make descriptive analytics more reliable, prescriptive analytics more actionable and predictive analytics more trustworthy. Redman (2023) stresses that poor definitions are the single biggest driver of data quality failures. DAMA-DMBOK (DAMA International,

2017) identifies modelling as a foundational discipline for governance, not an optional layer.

The paradox is that modelling feels least urgent just when it is most important. Like laying foundations for a house, it is slow, invisible and expensive. But without it, nothing built on top will stand.

### The cartographer's wisdom

Think of data modelling as drawing maps. Explorers may want to race ahead, but without a shared map, they lose themselves in the wilderness. A good map does not capture every tree or stone. It focuses on what matters: landmarks, boundaries, routes. In the same way, data models should not aim to document every data point, but to establish the structures that guide exploration and decision making.

### From burden to enabler

Organisations that treat modelling as a burden condemn themselves to endless debates and fragile analytics. Those that treat it as an enabler build durable systems, where new technologies can be integrated and trusted. Modelling is not a distraction from business value. It is the hidden scaffolding that makes value possible.

*Maxim:* Model early, or reconcile forever.

## Principle 14: Balance offence and defence in your projects

A good fitness programme works because it is balanced. You do not only train arms or legs, you strengthen the whole body. Ignore one set of muscles, and you invite injury. The same is true for data work. An organisation that overinvests in offence, such as advanced analytics, ML and dashboards, without corresponding attention to defence, such as data quality, governance, data catalogs and stewardship, is building fragility into its system.

The imbalance is seductive. Offence is glamorous. Predictive models and AI demos win attention, while data catalogs and governance often feel mundane. But without a strong defensive core, offensive plays collapse. Bad data undermines ML. Inconsistent definitions erode trust in dashboards. Lack of governance makes regulatory compliance a ticking bomb.

### Lessons from industry

Healthcare offers a striking example. During the COVID-19 pandemic, governments invested heavily in predictive models for case surges and hospital capacity. In many countries the forecasts proved unreliable, not because of the models themselves but because of inconsistent and incomplete reporting from hospitals and testing centres. Later studies showed that when governments standardised definitions, improved data lineage and strengthened reporting governance, forecasting accuracy and policy usefulness increased significantly (Araja, Berkis and Murovska, 2022; Van Beusekom, 2024).

In retail, Walmart's analytics teams discovered that inventory optimisation algorithms were frequently undermined by poor product master data. Duplicate product codes and inconsistent attributes meant that forecasts were misaligned with reality. The company's response was to pair its advanced analytics investments with major initiatives in data quality and governance, leading to more accurate replenishment and improved margins (Redman, 2023).

Technology companies have learned the same lesson. Google's reliability engineering culture emphasises that sophisticated AI models are useless without defensive investments in logging, monitoring and observability. Sculley et al. (2015) describe how neglecting 'hidden technical debt' in data systems causes models to decay, with performance collapsing not because the algorithms are wrong but because the inputs are corrupted.

Across industries, the lesson is clear: offence cannot succeed without defence.

## Why balance matters

Redman (2023) argues that offensive gains from analytics cannot compensate for defensive weaknesses in data quality. Research supports this view. Studies show that organisations which balance governance and innovation tend to be more resilient and deliver stronger long-term performance. *MIT Sloan Management Review* highlights that companies integrating experimentation with structured governance frameworks achieve faster learning without compromising trust (Kiron et al., 2011). Similarly, Rogers (2016) observes that sustainable digital transformation depends on building innovation and control as complementary, not competing, forces.

## The athlete's core

Think of data initiatives like athletics. A runner who trains only their legs may run fast for a time, but without core strength, their stride collapses under stress. In the same way, an organisation that invests only in offence will stumble when the weight of poor data quality drags it down. Strength comes from balance.

## From imbalance to integration

Mature organisations design portfolios that pair offence with defence. Every analytics initiative is matched with an enabling investment. For every ML model, a data quality check. For every dashboard, a metric steward. For every new platform, a governance process. Offence and defence are not rivals; they are complements.

*Maxim:* Strong offence requires stronger defence.

CHAPTER 6

# A Model in Practice

David Castro-Gavino

## Introducing the model

Across decades in different industries and roles, we found ourselves asking the same question: there must be patterns and organisational set-ups that all successful data-driven companies share. In Chapters 1 and 3, we described how so much of the essential work is invisible, the hidden mass beneath the iceberg. Dashboards, models and tools sit at the tip, but without a foundation of governance, ownership and enablement, they cannot sustain their weight.

Like the MP3 format that compresses sound by removing inaudible frequencies while preserving what matters most, mature data organisations learn to reduce complexity without losing fidelity. They identify the structural signals that truly carry value and filter out the operational noise.

What lies at the bottom of the iceberg is not volume but clarity, the patterns and foundations that enable data to flow with rhythm and purpose.

As we reflected on this, we debated whether what we were building was a 'framework' or a 'mental model'. The difference is not semantic; it is practical, and you can have a look at Figure 6.1. Frameworks are prescriptive. They set out tasks and activities that can be followed step by step to reach a particular goal.

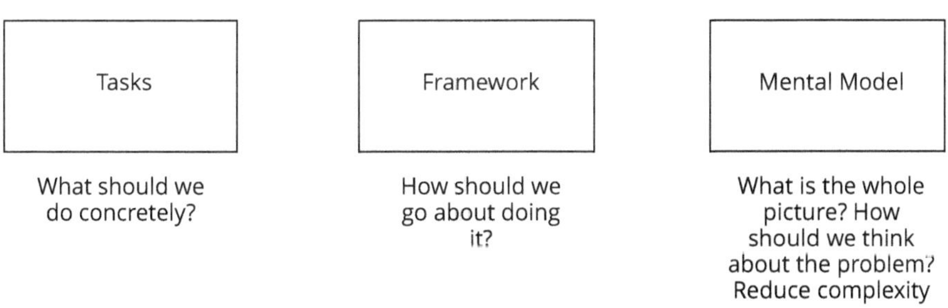


**Figure 6.1** *The differences between tasks, frameworks and mental models.*

In Boyan's earlier book, *Elements of Data Strategy* (Angelov, 2023), a framework is laid out for how to design a data strategy: three distinct phases of due diligence, design and delivery, executed in sequence. As Boyan wrote there: 'Frameworks are most useful when they provide clarity of action, showing practitioners what to do next in a complex environment.' Frameworks give direction. They answer the question 'what should we do?' But they can also carry the risk of becoming rigid.

A mental model, by contrast, answers a different question: 'How should we see?' It does not tell you every step to take, but it provides a new picture of an otherwise complex and opaque system. In that sense, it is similar to the approach of *Team Topologies* (Skelton and Pais, 2019), which also presents a mental model that helps teams to visualise and adapt organisational structures rather than prescribing rigid processes. By shifting perspective, a mental model allows leaders to adapt existing frameworks or design new ones in ways that fit the unique context of their organisation.

**What is the Enabling Data Model?**

The Enabling Data Model is a diagnostic system for aligning people, governance, technology and enablement so as to unlock scalable, trustworthy data value.

Unlike traditional maturity models, it does not measure static progress. Instead, it helps organisations to diagnose friction, clarify roles and activate sustainable insight through structure, not control.

It goes beyond typical maturity models by shifting the focus from static progress markers to dynamic, friction-based diagnostics. This enables organisations to understand not only where they are but also how to continuously evolve and optimise their data capabilities.

It is a blueprint for turning disconnected effort into coordinated momentum.

At its core, the Enabling Data Model is a mental model. It does not prescribe every action a data leader must take. Instead, it surfaces the invisible forces such as friction, trust, clarity and adoption that determine whether data efforts compound into momentum or collapse into inertia.

Our intent in shaping the model was not to add yet another abstraction to the already crowded data landscape. Instead, we wanted to codify what industry experience and research repeatedly confirm. Carruthers and Jackson (2018) emphasise that data strategy must be actionable and living, not static documents filed away. Davenport and Miller (2022) warn against cargo cult behaviours, where organisations adopt tools without adapting them to context (see Chapter 1). DAMA International (2017) stresses that sustainable value emerges only when technical, organisational and cultural dimensions are aligned. Bernard Marr (2017) highlights that data initiatives collapse when they fail to connect with business strategy and leadership commitment.

Industry research reinforces this point. McKinsey & Company reports that fewer than 30% of organisations achieve transformative business impact from their data initiatives (Chui et al., 2023). Gartner's 2023 survey found that less than half of data and analytics leaders (44%) believe their teams effectively provide value to their organisations (Gartner, 2023). The evidence is clear: the problem is not lack of effort, ambition or investment. The problem is incoherence. Effort without structure creates inertia and waste.

The iceberg metaphor helps to make this visible. What rises above the surface is only as stable as what anchors it below. Without a solid foundation, the visible achievements of data teams collapse under their own weight. The Enabling Data Model makes those foundations tangible, showing where friction accumulates and how it can be converted into forward motion.

In the following sections, we describe the model in detail, explore its four pillars and show how it can be applied in practice. Examples, such as the redesign of metadata practices, will be used to illustrate how the model moves from abstraction to lived reality. The focus, however, is not on a single case study. It is on the structure itself: a way of thinking and working that enables sustainable, scalable value from data.

## Why we need a model

In earlier chapters we explored the paradox that, despite significant investment, many organisations struggle to turn effort into durable value. Studies show that only a minority achieve meaningful impact (Gartner, 2023; McKinsey & Company, 2023).

This failure is not due to a lack of intent, investment or intelligence. It is due to a lack of structure. Without a coherent operating model, even the most advanced technologies create more noise than value. Carruthers and Jackson (2018) emphasise that data strategy must be actionable and living, rather than a static document filed away. Bernard Marr (2017) makes the same point from a business perspective: without alignment to strategy and leadership commitment, data initiatives collapse under their own complexity. Similarly, Davenport and Miller (2022) show that technology succeeds only when shaped by context and purpose.

This is the paradox that the Enabling Data Model was designed to address. Where most approaches focus on assessing maturity or prescribing best practices in isolation, the model offers something different: a pragmatic, cross-functional mental model designed not for static benchmarking but for operational momentum.

**Behind the model: why friction?**

The Enabling Data Model was born not in theory but in practice, shaped by the demands of transforming data capabilities inside fast-scaling, decentralised and federated organisations.

We did not begin with pillars. We began with pain points.

Over time, we found the same patterns repeating: trust gaps, unclear ownership and firefighting instead of forward planning, and tools that were present but inaccessible. These frictions appeared again and again, regardless of domain or team.

That experience led us to ask a different question: what if we diagnosed friction first, instead of measuring maturity later?

By starting with friction, we were able to surface the systemic causes of inefficiency, distrust and disconnection. The four pillars of the Enabling Data Model – People, Governance, Technology and Enablement – then emerged not as abstractions, but as the most persistent fault lines across which this friction travelled.

What resulted was not only a model but a rhythm: a way of locating friction, aligning intent and enabling teams to deliver sustainable value.

Incoherence is the enemy. Effort without structure leads to disconnected tools, redundant metrics and wins that do not scale. Carruthers and Jackson call this 'Data Theatre', visible motion without meaningful progress. The Enabling Data Model reframes the question. Instead of asking 'How mature are we?' it asks, 'How are we enabling sustainable, scalable insight across the organisation?'

The answer lies in connecting the four interdependent domains of People, Governance, Technology and Enablement. These are not silos but force multipliers. When aligned, they create what we call the Flywheel of Insight, a self-reinforcing system in which clarity, trust and capability compound over time.

**The Flywheel of Insight**

When the four pillars of People, Governance, Technology and Enablement, are aligned, they create a self-reinforcing cycle of value, the Flywheel of Insight:

- Clarity → shared definitions, role expectations and visibility into data assets
- Trust → belief in the data, the systems and each other
- Capability → the skills, tools and processes to deliver outcomes
- Adoption → consistent, confident use of data in decision making.

As each component strengthens, the flywheel accelerates. More clarity leads to greater trust, which fuels the development of capability. This in turn fosters adoption, creating a cycle that sustains itself and continually amplifies value across the organisation.

The Flywheel of Insight (Figure 6.2 Flywheel of Insight) builds on lessons from industry. Redman (2023) has shown that clarity in roles and processes directly improves trust in data, which in turn increases adoption. Gioia (2024) argues that decentralised teams succeed when systems are designed to compound capability, not simply to deliver isolated outputs. These perspectives reinforce the point that resilience in data organisations comes not from removing complexity but from embedding alignment and clarity within them.

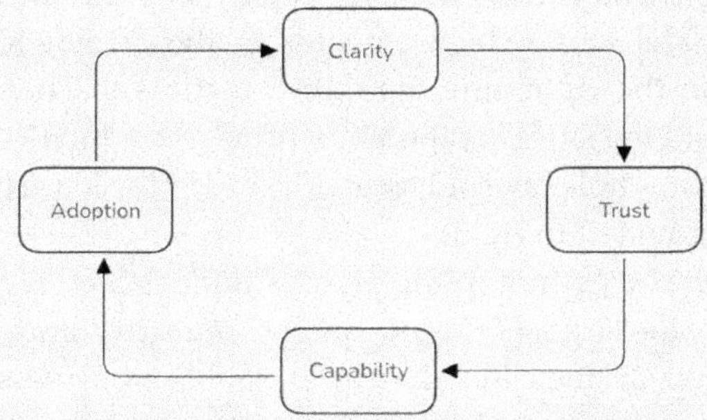


**Figure 6.2** *Flywheel of Insight.*

This is not a model for theoretical optimisation. It is a model for operational durability. Complexity in the modern data ecosystem is inevitable, but chaos is not. What distinguishes resilient data organisations is not the absence of complexity but the presence of clarity in how people work, how systems interoperate and how trust is cultivated and maintained.

The choice of the word 'enabling' is deliberate. This model does not seek to control or centralise. It seeks to empower. It recognises that the future of data is decentralised, but decentralisation without scaffolding leads to entropy. The answer lies not in more tools, roles or policies but in connecting the latent capabilities already present in an organisation through a shared operating model.

The Enabling Data Model, visually presented in Figure 6.3, is not a destination. It is a rhythm, a blueprint for sustained coherence, aligned behaviours and insight at scale.

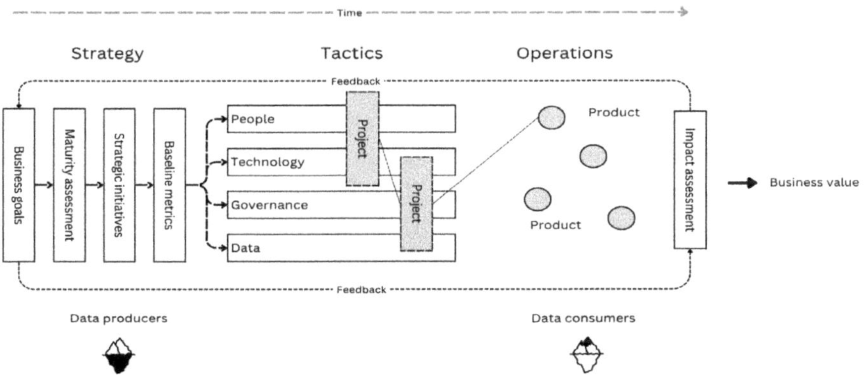


**Figure 6.3** *The Enabling Data Model.*

Let's go through its different elements step by step. On the highest level of abstraction the model has two big elements – on the left side we have the data producers and on the right side the data consumers. The former are the enabling pillars and the latter are the shiny products, which directly drive the business value. Our whole book advocates a shift to the left. This flow mimics the data lineage from left to right.

If we go deeper, the earliest in the process topic is Strategy: here we need to align with business goals, based on the maturity and context of the organisation, set up strategic initiatives and establish business metrics which can later support our performance. Then we move on to Tactics, where the enabling projects are split between the four pillars. Finally, in Operations, we can feed the value-driving products. Some of these, such as dashboards can have a relatively lightweight path through the model, while others – such as a churn model in salesforce – can have a longer one, and much more needs to be done on the data producer side to make them successful.

The final essential element in the model is the feedback loops between all components. This is a direct inspiration from StratOps, and allows organisations to quickly learn and adapt while the model is in action.

## A model for friction, not just maturity

Traditional data frameworks often rely on maturity models. They position organisations on a fixed scale, from novice to advanced, as if progress were a straight line. These models can be useful in highlighting broad capability gaps, but they risk creating a false sense of progress. They imply that once you reach a higher stage, the problems of earlier stages disappear. In practice, this is rarely true. Capabilities evolve unevenly, regress under pressure and require constant adjustment.

We came to see that maturity scores often mislead more than they guide. They encourage comparison instead of coherence. They create incentives to 'look mature' rather than to resolve the actual problems that slow down delivery or erode trust. This is why Carruthers and Jackson (2018) warn against treating maturity assessments as ends in themselves. They may reveal where an organisation stands in theory, but they do not explain why friction persists in practice.

Friction is different. Friction is the lived experience of dysfunction in a system. It is the delayed dashboard release, the duplicate metric, the missing owner or the broken pipeline that no one noticed until it failed. These moments reveal where trust is weakest and where efficiency is most compromised. They are not abstract stages, they are tangible signals.

By focusing on friction, the Enabling Data Model provides a dynamic way to guide investment and change. It does not score an organisation against an idealised benchmark. It helps leaders ask more practical questions:

- Where are the handoffs that consistently break down?
- Which definitions are most contested, and why?
- What ownership gaps create the most rework or firefighting?
- Which tools are most inaccessible to the people who need them?

This diagnostic approach turns friction into a compass. It shifts the focus from 'How mature are we?' to 'What is stopping us from moving faster, with more confidence, right now?'

**Maturity models vs friction diagnostics**

Maturity models:

- measure static progress along a linear scale
- encourage comparison between organisations
- risk rewarding appearances of advancement rather than solving problems
- often result in 'Data Theatre', the visible activity without meaningful impact.

Friction diagnostics:

- identify real obstacles in the flow of data work
- highlight where trust breaks down or efficiency stalls
- guide targeted interventions with immediate relevance
- create momentum by resolving what slows teams down today.

Davenport and Miller (2022) describe this as moving beyond 'cargo cult' data culture, where appearances of maturity mask unresolved structural gaps. Gioia (2024) shows that high-performing organisations embrace this dynamic view, treating complexity as natural but using diagnostic practices to keep it coherent. Redman (2023) emphasises that trust is not a maturity milestone but a continuous practice, renewed each time data is produced, transformed and consumed.

This is why the Enabling Data Model begins not with maturity but with friction. It recognises that data organisations are never finished. They are always evolving, sometimes unevenly, sometimes under strain. By surfacing friction, leaders can target the most impactful interventions, build momentum where it matters most and prevent wasted investment in appearances of maturity that do not translate into value.

## A model for enablement

As already noted, the term 'enabling' was chosen deliberately. The model is designed to empower decentralised teams by providing the scaffolding they need to succeed, turning latent potential into sustained, scalable capability.

Throughout our careers we have seen the limits of control-based approaches. Centralisation may offer short-term consistency, but over time it creates bottlenecks, erodes trust and constrains innovation. Decentralisation, by contrast, unlocks energy and ownership, but without structure it can drift into entropy. The Enabling Data Model seeks to resolve this tension. It is not about choosing one extreme or the other. It is about providing the right scaffolding so that autonomy and alignment can coexist.

**From model to method**

The Enabling Data Model is more than a conceptual architecture. It is supported by a diagnostic starting toolkit that may include the following methods:

- a four-level rubric to assess operational maturity
- a friction taxonomy to identify and label recurring pain points
- a persona framework to ensure real user needs are addressed
- a Platform Fit Canvas to align workloads and system capabilities
- Use Case Enablement Cards that link infrastructure with business value.

Each of these tools plays a critical role in putting the model into action. From assessing maturity and identifying friction to aligning platform capabilities with business needs, they provide the structure required not only to diagnose issues but to address them deliberately.

Use Case Enablement Cards provide a practical mechanism to connect data capabilities with business outcomes. They help teams frame use cases in terms of value, ownership, required data assets, enabling capabilities and measurable outcomes. In doing so, they prevent infrastructure work from becoming abstract and ensure that technical decisions remain anchored in clear business intent.

Together, these methods form a pathway for transforming data from a reactive function into a strategic enabler.

Having explored the rationale behind the Enabling Data Model, we now turn to its practical architecture, supported by the four interdependent pillars of People, Governance, Technology and Enablement. Addressed in isolation, these domains often generate misalignment and friction. But when orchestrated together, they form a self-reinforcing system, what we earlier described as the Flywheel of Insight, where clarity builds trust, trust strengthens capability and capability accelerates adoption.

The model was born not from abstraction but from necessity. It was shaped through the lived experience of fragmented platforms, eroded trust and organisational fatigue. Its goal is simple: operational durability through aligned behaviours, not theoretical elegance. As Gioia (2024) observes, resilient organisations thrive not because they remove complexity, but because they embed clarity and coherence into it. The Enabling Data Model provides that coherence by connecting what already exists inside organisations and turning it into a rhythm that sustains progress.

What makes this diagnostic layer powerful is its adaptability. A start-up may rely on the persona framework to ensure that scarce data resources are directed to the highest-value user needs. A multinational enterprise, by contrast, may use the Platform Fit Canvas to align workloads across multiple regions and prevent redundant investment. In both cases the principle is the same: friction is turned into signal and signal is translated into deliberate design choices.

This reflects a broader pattern across the field. DAMA International (2017) underscores that sustainable transformation comes when technical, organisational and cultural dimensions are synchronised. Gartner (2023) reports that fewer than half of data and analytics teams effectively provide value to their organisations, emphasising that technology investment must be accompanied by governance, enablement and clear business alignment. The Enabling Data Model provides the scaffolding for this synchronisation, while the diagnostic toolkit supplies the method to embed it in day-to-day practice.

## The first pillar: People

At the heart of any data transformation are not tools or platforms, but people. Data engineers, analysts, PMs, marketers and decision makers each play a distinct role in the lifecycle of data, yet too often their efforts remain fragmented. When responsibilities are unclear, capabilities uneven or incentives misaligned, even the most sophisticated infrastructure will falter.

The People pillar of the Enabling Data Model addresses this foundational challenge. It calls for clarifying responsibilities across disciplines and enabling a shared fluency in the language and practices of data work. More than technical skill, this pillar recognises the critical importance of aligned behaviours, continuous learning and cultural reinforcement. Carruthers and Jackson (2018) place culture at the centre of data value. Without organisational alignment, data initiatives struggle to scale beyond pockets of excellence. As Peter Senge argued in *The Fifth Discipline,* lasting transformation requires people to share a common language and purpose, rather than operate in silos (Senge, 2006).

## Why people come first

Every major study on data transformation places people and culture at the centre of success or failure. McKinsey has shown that the top barriers to scaling analytics are not technical limitations but cultural resistance and lack of front-line adoption. Gartner (2025) highlights data literacy as a persistent barrier to successful data programmes. Accenture (2020) similarly found that, despite large-scale investments in platforms and AI, only 32% of organisations are able to create measurable value from data, and just 27% report that their analytics initiatives produce actionable insights. The constraint is not technology alone, but how effectively people are able to understand, trust and act on the data available to them.

Our own careers have underscored this truth. Ownership gaps, onboarding bottlenecks and misaligned incentives created more friction than any missing tool. Conversely, once roles were clarified, literacy embedded into induction and incentives aligned with trust, progress accelerated. Industry examples reinforce this dynamic. Procter & Gamble's Decision Cockpit (Henschen, 2012), for instance, delivered value only after cultural investment in literacy and ownership caught up with technology. Redman (2018) also highlights that data quality improvements sustain only when people see stewardship as part of their daily work, not as an extra burden.

This is why we call the People pillar the first among equals. It determines whether governance will be respected, whether technology will be adopted and whether enablement will stick. Without people, the rest remains architecture on paper. With people aligned, the Flywheel of Insight begins to turn.

## Centrality of change management

Enabling people also means enabling change. Every transformation asks individuals and teams to let go of old habits and adopt new ones. Without structured change management, even the most carefully designed model risks rejection or indifference.

Prosci's research shows that projects with excellent change management are six times more likely to meet their objectives than those with weak practices (Creasey, 2021). In the data context, this translates directly into adoption. New data catalogs, governance processes or self-service platforms take root only when supported by clear communication, leadership sponsorship and ongoing reinforcement.

In practice, many of the most effective interventions we have seen were as much about change as they were about design. The introduction of trust champions, for example, worked because it gave people visible peers who made adoption feel local rather than imposed. Embedding data literacy into onboarding was not only a skills initiative but a cultural signal that data was now part of the organisation's DNA. As John Kotter (2012) has long observed, transformation depends on creating urgency, building coalitions and reinforcing wins until they become habits. The same applies in data work.

## Dimensions of the People pillar

To enable sustainable and scalable value from data, the People pillar must be assessed along several interdependent dimensions:

- *Role clarity and ownership:* Clearly defined responsibilities across the data lifecycle ensure accountability and reduce friction. Domain-oriented approaches such as data mesh depend on formalised stewardship and clear interfaces between producers and consumers.
- *Data literacy and cross-functional fluency:* Data literacy is no longer a specialist competency but a baseline expectation. High-performing organisations foster fluency across disciplines so that domain experts, analysts and engineers can collaborate using shared vocabulary and mutual understanding.
- *Capability development and career architecture:* Developing talent requires more than ad hoc training. It demands career paths, mentoring and structures that balance technical depth with horizontal collaboration. Sustained investment in skills keeps momentum alive.
- *Incentives and cultural alignment:* What is rewarded shapes culture. If teams are measured solely on throughput, silos will persist. Incentives must reinforce collaboration, stewardship and trust. Misaligned goals and KPIs remain silent killers of data programmes. Microsoft has shown how shared OKRs across teams can break silos and align incentives around system-wide outcomes rather than local optimisation.
- *Ways of working and delivery integration:* Data must be integrated into the operating rhythm of the organisation. Applying agile and DevOps principles ensures that rituals such as retrospectives, sprint planning and adoption reviews become part of the collaborative fabric. DevOps, a set of practices that brings development and operations teams together to deliver, test and run systems continuously, improves speed, reliability and collaboration.

## Bridging story and principle

In the HelloFresh story, this became clear during the early delivery phase, when trust champions and structured onboarding rituals began to shift adoption in practice. The impact was immediate, but the lesson was deeper: sustainable data transformation starts with people, not platforms.

But this lesson is not unique to one company. Organisations across industries face the same challenges of fragmented roles, uneven literacy and cultural resistance. Whether in retail, healthcare, finance or manufacturing, the same patterns repeat. Success comes when leaders treat people as the foundation: clarifying ownership, embedding literacy, aligning incentives and managing change deliberately.

That is why the People pillar is written not as a case-specific observation but as a universal principle. It distils what we have lived into a model that any organisation can use to locate friction, design interventions and build durable cultural scaffolding for data.

**People pillar summary**

The People pillar provides the human scaffolding of the Enabling Data Model. It recognises that trust, fluency and aligned ownership are not peripheral to data success; they are central to it. As shown in the HelloFresh delivery phase, particularly during the introduction of trust champions and the Data Academy onboarding programme, reducing onboarding time, embedding literacy into induction and making ownership visible became the foundations of adoption. Those examples were not side benefits, they were the core of transformation.

The lesson is simple. Technology may scale pipelines, but it is people who scale trust.

## The second pillar: Governance

Good governance is not bureaucracy, it is the foundation of trust. In fast-moving organisations, data evolves faster than documentation. Metrics drift. Definitions fork. Compliance becomes reactive. Without governance, decentralisation collapses into chaos.

The Governance pillar of the Enabling Data Model introduces coherence into complexity. It provides the structures, agreements and expectations that allow decentralised teams to move quickly without fragmenting. Governance is not about control for its own sake; it is about establishing a shared baseline of accountability, discoverability and quality. Carruthers and Jackson (2018) frame governance as essential to making data useful, rather than as a control mechanism in its own right.

### Why governance matters

Across industries, organisations consistently underestimate governance. Gartner's (2023) enterprise maturity research shows that companies with robust governance achieve higher business value from analytics than those without it. McKinsey likewise finds that effective governance directly supports trusted, scalable analytics, while its absence leads to redundancy, shadow reporting and eroded confidence in data-driven decisions (McKinsey & Company, 2020b). Our experience confirmed this. In one global programme, glossary definitions diverged across markets to the point that identical terms carried conflicting meanings. Business leaders found themselves debating semantics rather than decisions. Similarly, ownership gaps left certified assets unmanaged long after their creators had departed. In each case, the absence of governance generated friction and distrust far beyond the data team.

Yet governance is not just about compliance. At its best, governance is also about understanding processes: how data is created, how it flows and how it is used to make decisions. Without this process lens, data remains abstract, disconnected from its operational reality and difficult to enable. As Davenport and Redman (2022) have shown, effective data management combines technical and human systems so that trust and quality are embedded in how data is created, moved and used. A well-governed organisation not only documents definitions, it makes the links between process, policy and platform visible so that teams can act with confidence.

Industry practice echoes this shift from rules to rhythms. Airbnb's Data University embedded shared definitions and expectations into training so that analysts spoke the same language (Feng, Coffman and Grewal, 2017). Examples across industry, from manufacturing to retail, show that federated stewardship and process improvement reduce cost and error when engineering and operational teams share accountability for data quality. Data mesh practitioners likewise highlight that federated governance requires small, accountable domain teams and cross-domain alignment so that autonomy does not fragment meaning (Dehghani, 2022).

Thomas Redman has long warned that invisible governance gaps surface only at the point of failure, often when regulatory or reputational damage has already been done (Redman, 2023). By making governance visible, explicit and process aware, organisations avoid the silent drift into data theatre: dashboards that look good but are disconnected from the reality of how the business runs.

## Dimensions of the Governance pillar

To achieve operational durability and analytical confidence, the Governance pillar must be assessed across several interdependent dimensions:

- *Ownership and stewardship structures:* Every asset, whether a metric, model or pipeline, must have both a technical and a business steward. The DAMA perspective stresses that lineage without business context is insufficient (DAMA International, 2017). Mature organisations embed stewardship across domains, balancing local autonomy with central clarity.

- *Standards and definitions (semantic governance):* Without shared meaning, speed becomes risk. Consistency in metric definitions, dimensional hierarchies and naming conventions is essential. The absence of semantic governance leads directly to fractured analytical experiences and incompatible data products.
- *Process understanding and operational mapping:* Governance must capture not only what data means but how it flows through processes. Data is never created in a vacuum; it is generated, transformed and consumed as part of business processes. If those processes are poorly understood or undocumented, governance risks becoming a catalog of definitions with little operational meaning.

For example, an organisation may carefully define 'on-time delivery' in its reporting layer. Yet, if the underlying process steps in logistics such as order picking, carrier handoff and customer confirmation are not mapped, the data will drift. Each team may apply its own interpretation of when delivery counts as 'on time', leading to fractured metrics and disputes in executive meetings.

This pattern is not unique to logistics. In financial services, inconsistent mapping of revenue recognition processes has led to regulatory breaches where the data was technically accurate but misaligned with accounting rules. In healthcare, mismatched interpretations of patient journey steps have produced duplicated or missing data in EHRs, directly impacting on care quality. These cases highlight that data governance cannot stop at semantics; it must extend into process governance.

Understanding processes provides the connective tissue between governance and enablement. When teams know not just what a metric means but where in the process it is captured and how it flows, they are better able to trust and apply it. This linkage makes governance actionable: lineage diagrams become more than technical maps – they become operational blueprints that guide improvement.

As Redman (2023) notes, the costliest data errors rarely come from systems; they come from misaligned processes that no one thought to examine. By embedding process understanding into governance, organisations prevent errors from becoming systemic, reduce rework and accelerate enablement.

- *Data contracts and interoperability agreements:* Modern governance enforces not only schema consistency but behavioural guarantees. Data contracts – explicit agreements between producers and consumers – create modularity and trust. They specify service levels, freshness expectations and change management protocols so that teams can evolve without breaking each other.

- *Lineage and observability:* Traceability is a precondition for trust. Teams must see where data originates, how it is transformed and who relies on it. Automated lineage and observability tools are now essential for enabling trusted self-service at scale.
- *Policy enforcement and regulatory alignment:* Governance must also fulfil its traditional obligations: privacy, compliance and security. This involves embedding role-based access controls, GDPR and CCPA alignment, audit trails and automated policy enforcement into daily workflows, rather than layering them on as afterthoughts.

### Bridging story and principle

Earlier in this book we showed how inconsistent glossary ownership and fragmented lineage created daily friction, eroding trust across teams. Those episodes illustrated the same truth that the Governance pillar formalises: coherence is not a luxury but a necessity. The mechanisms we introduced there, such as stewardship roles, domain-led certification and visible trust indicators, were not about bureaucracy. They were about making process visible and trust operational.

This is not limited to one organisation. Whether in financial services subject to regulatory scrutiny; in healthcare, where data quality impacts on patient safety; or in retail, where inconsistent metrics distort performance, the absence of governance generates the same downstream costs. The Enabling Data Model positions governance not as a centralised bureaucracy but as the scaffolding that allows decentralised teams to move fast without breaking trust.

**Governance pillar summary**

The Governance pillar transforms ambiguity into confidence. It ensures that data assets carry ownership, meaning, reliability and accountability. As shown in the HelloFresh delivery phase, particularly through the introduction of trust champions and federated certification workflows, governance shifted from perceived overhead to a practical enabler.

The lesson is clear. Technology may accelerate access, but only governance can make speed safe.

## The third pillar: Technology

Technology is the most visible part of a data organisation. It is where investment is most concentrated and where expectations are highest. Yet, too often, platforms are introduced with the hope of solving strategic problems, only to become abandoned, underused or misaligned because they were not connected to people, governance or process. Tools alone do not create value. It is the architecture, accessibility and alignment of technology that make it enabling.

The Technology pillar of the Enabling Data Model reframes the role of platforms. Their purpose is not sophistication for its own sake, but acceleration: shortening the time from data to decision, reducing cognitive load and embedding trust in daily work. As Bernard Marr (2017) argues, the purpose of data technology is not to be the most advanced, but to be the most useful. Similarly, Strengholt (2024) emphasises that modern data fabrics are valuable not because they are fashionable, but because they enable composability and agility across a decentralised ecosystem.

## Why technology matters

Across industries, the biggest failures in data transformation are rarely due to lack of investment in tools. McKinsey found that around 70% of transformation programmes fail, not because of inadequate platforms but because organisational structures, behaviours and incentives are not aligned to make use of them (Ewenstein, Smith and Sologar, 2015). This reinforces a critical truth: technology is not the issue, but how it is chosen and applied.

Too often, organisations fall into the trap of 'silver bullet' thinking. A new data warehouse is procured to solve governance gaps. An ML platform is introduced to offset poor data quality. A catalog is rolled out in the hope that it will impose trust by itself. Each time, the result is disappointment, because the underlying issues are not technical but organisational.

One of the clearest lessons came from our own metadata work. Earlier catalog initiatives failed despite heavy investment. When reframed as a product, designed around people and workflows, adoption finally accelerated. The point was never the tool, it was the fit.

## Dimensions of the Technology pillar

To move from patchwork tooling to strategic infrastructure, the Technology pillar must be evaluated across several interdependent dimensions:

- *Architecture and modularity:* Composable architecture is the foundation of scalable ecosystems. Rather than monolithic platforms, modern organisations adopt interoperable components like warehouses, orchestration engines, data catalogs and APIs that evolve with needs.
- *Self-service design and usability:* A platform that requires engineering mediation for every query is not enabling. Interfaces must support analysts, product owners and business stakeholders in finding and using data directly, with clear onboarding and accessible documentation.

- *Lifecycle coverage and extensibility:* Technology must support the full data lifecycle, from ingestion and modelling to distribution and monitoring. Gaps create duplication and delays. Extensible platforms allow new capabilities to be added without replacing the foundation.
- *Reliability, observability and resilience:* Trust is earned through performance. Uptime, latency, data freshness and schema stability must be observable and governed by service level agreements (SLAs). Without this, confidence in platforms collapses quickly.
- *Security, compliance and data protection:* As access scales, protection must scale too. Role-based access, encryption, audit logs and privacy-by-design controls are non-negotiable foundations for enabling safe use.
- *Build vs buy: strategic differentiation:* This is one of the most common pitfalls. Start-ups and scale-ups often default to building everything in-house, motivated by speed, control or the belief that their needs are unique. While this can create agility in the short term, it often leads to high maintenance costs, talent dependencies and systems that cannot scale.

**Build vs buy: a decision lens for technology**

The build vs buy decision is one of the most consequential in data strategy. Both paths carry risks if pursued without discipline.

- Start-ups and scale-ups often lean towards build. This creates early flexibility and ownership, but at scale it can result in brittle, costly systems that depend on scarce talent. As Zhamak Dehghani (2019) observed in her work on data mesh, organisations that overbuild without governance often end up with bespoke silos that cannot interoperate.
- Large enterprises often default to buy. Public benchmarks show significant waste and underutilisation across bought platforms and tools: companies use only about half of their provisioned SaaS licences on average (Zylo, 2024), and a majority report difficulty managing and optimising cloud spend at scale (Flexera, 2025). Despite sustained investment, most firms still struggle to realise business value from data initiatives (Wavestone, 2024).
- Balanced approaches evaluate whether the capability in question is core to competitive differentiation. Davenport and Miller (2022) argue that organisations should build only where a capability directly supports unique advantage. Everything else should be bought, but bought with careful attention to integration, usability and lifecycle cost.

Decision lens for leaders:

1 Is the capability core to competitive advantage? If yes, build or co-develop.
2 Is there a mature market solution that meets 80% of needs? If yes, buy and focus energy on integration.
3 What are the total lifecycle costs from maintenance, migration and adoption over five years?
4 How will this choice scale with people, governance and process, not just technology?

The key is not whether you build or buy, but whether you make the choice intentionally, aligned to strategy and supported by governance and enablement.

Large enterprises often fall into the opposite trap, continually buying new technology without fully understanding integration costs, adoption needs or long-term implications. This can result in expensive migrations, overlapping licences and fragmented ecosystems.

The Enabling Data Model emphasises pragmatic evaluation: build when the capability is core to competitive differentiation, buy when mature solutions exist, and always prioritise integration, usability and sustainability over novelty. Technology choices must be made with both the short- and long-term consequences in mind.

## Bridging story and principle

In the HelloFresh story, this became clear when brittle supply chain pipelines were rebuilt into modular products and static dashboards evolved into real-time analytics. These moments reinforced a simple truth: technology must be designed to enable, not to impress.

The catalog case provided a further demonstration. When earlier catalog initiatives failed, the instinct could have been to try another tool. But the breakthrough came when technology was no longer treated as the silver bullet, and the focus shifted to workflows, governance and enablement. Technology became the delivery layer for trust, not the starting point.

This insight holds true across industries. In financial services, cloud and third-party deployments must be integrated into risk and compliance operating models, as set out by the UK Prudential Regulation Authority's (2021) guidance on outsourcing and third-party risk management. In healthcare, EHR initiatives falter when usability is weak and burdensome, which is linked to workflow disruption and clinician burnout (Holmgren, Hendrix and Maisel, 2024). In retail, marketing stacks fragment when tools are added without alignment to business processes. Success comes when technology is treated not as a stack, but as an ecosystem designed for people, processes and outcomes.

**Technology pillar summary**

The Technology pillar ensures that platforms empower rather than encumber. It is not about chasing innovation for its own sake, but about building composable, resilient and user-centred infrastructure. As shown in the HelloFresh story, through modular forecasting, refactored pipelines and integrated platforms delivered measurable improvements in speed and trust.

The lesson is clear. People may scale trust, governance may scale coherence, but only technology can scale possibility.

## The fourth pillar: Enablement

If governance defines the rules and technology builds the roads, then enablement is the on-ramp. It is the lantern that lights the way, turning architecture into adoption and potential into value. Without enablement, the other pillars stand as structures on paper. With enablement, they move together, carrying the weight of the model into action.

The Enablement pillar of the Enabling Data Model is concerned with the human–system interface. It ensures that people can find, understand and work with data without bottlenecks or gatekeeping. It encompasses the playbooks, catalogs, onboarding guides, certification rituals and training mechanisms that turn platforms into products and products into outcomes. It removes ambiguity and replaces it with discoverability, fluency and confidence.

Critically, enablement is not a one-off initiative. It is a cultural and operational commitment to reducing the friction of delivering value. As Redman (2023) argues, organisations create mistrust and delay when they fail to make data understandable, well-defined and usable in everyday work. A well-enabled organisation does not just grant access, it removes the cognitive load required to interpret, apply and scale insight.

As Peter Weill and Stephanie Woerner at MIT have observed, successful digital transformations are distinguished not by their architecture, but by the way they embed practices into everyday work. The same principle applies here: enablement is what makes the other pillars real (Weill and Woerner, 2018).

Where access is easy but understanding is hard, teams hesitate. Where both are fluid, they move.

### Why enablement matters

Enablement is often overlooked. Organisations pour investment into platforms and governance, yet adoption stalls when people cannot navigate the system, or when trust signals are invisible. As McAfee and Brynjolfsson (2008) explain, IT delivers competitive advantage only when organisations combine it with complementary changes in business processes, skills and culture. In practice, adoption is not driven by feature depth but by fluency: how quickly a new analyst can find a trusted metric, how confidently a PM can explore, how easily an engineer can trace lineage.

We saw this vividly in our own work. At one point, onboarding a new analyst took weeks, not because tools were missing but because guidance was fragmented across Slack threads, Confluence pages and word of mouth. Once we embedded literacy into induction, created certification rituals and made ownership visible through trust champions, adoption accelerated dramatically.

Suddenly, analysts reported spending less time searching for meaning and more time delivering insight.

Industry peers show that the most successful organisations treat enablement as the true accelerator of change. Netflix scaled its data culture not by building the biggest platform but by investing in metadata-driven discovery and self-service tools that made trust visible in daily work. Airbnb created its Data University to help thousands of employees, ensuring that even non-specialists could explore and apply data with confidence. Spotify's 'data jam sessions' normalised experimentation and made new practices feel safe. Shopify halved onboarding time by developing playbooks and documentation that lowered the barrier to entry. JP Morgan paired governance investments with structured enablement so that compliance rules were not only written but lived. The UK NHS, meanwhile, illustrates the opposite: the absence of enablement in clinical data systems slowed the adoption of EHRs, proving that even with technology in place, without usability, adoption falters.

Together these examples show a simple truth: technology may open the door, but only enablement invites people to walk through.

**Enablement as the bridge between pillars**

Enablement is also where the four pillars converge.

- People bring ownership, but enablement makes that ownership visible and reusable. A steward's knowledge becomes accessible through catalogs, playbooks and embedded documentation.
- Governance provides trust, but enablement turns trust into action. Definitions and contracts move from PDFs into dashboards, workflows and search results.
- Technology supplies capability, but enablement ensures capability is applied. Tools become products, interfaces and experiences that reduce friction rather than create it.

This is why we call enablement the bridge of the model. It connects intention with practice, ensuring that investments in people, governance and technology translate into value. It is also where the Flywheel of Insight begins to accelerate: clarity becomes usable, trust becomes operational and adoption becomes scalable.

## Dimensions of the Enablement pillar

To build durable capability and scalable adoption, the Enablement pillar must be assessed across several interdependent dimensions:

- *Documentation, playbooks and system literacy:* Enablement begins with clarity. Teams need access not only to data, but to the context that defines how to use it. Documentation is not peripheral; it is part of the user experience. Organisations that invest in playbooks, lineage maps and catalogs create the conditions for self-navigation and fluency.

- *Onboarding and certification pathways:* How new joiners are introduced to data is one of the strongest predictors of success. Scalable enablement depends on structured learning that is embedded into daily work and evolves with each role. The most mature models create certification pathways that reinforce confidence through continuous practice, not one-off training.
- *Embedded help and support systems:* Anticipating questions reduces dependency on central teams. Contextual help embedded in tools, cohort-based learning and in-app guidance transform adoption from a struggle into a habit. Treating data support with the same rigour as product support is essential to making platforms stick.
- *Measurement and feedback loops:* Enablement must be managed like a product. Adoption data, satisfaction scores and time-to-competency metrics reveal what is working and where friction remains. Continuous feedback ensures that the system evolves with its users.
- *Cultural reinforcement and ritualisation:* Finally, enablement is cultural. It thrives through rituals such as showcase days, office hours, onboarding ceremonies and certification forums. As Edgar Schein (2010), the father of organisational culture studies, observed, repeated behaviours are what embed new norms.

## Bridging story and principle

Earlier in this book we showed how enablement turned abstract catalogs into living systems, where onboarding time dropped, duplicated queries fell and trust became visible. Those episodes illustrated the same truth that this pillar formalises: without enablement, the other pillars remain potential; with enablement, they become performance.

But this is not limited to one organisation. Whether in retail, healthcare, banking or technology, adoption is what separates shelfware from capability. A well-governed, well-architected platform that no one uses is no more valuable than one that does not exist. Enablement is the condition that breaks the iceberg, surfacing the invisible foundation and making it usable.

**Enablement pillar summary**

The Enablement pillar of the Enabling Data Model bridges intention and adoption. It lowers the activation energy required to work with data by embedding clarity, confidence and continuous learning into the organisational fabric. Enablement is not just about making data accessible, it is about making it usable, trusted and ultimately transformative.

The lesson is simple. Governance may provide safety, technology may provide scale and people may provide ownership, but only enablement ensures that the system is lived. It is the lantern that makes the path visible, the bridge that carries the pillars into practice and the rhythm that turns structure into value.

## Making it real: diagnostic toolkit

The four pillars describe the structural foundations of the Enabling Data Model. But structures alone do not move. To translate them into practice, organisations need a way to diagnose friction, align investment and prioritise what matters most. This is where the diagnostic toolkit comes in. It is the practical companion to the model, giving leaders the instruments to locate gaps, and teams the guidance to act on them.

We often say that the model provides the rhythm, but the toolkit provides the score. It makes the abstract concrete, ensuring that the pillars are not only understood but lived in daily work.

### Personas in practice

Friction is always experienced by someone, not in the abstract. An analyst might feel it as wasted hours searching for definitions, while an engineer experiences it as firefighting broken pipelines. Personas bring these experiences into focus. By mapping each pillar through the lens of roles such as Analyst, Engineer, Scientist and Product Owner, leaders can see where ownership is unclear, where governance feels like overhead or where technology does not serve.

Industry practice reinforces this. Airbnb's Data University tailored learning paths to different roles, ensuring that adoption did not stall at a one-size-fits-all training programme. Netflix similarly invested in persona-based discovery frameworks to ensure that metadata searches reflected the needs of engineers as much as PMs. By expressing friction in human terms, personas turn diagnostics into action.

### Use case and data catalog maturity

Too many data catalogs fail because they prioritise coverage over value. Counting the number of datasets ingested tells you little about whether the platform is trusted or used. What matters is alignment with use cases. A catalog that certifies the metrics used in quarterly reviews, or the pipelines that drive customer communications, will always create more impact than one that indexes tables no one touches.

Research from McKinsey & Company (2022b) shows that organisations achieve the highest returns on data investment when they anchor platform development in business use cases that create measurable impact. Shopify is an instructive example: it deliberately linked documentation and playbooks to high-value product analytics cases, cutting onboarding time for new analysts by half. Use case maturity ensures that adoption is anchored in outcomes, not in the false comfort of volume.

## Platform Fit Canvas

Platform debates often collapse into vendor comparisons or feature wish lists. The Platform Fit Canvas reframes the conversation. Instead of asking which tool has the most connectors, it asks whether the architecture fits the workloads, latency needs and user personas it is meant to serve. Does it support real-time decisions where needed? Does it give analysts fluency without dependence on engineers? Does it align with governance requirements across markets?

Spotify's platform evolution is a case in point. By focusing on how well systems served developers and analysts, rather than chasing the most advanced vendor features, it built a platform that was not only technically sound but culturally aligned. Similarly, JP Morgan used capability-fit frameworks to ensure that compliance and usability were considered together, avoiding costly migrations that arise when tools are chosen in isolation.

## Use Case Enablement Cards

If personas explain who experiences friction, and the Platform Fit Canvas explains whether the architecture is fit for purpose, Use Case Enablement Cards make clear why the work matters.

Each card links a business use case to the data capabilities required to enable it: the decision or process being improved, the data assets involved, the owners accountable for them, the governance conditions required, the platform capabilities needed and the measurable outcome expected. In this sense, the cards act as the bridge between the left side of the model, where enabling capabilities are built, and the right side, where business value is realised.

For example, a churn reduction use case might link customer event data, ownership in the CRM domain, governance through certified definitions and platform capabilities such as real-time pipelines, all tied to a measurable reduction in customer attrition.

This prevents teams from funding generic platform work in the abstract. Instead, it asks a sharper question: what capability must be enabled so that this use case can create value? This approach aligns with broader work on data-driven ideation, where structured canvases help teams connect technical possibilities with business value (Kronsbein and Müller, 2019).

Taken together, these tools form the operational lens of the Enabling Data Model. They ensure that each pillar is not left to theory, but tested against the lived reality of teams and the practical demands of the organisation. Personas make friction human. Use cases tie adoption to value. The Platform Fit Canvas ensures that architecture serves rather than distracts. Use Case Enablement Cards connect capability to outcome.

The lesson is simple. Models may inspire, but only methods make them real. The diagnostic toolkit is what turns the structure of the pillars into the rhythm of adoption.

## What good looks like: outcomes

The real test of any model is not whether it sounds convincing but whether it changes outcomes. The Enabling Data Model has always been designed with this in mind. By embedding its rhythm into daily practice, organisations begin to see shifts that go beyond systems and touch behaviours, decisions and culture.

- *Faster time to insight:* Time to insight is one of the most sensitive indicators of data maturity. When friction is left unaddressed, analysis slows to a crawl, with weeks spent searching for definitions or rebuilding duplicated logic. Once friction is diagnosed and reduced, those weeks collapse into days. In our work we saw how embedding catalogs, playbooks and trust signals cut average onboarding effort by hours per week.

**Case in point: Procter & Gamble**

Procter & Gamble's Business Sphere and Decision Cockpits are widely cited as examples of reducing decision latency by streamlining access to trusted key performance indicators. For example, Procter & Gamble reported retiring over 80% of its standardised BI reports after deploying the Decision Cockpit, shifting focus from generating reports to making decisions (Henschen, 2012).

- *Increased trust in data:* Trust is the currency of data. Without it, even the most sophisticated platforms go unused. We witnessed how the 'three churn numbers' problem – different teams producing different answers for the same metric – eroded confidence rapidly. Recovery came only when stewardship was clarified, lineage was made visible and certification rituals were embedded.

**Case in point: Capital One**

In financial services, Capital One has been widely recognised for combining strong governance with active enablement. Its data management approach on AWS embeds ownership, observability and automation into daily workflows, creating a culture where compliance and innovation reinforce each other. By aligning governance frameworks with enablement practices, Capital One built a data-driven culture that balances control with creativity (Amazon Web Services, 2025).

- *Scalable enablement:* Enablement is the lever that converts potential into performance. Once certification pathways, onboarding rituals and literacy programmes were introduced, new analysts became productive in days rather than weeks.

**Case in point: Airbnb**

Airbnb's Data University trained thousands of employees across the company, ensuring that even non-specialists could work confidently with data. Its tiered curriculum, aligned to roles and responsibilities, embedded literacy into the organisational fabric and scaled adoption far beyond the data team (Feng, Coffman and Grewal, 2017).

- *Improved cross-functional alignment:* One of the most visible outcomes of applying the model is the reduction in wasted time debating metrics rather than decisions. Shared definitions, clear ownership and visible rituals shift the conversation from semantics to strategy.

**Case in point: NHS Digital**

In healthcare, NHS Digital's work on EHRs shows how aligning data governance to clinical processes improves both quality and trust. Early systems suffered from inconsistent data entry and unclear ownership, leading to duplication and reporting errors. By introducing national data standards and clearer accountability, NHS Digital improved record accuracy and the confidence of clinicians using them (Martin, 2019).

- *Clearer investment decisions:* Finally, the Enabling Data Model strengthens how leaders prioritise scarce resources. Scoring each pillar and using Use Case Enablement Cards helps organisations direct investment where it will have the greatest impact, not where the loudest voices are. This prevents cycles of 'shiny object syndrome', where tools are bought without solving root problems.

**Case in point: McKinsey & Company**

McKinsey has shown that technology investments deliver value only when paired with organisational practices that make them usable by the front line. Platforms alone do not create advantage; adoption, process and governance are what turn them into capabilities (McKinsey & Company, 2022b).

These outcomes are not hypothetical. They are lived, tested and repeated across industries and contexts. Together they demonstrate that the Enabling Data Model is not a static framework but a rhythm that translates effort into momentum and momentum into impact.

## Bridging the gap from model to value

The Enabling Data Model turns the abstract ambition of being 'data driven' into something operationally grounded. It translates vision into behaviours, embedding clarity, ownership, interoperability and usability across the ecosystem. Where other approaches often remain static or descriptive, this model is designed to be lived, tested and adapted under real organisational pressure.

Unlike maturity models that measure progress against an idealised end state, the Enabling Data Model embraces the uneven, non-linear reality of transformation. Capabilities do not evolve in lockstep, and trust is not created by ticking boxes. It grows in rituals, in repeated decisions and in the daily reinforcement of shared practices.

This is also where the iceberg metaphor comes full circle. Earlier we argued that most organisations only see the tip: dashboards, models, reports. The Enabling Data Model uncovers the submerged structure, the alignment of people, governance, technology and enablement that supports durable value. The Flywheel of Insight shows how that structure moves, turning alignment into momentum.

Industry examples reinforce this point. Lyft's metadata-driven data discovery platform, Amundsen, shows how embedding trust and search directly into engineers' daily workflows increases adoption and reuse (Grover, 2019). Airbnb's Data University translates principles of governance and literacy into practice, enabling thousands of employees to participate confidently in data work (Christian, 2017). Capital One's data governance and enablement model on AWS demonstrates how embedding ownership and automation into everyday workflows can reduce risk and accelerate innovation (Amazon Web Services, 2025).

The Enabling Data Model provides both a way to diagnose friction across the pillars and a rhythm to transform alignment into accelerating value. In practice, this is how the iceberg breaks. What was once hidden, fragmented or fragile becomes visible, connected and durable. The model does not promise the absence of complexity, but it does provide coherence. And coherence is what turns data from potential into performance.

## Reflection

The Enabling Data Model is not simply a tool for diagnosing friction. It is a way of thinking about how organisations grow through clarity, trust, capability and adoption. By making the hidden structure of the iceberg visible, it turns complexity into coherence and effort into momentum.

In our careers we have seen too many frameworks that looked elegant but failed to live. They offered diagrams without rhythm, vision without pathways into daily work. Our intent here has been different. We set out not to add another model to the shelf, but to capture the practices that allow data to flow, trust to take root and value to scale.

The lesson is clear. Effort without structure creates inertia. Structure without rhythm remains static. The Enabling Data Model provides both structure and rhythm, offering leaders a way to move from potential to performance.

And yet this is only part of the story. A model alone is not enough. To embed these lessons more widely, organisations also need shared principles that transcend any single company or programme. That is where we now turn: from model to manifesto, from operating rhythm to enduring values.

# Conclusion

Boyan Angelov and David Castro-Gavino

When Tom Redman set the stage in his Foreword, he asked three deceptively simple questions: What has changed? How do we make data first class? How do we prepare to capture the real value that AI promises?

This book has been our answer to those questions, not through theory alone but through lived experience, reflection and an insistence on seeing the whole system as more than the sum of its parts. We began with the problem, a world flooded with technology yet starved of enablement. We explored the illusion of progress created by pilot projects, frameworks and merchants of complexity. And we examined why so many organisations, despite their ambition, remain stuck at the surface of the iceberg, heading for disaster.

Then we went deeper, to the invisible work that sustains everything above it. Through the HelloFresh transformation, we saw how data can move from chaos to coherence, from asset to enabler, from a technical function to a shared capability. From that experience emerged the Enabling Data Model, a way to describe, diagnose and ultimately deliver what 'data driven' truly means.

So, have we answered Tom's challenge? We believe we have shown that what has changed is not the technology, but our understanding of what matters. We have made the case that data becomes first class not by demanding attention but by earning trust. And we have argued that preparing for AI is not about chasing disruption but about building the foundations that make transformation possible.

Yet no book can finish this work for you. The final step belongs to every reader who chooses to act, who decides to see the iceberg, to invest in the unseen layers and to lead with intent rather than imitation. If we do this together, we can finally move beyond the recurring Groundhog Day of data. We can replace complexity with clarity, fragmentation with flow and slogans with substance.

The challenge remains as Tom described it: demanding, urgent and human. But the path forward is now clearer than ever: enable your people, govern with confidence, design for trust and never lose sight of why we started. Because when data is truly enabled, it stops being just a department and becomes the bloodstream of the organisation. And that is how we turn the promise of AI into practice – not as an aspiration, but as a new way of working, thinking and leading.

## Closing reflection

Every transformation begins quietly. It starts when one leader decides to look beneath the surface, to value the work that few can see but all depend on. The iceberg will always be there, but it no longer needs to be a threat. It can become a reminder of what lies beneath every successful organisation: structure, discipline and purpose. The future of data will not be built by those chasing complexity, but by those who enable clarity. That is the work ahead of all of us.

# Appendix 1: Applying the Enabling Data Model

David Castro-Gavino

## How to use this section

This section is not intended to be a step-by-step manual that dictates exactly how you should build a data catalog, design a platform or run a data team. Our intent in this book has not been to provide a rigid 'how-to' guide that you simply follow without thought. Instead, the aim is to show you what 'fishing' looks like in the holistic sense: how to understand the river you are in, how to read the conditions, how to select the right tools for the environment you are facing and how to build the habits and reflexes that allow you to adapt over time.

In other words, we are not here to hand you a set of instructions and say 'do this and you will succeed'. Rather, we want to shift your way of thinking so that you can apply the principles of the Enabling Data Model in a way that is sensitive to your organisation, your culture and your particular challenges. Every organisation is different, every team is shaped by its own history and incentives and every data landscape has its own points of friction. What works in one environment may not work in another. The intent of this section is therefore to provide an application framework, a way of seeing and listening, that you can use to make sense of your own setting and decide what moves to make.

The Enabling Data Model is designed to be that compass. It does not dictate which road to take, but it helps you to orient yourself so that you can see clearly where friction is holding you back, where alignment is missing and where capability must be strengthened. It helps you to listen before you act, diagnose before you prescribe and design with intent rather than react with haste.

In what follows you will find two kinds of content:

- *The Toolkit.* This includes frameworks, diagnostic rubrics and canvases. Each of these can be applied in practice to surface friction, align

stakeholders and shape investment priorities. They are not intended as one-size-fits-all solutions, but as structures that can be adapted and scaled to fit your organisation.
- *Model in Practice call-outs.* Alongside the toolkit we present short, real-world examples of how these tools have been applied in practice. These are not brand-specific case studies, but anonymised scenarios that show how a concept moves from abstraction to reality. They will help you to see the kinds of insights the toolkit can surface, and how those insights can be turned into decisions.

A more detailed, end-to-end narrative is provided in Appendix 2, where we bring the toolkit together through a full example of how metadata was treated as a product in a complex, multi-market organisation. This illustrates the rhythm of application in practice, from diagnosis to design to adoption.

It is also important to stress that the toolkit we share here reflects what we have used in practice. It is grounded in real experience and proven to unlock adoption and trust, but it is not the only way. There is a wealth of literature available, with excellent methods, templates and how-to guides on data maturity, governance frameworks, agile data practices and more. Think of this as one set of tools in your belt. The value lies not in limiting yourself to these pages, but in learning to combine approaches and build your own set of instruments that fit your organisation's needs.

Promise to the reader: If you take the time to work through this section and adapt the tools to your context, by the end you will have achieved three things. First, you will have surfaced the specific points of friction within your organisation, not as vague complaints but as structured and diagnosable challenges. Second, you will have created a prioritised plan for where to act, making trade-offs explicit and aligning stakeholders on what matters most. Third, you will have established a measurable path to adoption, allowing you to track whether your changes are creating real impact and building trust.

The purpose of this section is therefore practical, but not prescriptive. Use it as a compass, not as a map. The value lies not in ticking off steps, but in learning to see your organisation with new clarity and using that clarity to design capabilities that will last.

## Listening before leading

In his widely cited book *The First 90 Days*, Michael Watkins (2003) warns that leaders cannot fix what they have not yet understood, and that the instinct to act early often comes at the cost of deeper alignment.

This principle resonates strongly with our own experience. Both of us, as consultants and later as leaders stepping into new roles, have felt the pressure to prove ourselves quickly. The request from sponsors is often framed as urgent: 'clean up the data', 'build the dashboard', 'stand up the platform'. It is natural to want to respond with action. Yet, time and again we have learned that the most powerful first act is restraint. To pause, to listen and to diagnose before prescribing.

Listening is not only about humility, though that matters. It is also about effectiveness. Every organisation carries hidden assumptions, legacy scars and embedded ways of working. These are rarely visible in the glossy strategy deck or the onboarding notes. They live in the unwritten rules of who answers Slack questions, in the shadow systems analysts maintain, in the definitions that exist in three different places with three different owners. If you rush into solution mode without uncovering these subtleties, you risk building on sand.

Edgar Schein's *Humble Inquiry* (2013) captures this stance well. He describes listening not as passive but as an active practice of curiosity, designed to surface what others may take for granted. Amy Edmondson, in *Teaming* (2012), extends this point by showing that high-performing organisations create psychological safety for people to voice problems and concerns. Listening is therefore not only diagnostic but relational. It tells people that their pain matters and that their lived experience is valued.

It is also important to recognise that listening is not confined to new jobs or executive transitions. The same principle applies whenever you begin a new project, a new programme or a new piece of infrastructure. Each time, there is a risk of assuming too much, carrying forward mental models from the last initiative or over-indexing on what you believe worked elsewhere. Chris Argyris (1991) called this the trap of 'single-loop learning', acting to correct visible problems without questioning the underlying assumptions that shape them. Listening expands the loop, allowing you to test assumptions before they derail the outcome.

In practical terms, listening means deliberately slowing down. It means resisting the urge to produce an architecture diagram in week one or launch a pilot in month one. Instead, it means investing time in discovery: interviews, workshops, shadowing, telemetry analysis and reviewing artefacts. It is not glamorous, and it can feel slow in environments addicted to velocity. But this restraint is what creates the clarity that later enables speed without chaos.

### Checklist for leaders starting out

- Map the transition type. Ask whether you are facing a start-up, a turnaround or a realignment. Context changes the play.
- Identify five to seven pivotal stakeholders. These are the people closest to the work and the friction. Their perspectives are non-negotiable.
- Collect three kinds of evidence. Gather lived pain, telemetry and artefacts. Together, these form a triangulated picture.
- Restrain the impulse to act. Hold back from declaring fixes or drawing target architectures until the diagnosis is complete. The discipline of restraint is what builds credibility.

**Model in practice: vignette**

When one large digital operator began its metadata programme, the instinct from leadership was to procure a new catalog immediately. Previous tools had failed to gain traction, and the reflex solution was to swap platforms. The team chose to pause. Instead of rushing, they opened with structured interviews and shadowing. Analysts described spending hours asking the same metric questions in Slack, while engineers admitted lineage was assembled by memory and manual tracing. Leaders voiced frustration with competing definitions of critical KPIs. These observations were confirmed by telemetry: fewer than 25% of glossary entries had been updated in the past year, adoption was low and incident tickets were climbing. Artefacts told the same story, that multiple definitions of 'active customer' lived side by side, none of them reconciled. By listening first, the team surfaced the unspoken assumptions that had undermined previous efforts and created a shared sense of urgency that became the foundation for redesign.

Sounds familiar.

## Why a diagnostic approach?

The Enabling Data Model is not a maturity assessment. It is a diagnostic operating model. That distinction matters.

Maturity models have been popular in data for over two decades, and they have their uses. They can provide a broad sense of whether an organisation is at a 'nascent' or 'advanced' stage and can be helpful in tracking progress at a very high level. But, as Argyris (1991) argued in his work on organisational learning, single-loop approaches correct surface problems without interrogating deeper causes, which is rarely sufficient. A maturity score may tell you that you are at 'level two', but it does not tell you why, or where to act first. In our own consulting careers, we saw this pattern repeatedly. Leaders pinned a number to their data function, declared a desire to move to the next level and then became frustrated when the same structural frictions kept resurfacing.

Complex organisations rarely suffer from too little investment in data. More often, they suffer from misalignments: incentives that reward the wrong behaviours, platforms that become unwieldy as they grow, ownership models that fracture under scale or governance practices that look robust on paper but are ignored in practice. These frictions do not announce themselves neatly. They live in subtle patterns: analysts recreating the same metric in five different ways, engineers firefighting without observability, business leaders quietly keeping their own 'shadow numbers'.

This is why diagnosis matters. A diagnostic approach reframes complaints, aligns evidence and creates clarity for design. It offers three core advantages:

1. It reframes complaints as evidence. Instead of hearing 'the data is a mess' as a vague frustration, you can classify it as a governance gap, a people challenge or a technology misfit. Once categorised, complaints become usable evidence.
2. It connects evidence to design. Each friction identified through the diagnostic links directly to a capability that can be built or adjusted. Frustrations stop being noise and become inputs for prioritisation.
3. It builds alignment through shared language. Once teams see their pain mapped onto clear dimensions, they can agree on what the real issues are and stop arguing over symptoms.

We have both stepped into organisations where the instinct was to act first, to procure a tool, launch a dashboard or restructure a team. And we have both seen how these well-intentioned moves can backfire if they are not grounded in diagnosis. The assumptions that underpin quick actions are often invisible: assumptions about what people know, about how roles are structured, about whether governance processes are actually followed. Without diagnosis, those assumptions quietly derail the work.

## Friction is not uniform

One of the insights we have learned, across consulting and leadership roles, is that friction is not evenly distributed. Two teams can sit in the same company, use the same stack and yet live completely different realities.

For analysts, the blocker may be inconsistent definitions and opaque documentation. For engineers, it may be fragile pipelines that break without warning. For business leads, it may be uncertainty about which KPI is authoritative. Friction is contextual. Unless you can name and map it, you cannot design capabilities to relieve it.

The Enabling Data Model addresses this by offering a Friction Taxonomy across its four pillars. This taxonomy is not exhaustive, but it captures the recurring patterns we have seen across multiple organisations.

## Friction Taxonomy

*People*

- Ambiguity of ownership: no clear accountability for key assets
- Over-reliance on experts: knowledge trapped in a few individuals
- Uneven data literacy: some functions fluent, others left behind
- Misaligned incentives: KPIs that reward volume of output rather than trusted outcomes

*Governance*

- Metric sprawl: duplicated definitions across domains or markets
- Outdated glossaries: knowledge bases frozen in time
- Fragile contracts: handshake agreements rather than defined interfaces
- Inconsistent certification: assets marked as 'trusted' without clear criteria or review

*Technology*

- Disconnected tools: lineage and metadata trapped in silos
- Reactive engineering: impact of changes discovered only after breakages
- Lack of observability: failures spotted by users, not systems
- Monolithic platforms: slow to adapt, expensive to scale

*Enablement*

- Poor onboarding: new joiners losing hours searching or recreating assets
- Low adoption: data catalog or governance tools ignored in practice
- Documentation theatre: artefacts created for compliance, not for use
- Missing feedback loops: no visibility on whether assets are used, trusted or valuable

**Model in practice: friction snapshot**

When one diagnostic exercise was run inside a high-growth enterprise, four frictions stood out. Analysts confessed that glossary terms were duplicated and often contradictory, a clear case of Governance, Standards and Definitions. Engineers highlighted that lineage between transformation and BI layers was unreliable, a gap in Technology, Observability and Resilience. Business leads admitted they could not tell which KPIs were official, showing a weakness in Enablement, Use Case and Data Catalog Maturity. Finally, ownership of critical datasets had drifted as people moved roles, leaving a vacuum in People, Role Clarity and Stewardship. Individually, these might have looked like disconnected complaints. Seen through the Enabling Data Model, they formed a coherent pattern: a system where trust could not take hold because friction accumulated at every pillar.

## Diagnostic rubric: the backbone

The diagnostic rubric is the backbone of the Enabling Data Model. It provides the structure that turns listening into evidence and evidence into design. Without a rubric, discovery sessions risk becoming a series of anecdotes. These stories are important, but unless they can be organised, compared and shared, they rarely lead to alignment. The rubric creates that common frame. It allows leaders to ask not only 'What is happening?' but 'Where does it sit, why is it happening and how might we change it?'

The rubric is structured across the four pillars of the Enabling Data Model: People, Governance, Technology and Enablement. Each pillar is broken down into dimensions that capture the most critical levers of capability. Each dimension is scored on a four-point scale of operational maturity.

**Table A1.1** *The four-point scale of operational maturity*

| Level | Descriptor |
|---|---|
| 1 Nascent | Fragmented or ad hoc |
| 2 Emerging | Defined but inconsistent |
| 3 Scaling | Embedded with growing consistency |
| 4 Operationalised | Scaled and durable |

The purpose of this scale is not to label teams as 'good' or 'bad'. Its purpose is to surface where friction lives, to show where strengths already exist and to provide a common language for improvement.

### How to score

1 Score by persona, not in aggregate. An analyst may experience 'Self-service and usability' as level 1, while a data engineer may score it at level 3. Both views matter.
2 Capture the 'why'. For every score, write one sentence explaining the reason. This narrative context is as valuable as the number.
3 Look for patterns. Alignment emerges when you see friction clustering across pillars.
4 Heatmap your findings. Capture a baseline and then map your target state for the next two to three quarters. This creates a visual prioritisation tool.

Tables A1.2–A1.5 are on the following pages.

## Full enabling data diagnostic rubric by pillar

**Table A1.2** *People*

| Dimension | 1 Nascent | 2 Emerging | 3 Scaling | 4 Operationalised |
|---|---|---|---|---|
| Role clarity and ownership | Roles undefined or siloed | Some roles defined, unclear ownership | Clear roles with partial accountability | Roles well defined across lifecycle, clear interfaces |
| Data literacy and fluency | Reliance on specialists | Inconsistent fluency across functions | Growing baseline and vocabulary | Organisation-wide fluency and shared language |
| Capability development | No clear skill progression | Ad hoc training or mentoring | Defined paths and internal learning models | Structured growth tracks and mentorship systems |
| Incentives and cultural alignment | Conflicting KPIs or goals | Some shared OKRs, limited alignment | Incentives support collaboration and trust | Outcomes-based reward structure, cross-functional KPIs |
| Ways of working and integration | Reactive, siloed workflows | Partial integration with delivery | Embedded rituals (sprints, reviews, retrospectives) | Agile-compatible, consistent integration practices |

**Table A1.3** *Governance*

| Dimension | 1 Nascent | 2 Emerging | 3 Scaling | 4 Operationalised |
|---|---|---|---|---|
| Ownership and stewardship | Undefined, centralised | Partial assignment of roles | Federated ownership with central standards | Stewardship embedded in all teams |
| Standards and definitions | Metric sprawl, conflicting logic | Some standardisation via consensus | Central glossary with working groups | Certified metrics with embedded governance workflows |
| Data contracts and interopera-bility | Fragile, undocumented links | Some handshake agreements | Informal contracts with evolving accountability | Formalised SLO-backed contracts between domains |
| Lineage and observability | No visibility, reliance on tribal knowledge | Basic cataloguing or lineage views | Lineage tracked, freshness alerts in place | Real-time observability with monitoring and alerting |
| Policy enforcement and compliance | Manual processes, gaps in coverage | Reactive compliance | Partially automated policy management | Full automation of data policy and privacy enforcement |

**Table A1.4** *Technology*

| Dimension | 1 Nascent | 2 Emerging | 3 Scaling | 4 Operationalised |
|---|---|---|---|---|
| Architecture and modularity | Monolithic or legacy | Hybrid with limited flexibility | Service oriented and partially modular | Fully composable architecture integrated across stack |
| Self-service and usability | Engineer-dependent pipelines | Partial self-service with friction | Easy access with growing usage across teams | Intuitive, role-based self-service with training built in |
| Lifecycle coverage and extensibility | Ingestion-focused, fragmented | Covers modelling or visualisation | Supports end-to-end use cases | Full lifecycle platform with extension hooks |
| Observability and resilience | Failures discovered downstream | Some alerts for failure/freshness | Monitored SLOs with alerting and rollback options | Resilient pipelines with root cause and proactive observability |
| Security and privacy | Manual permissioning, access issues | Role-based access in place | Fine-grained controls, access logs | End-to-end security model with policy-as-code enforcement |
| Build vs buy strategy | Opportunistic and ad hoc | Vendor tools adopted as quick fixes | Selective build/buy with some reuse | Clear build vs buy logic aligned to strategic capability |

**Table A1.5** *Enablement*

| Dimension | 1 Nascent | 2 Emerging | 3 Scaling | 4 Operationalised |
|---|---|---|---|---|
| Documentation and literacy support | Tribal knowledge, outdated documentation | Scattered documentation, some guides | Playbooks and documentation used in onboarding | Systematic documentation embedded in workflow |
| Onboarding and certification | No formal onboarding | Tool-focused walkthroughs | Role-based learning plans | Certification pathways aligned to user journeys |
| Embedded help and support | Ticket-dependent support | Slack channels, some FAQs | Embedded guides, curated examples | Product-style help embedded in tooling |
| Measurement and feedback loops | No tracking of adoption | Anecdotal feedback only | Usage telemetry, periodic surveys | Feedback loops drive continuous improvement roadmap |
| Cultural rituals and reinforcement | No shared data rituals | Some showcases or knowledge shares | Recurring ceremonies to embed data values | Embedded rituals, office hours, showcase weeks |
| Use case and data catalog maturity | No catalog or documentation of use cases | Informal tracking of some reusable data sets | Catalog aligned to working data sets and use cases | Certified, discoverable, curated catalog aligned to persona needs and business outcomes |

## Making the rubric actionable

The rubric becomes powerful only when it is applied with discipline. Two practices are essential. First, score by persona, not only in aggregate. A product analyst, a data engineer and a business lead will each experience friction differently. By capturing their scores separately, you reveal where perspectives diverge – and those divergences are often the richest insights. Second, capture a one-sentence 'why' for every score. Numbers without explanation are empty. A short narrative for each score transforms abstract data into grounded evidence.

Once scores are collected, the next step is to visualise them as a baseline heatmap. This shows not only today's reality but also the ambition for the next two to three quarters. The heatmap makes priorities clear. Baseline reveals where you are starting. Target shows what good looks like in your context. Delta, the gap, becomes the focus for design and investment. The purpose of the heatmap is not to demand perfection but to create a shared view of where progress matters most.

### Example: baseline vs target heatmap

A sample baseline heatmap across selected dimensions might look as shown in Figure A1.1.

Baseline vs Target Heatmap (Sample)

| **Pillar** | **Dimension** | **Baseline Score** | **Target Score (2–3 Quarters)** |
|---|---|---|---|
| People | Role Clarity & Ownership | 1 | 3 |
| Governance | Standards & Definitions | 2 | 3 |
| Technology | Observability & Resilience | 1 | 3 |
| Enablement | Onboarding & Certification | 2 | 3 |
| Governance | Lineage & Observability | 2 | 3 |
| Technology | Self-service & Usability | 2 | 4 |

**Figure A1.1** *Baseline vs target scores for selected dimensions. Each score reflects how a specific persona experienced the system at the time of assessment.*

**Model in practice: baseline heatmap**

When one enterprise applied the rubric to its metadata programme, analysts scored Role Clarity and Ownership at level 1, noting that they were still reliant on Slack channels to identify data owners. Engineers placed Observability and Resilience at level 1, explaining that 'we only know a pipeline has failed when a stakeholder shouts'. Meanwhile, governance leads gave Standards and Definitions a level 2, acknowledging partial glossaries but admitting duplication and drift.

The surprise was not the low scores but the mismatch between groups. Executives had assumed that catalog and lineage investments were already delivering value. The heatmap revealed that for front-line users, those investments had yet to translate into trust or efficiency. This alignment of perception and evidence became the foundation for a redesigned approach.

## Toolkit in action: personas

### Why personas matter

One of the most common mistakes in data transformation is designing in abstraction. Teams launch platforms, roll out catalogs or define governance frameworks as if the user is a generic 'analyst' or 'engineer'. In reality, no two users experience the same friction in the same way. A business sponsor struggling with conflicting dashboards does not share the same pain as a data engineer firefighting fragile pipelines. A product owner may be paralysed by KPI misalignment, while an operational manager on the shop floor may never see a dashboard at all but still feels the consequences of poor data through delayed processes or missed targets.

The Enabling Data Model encourages leaders to look at transformation through the eyes of their personas. Personas are not abstract demographics. They are role-based archetypes that surface lived experience. They capture goals, frictions, critical dimensions and a clear 'definition of done'. By grounding strategy in personas, you avoid designing for 'the average user' and instead build targeted capabilities that unlock adoption, trust and business value.

It is also important to broaden the frame. Your organisation's data ecosystem impacts on more than analysts and engineers. A sales executive, a plant operator or a customer service representative may all rely on outputs shaped by data, even if they never log in to a dashboard. Understanding these secondary personas is often where hidden frictions surface; for example, the plant operative waiting on a batch quality report, or the customer care agent lacking timely context on churn risk.

### Core personas

1. The decision maker (executive or business sponsor)
    - Goal: Make fast, confident decisions that drive strategy and performance.
    - Top frictions:
        - Conflicting numbers across dashboards create credibility gaps.
        - Delayed insights mean decisions are made with outdated information.
        - Lack of trust in data leads to reliance on intuition or shadow reporting.
    - Critical rubric dimensions:
        - Governance: Standards and Definitions, Certification and Stewardship.
        - Enablement: Use Case and Data Catalog Maturity, Ritual Reinforcement.

- Definition of done:
  - Board or leadership meetings spend less time debating numbers and more time discussing actions.
  - A small set of certified KPIs underpins all critical decisions.
  - Executives report confidence in the numbers they use.

2 The business manager (operational leader or product owner)

- Goal: Run teams effectively, align KPIs with strategy and meet delivery commitments.
- Top frictions:
  - KPIs are inconsistent across functions such as finance, operations and product.
  - Data arrives too late to inform weekly or daily cycles.
  - Ownership of metrics or dashboards is unclear.
- Critical rubric dimensions:
  - People: Role Clarity and Ownership, Cultural Alignment.
  - Enablement: Documentation, Onboarding and Certification.
- Definition of done:
  - Dashboards reflect agreed OKRs and are updated on agreed cycles.
  - Misalignment disputes are rare, resolved quickly through clear governance.
  - Managers can explain the meaning of key metrics without caveats.

3 The data consumer (analyst or domain expert)

- Goal: Translate data into insight and deliver answers to business questions.
- Top frictions:
  - Duplicate metrics across dashboards and teams.
  - Hard-to-find definitions and lineage.
  - Reliance on engineers for access to core datasets.
- Critical rubric dimensions:
  - Governance: Standards and Definitions, Lineage and Observability.
  - Enablement: Documentation and Help Systems, Data Catalog Maturity.
- Definition of done:
  - Able to locate and trust a certified metric in under one minute.
  - Reduced reliance on Slack or ticket queues for basic questions.
  - More time spent on analysis than searching or rework.

4 The data builder (engineer or data scientist)

- Goal: Deliver reliable pipelines, models and datasets for others to consume.
- Top frictions:
  - Firefighting failures due to poor observability.

- Pressure to reinvent solutions for every request.
- Ambiguity around ownership and accountability across teams.

- Critical rubric dimensions:
  - Technology: Observability and Resilience, Lifecycle Extensibility.
  - Governance: Stewardship, Data Contracts.
- Definition of done:
  - Failures detected and resolved through system alerts, not user complaints.
  - Reusable components cover the majority of requests.
  - Contracts and SLAs define expectations clearly between producers and consumers.

5 The extended persona (operational or customer-facing staff)
- Goal: Execute front-line tasks effectively in manufacturing, customer service, logistics, or retail operations.
- Top frictions:
  - Reports arrive too late to inform daily work.
  - Data is presented in formats that do not map to workflows.
  - Feedback on errors or gaps never makes its way back upstream.
- Critical rubric dimensions:
  - Enablement: Documentation in context, Feedback Loops.
  - People: Incentives and Cultural Alignment.
- Definition of done:
  - Operators see data in real time, in formats that match their environment such as dashboards on factory screens or alerts in workflow apps.
  - Errors are reported once and resolved at source, not repeatedly downstream.
  - Performance improvements are visible and attributable to better data.

## Interview prompts by persona

Decision maker:

1. What number do you most hesitate to quote in a board meeting, and why?
2. How often do you receive conflicting reports?
3. Which dashboards do you rely on most, and how confident are you in them?
4. When did data last accelerate or delay a critical decision?
5. What would make you trust your KPIs without qualification?

Business manager:

1 Which KPIs are most critical for your team, and do they align with OKRs?
2 How often do you see delays in receiving data you need?
3 What happens when KPIs conflict across teams?
4 Who do you turn to when you cannot interpret a metric?
5 What decision would be easier if you had data in real time?

Data consumer (analyst):

1 How long does it take you to find the metric you need?
2 When was the last time you reused a certified dataset?
3 Which definitions or terms cause the most confusion?
4 How many hours a week do you spend chasing clarity from others?
5 What would make your analysis faster and less stressful?

Data builder (engineer or scientist):

1 How do you usually discover when something breaks?
2 Which requests feel like reinventing the wheel?
3 How many times have you rebuilt the same pipeline or feature?
4 How clear are ownership boundaries with upstream and downstream teams?
5 What observability signals or contracts would give you peace of mind?

Extended persona (operational staff):

1 When do you receive the data you need for your daily work?
2 How is the data presented, and does it fit your workflow?
3 What happens when the data is wrong, and how do you flag it?
4 Does the feedback ever come back to you with a resolution?
5 What would make your job easier if data worked better?

**Table A1.6** *Model in practice: persona voices*

| Persona | Before | After |
|---|---|---|
| Decision maker | 'Every report came with a caveat. We wasted half our leadership meetings debating whose numbers to trust.' | 'Now we have one KPI set. Debates are shorter, and the focus is on decisions, not definitions.' |
| Data consumer | 'I had three tabs open – Slack, JIRA, Confluence – just to find which revenue number was safe.' | 'Now I can search the catalog. I find the definition in seconds, with ownership and certification visible.' |
| Extended persona, plant operative | 'By the time I got the report, the batch had already moved on. I could not correct the issue.' | 'Now the data appears on a screen above the line. I can see issues immediately and act before they escalate.' |

## Assessing platform fit: from friction to architecture

Personas tell us *who* experiences friction. The Platform Fit Canvas tells us *why*. It takes the lived experience of users and traces it back to the system layers where capability is either enabling or blocking outcomes.

In most organisations, platform debates are dominated by feature checklists and vendor comparisons. Leaders ask, 'Does this tool integrate with Snowflake?' or 'How many connectors does it have?' While these questions matter, they do not tell us whether the platform actually supports the *workloads* that users rely on every day.

The Platform Fit Canvas shifts the conversation. Instead of features, it focuses on capability alignment: does the platform enable the interaction that a persona needs to deliver value? A platform may look strong in ingestion but weak in observability. It may be robust for analysts running SQL queries but fragile for scientists deploying models. Without this mapping, teams risk investing in tools that are technically impressive but experientially unfit.

### How to use the Platform Fit Canvas

The process typically unfolds in four steps:

1. *List critical workloads.* These are not generic 'use cases' but recurring patterns of work that matter most to your business: ingestion, model development, experimentation, reporting, metadata search.
2. *Map personas to workloads.* Identify who interacts with each workload and how. An analyst's 'exploratory analysis' looks different from a scientist's 'model development'.
3. *Trace capability layers.* For each workload, identify which parts of the stack are involved: ingestion, transformation, storage, semantic, reporting, modelling, experimentation or collaboration.
4. *Capture friction and ideal state.* Document the observed pain points (evidence from personas, telemetry, artefacts) and describe what an ideal experience would look like.

The result is a structured snapshot of where the platform fits, where it fractures and where investment will have the most impact.

See Table A1.7 on the next page.

**Table A1.7** *Platform Fit Canvas with example*

| Workload type | Primary personas | Interaction mode | Platform capability layer(s) | Observed friction | Ideal experience / gaps to close |
|---|---|---|---|---|---|
| Batch ingestion | Data engineers | Scheduled or event-driven pipeline development | Ingestion, Transformation, Storage | Failures not observable, unclear handoffs | Resilient pipelines, ownership visibility |
| Exploratory analysis | Analysts, domain experts | SQL-based or visual query tooling | Semantic layer, Query engine | Inconsistent metric logic, slow performance | Certified metrics, fast query paths |
| Model development | Data scientists | Notebook-based development | Modelling, Feature management | Poor feature discoverability, unclear handoffs | Feature registry, model tracking, retraining signals |
| Real-time analytics | Product or operations teams | Event-based or stream processing | Event collection, Stream transport | Latency unknown, no change control | Freshness SLAs, schema governance |
| Experimentation | PMs, analysts | A/B design and evaluation tooling | Experiment layer, Metric attribution | Duplicated logic, no standard evaluation model | Shared logic library, metric certification |
| Business reporting | Finance, executives | Dashboard consumption, KPI monitoring | Reporting layer, Semantic governance | Conflicting numbers across dashboards | Certified KPIs, governed reporting layer |
| Metadata experience (example) | Analysts, engineers, business managers | Search, browse, collaborate | Transformation, Orchestration, Storage, BI, Collaboration tools | Trust signals absent, metadata fragmented across systems, adoption low | Trust indicators visible in context (certification, owner, SLA), unified search across stack, usage telemetry closes adoption gaps |

## Platform capability layers (sample definitions)

- *Ingestion layer:* Enables collection and transport of raw data from source systems.
- *Transformation layer:* Applies business rules; joins, cleanses and prepares datasets.
- *Storage layer:* Manages persisted raw, working or curated data states.

- *Semantic layer:* Serves consistent metrics and joins to query tools or dashboards.
- *Modelling layer:* Supports training, evaluating and deploying ML models.
- *Experimentation layer:* Enables structured testing and performance attribution.
- *Reporting layer:* Visual delivery and aggregation of insights to non-technical consumers.
- *Collaboration layer:* Connects metadata, documentation and workflow tools to daily practice.

## Narrative in practice

When one digital operator ran its first platform fit workshop, the instinct was to jump into vendor comparisons. Instead, the team slowed down and began with workloads. Analysts described exploratory analysis that took hours longer than it should because definitions of core KPIs were inconsistent. Engineers highlighted that ingestion pipelines failed silently, with the first signal of an issue coming from a business stakeholder's Slack message. Business managers admitted that they often could not tell which dashboard carried the authoritative KPI.

By mapping these frictions onto workloads, the conversation changed. The canvas revealed that ingestion and observability were weak links for engineers, while semantic consistency was the gap for analysts and managers. The metadata experience row was especially revealing: the organisation had three separate glossaries, none updated and no way to see certification or ownership in context.

The ideal experience was reframed: metadata should be discoverable, searchable across the stack and visibly carry trust indicators such as certification status, owner and SLA. When the first pilots introduced these signals directly into BI tools and search results, the difference was immediate. Analysts stopped asking the same metric questions repeatedly, engineers could trace issues faster and managers expressed greater confidence in their dashboards.

**Model in practice: platform fit excerpt**

| Before | After |
|---|---|
| 'I would open three tabs: Confluence, JIRA and Slack, just to find out if a metric was trustworthy.' | 'Now when I search the data catalog, I see the certification badge, the owner and the SLA in the result. I do not need to ask anyone. I just know.' |

## From diagnosis to design principles

Diagnosis maps friction, but design intent is what converts that insight into action. Too often, organisations stop at the diagnosis stage: they know where the pain lives, but they rush into tactical fixes without clear principles to guide trade-offs. The result is predictable: more tools purchased, more dashboards built and more committees formed, but the same structural frictions remain.

The Enabling Data Model helps to bridge this gap by translating diagnostic evidence into design principles. These principles act as guardrails that steer decisions, especially when pressure builds to deliver speed over sustainability. They are deliberately simple, but they carry profound implications. They are not invented abstractions. They come from patterns observed repeatedly in our work and align with the enduring principles captured in the Data Manifesto (Chapter 5).

## Six design principles

### *Trust before scale*

*Rationale:* It is tempting to aim for completeness, to catalog every table, document every metric and tag every field. But completeness without trust is meaningless. A small set of reliable, high-value assets creates more impact than a sprawling collection that no one believes in.

*What this changes in practice:* Teams focus on a small set of high-value assets first, often the top 10 to 20 metrics or datasets that underpin core decisions. Adoption grows because people see immediate value. Scale follows trust, not the other way around.

### *Enablement over enforcement*

*Rationale:* Governance fails when it is experienced as bureaucracy. Amy Edmondson's (2012) work on psychological safety shows that people engage with rules and feedback loops only if they believe they are supported, not punished. The role of governance is to make the right path easier, not harder.

*What this changes in practice:* Instead of central sign-off queues, organisations embed guidance inside workflows. Examples include in-tool prompts in BI dashboards, automated lineage displays in pipeline tools or glossary links in query editors. Compliance becomes almost invisible because it is the most efficient way to work.

### Lifecycle, not snapshot

*Rationale:* Many governance initiatives assume that assets, once defined, stay trusted forever. In reality, definitions drift, pipelines break and people move roles. Chris Argyris's (1991) distinction between single-loop and double-loop learning is relevant here: static controls only correct surface issues, while lifecycle thinking revisits assumptions and adapts over time.

*What this changes in practice:* Every trusted artefact is given an expiry or review cycle. Glossary terms must be recertified, dashboards must be reviewed quarterly and contracts must evolve with schema changes. Trust is treated as dynamic, not permanent.

### Federate stewardship

*Rationale:* Trust does not scale from the centre. As Elinor Ostrom's Nobel prize-winning research on commons governance showed, local stewardship outperforms central policing when resources are distributed and complex (Ostrom, 1990). The same holds true for data. Ownership must sit at the edges, with central teams offering light coordination.

*What this changes in practice:* Domains nominate trust champions, who run certification locally. Instead of waiting for central approval, assets are certified and maintained at source. The centre provides playbooks and telemetry, but trust is embedded where the work happens.

### Measure adoption, not volume

*Rationale:* Volume is a vanity metric. Counting catalog entries, dashboards or models built tells you nothing about value. What matters is whether the artefacts are used, trusted and enable faster, better decisions. As Davenport and Prusak (1998) argued, knowledge has no value unless it is applied.

*What this changes in practice:* Metrics shift to usage telemetry such as searches, views, recertification rates, time saved in onboarding or debugging and adoption trends across domains. Leaders stop celebrating ingestion milestones and start celebrating adoption milestones.

### Make correctness the path of least resistance

*Rationale:* Behavioural economics has long shown that defaults shape behaviour more than rules (Thaler and Sunstein, 2008). If it is easier to duplicate a metric than to certify one, duplication will win every time. The design challenge is to make the correct action the easiest one.

*What this changes in practice:* Systems are designed so that certified metrics appear first in search, lineage is one click away and certified dashboards load faster or with fewer steps. People do not comply because they are told to. They comply because it is faster and easier.

**Model in practice: principle to decision**

When one enterprise redesigned its metadata programme, these principles turned into concrete decisions.

- *Federate stewardship* → Introduced domain trust champions who owned certification workflows, reducing approval times from weeks to days.
- *Measure adoption, not volume* → Stopped reporting 'number of catalog entries' and instead tracked active searches, usage per certified asset and onboarding time saved.
- *Make correctness the path of least resistance* → Surfaced certification badges, owner details and SLA indicators directly in BI dashboards. Analysts naturally chose certified metrics because they were easier to find.

## Intervention Catalog (by pillar)

Diagnosis and design principles give you clarity, but clarity alone does not shift behaviour. Leaders often ask, 'What do I do on Monday morning?' The Intervention Catalog answers that question. It is not exhaustive, nor is it intended as a rigid blueprint. Think of it as a menu of high-leverage moves. Each intervention is small enough to trial quickly, but designed to unlock systemic change when applied consistently.

The value of this catalog lies not in following every item, but in selecting the ones that match the friction surfaced in your diagnostic. For some organisations, the biggest gains will come from governance fixes. For others, enablement will move the needle first. The discipline is to choose deliberately, pilot surgically and measure outcomes in adoption and trust.

## People: shaping ownership and fluency

Friction often lives in people rather than platforms. Analysts rely on informal experts, ownership drifts as roles change and new joiners lose weeks just learning where to look. People-focused interventions are about making ownership explicit, building confidence in roles and equipping teams to contribute without bottlenecks.

### *Trust champions*

- *When to use:* Early in programmes where credibility is low and central teams are overloaded.

- *What to change:* Appoint visible stewards inside domains. These are not bureaucratic gatekeepers but peers with enough respect and fluency to certify assets and answer questions.
- *How to measure:* Growth in certified assets, time from request to certification, recognition of champions in team retrospectives.

#### *Explicit ownership on high-value assets*

- *When to use:* When everyone uses the KPI but no one maintains it.
- *What to change:* For every high-value dataset or dashboard, assign a named producer, a primary consumer and a clear escalation channel.
- *How to measure:* Share of executive KPIs with named owners, mean incident resolution time, reduction in 'who owns this?' messages.

#### *Role-based onboarding tracks*

- *When to use:* When analyst or engineer onboarding is inconsistent and turnover is high.
- *What to change:* Replace tool tours with role-specific paths. Analysts learn how to use the catalog and certified assets. Engineers learn how to trace lineage and update contracts.
- *How to measure:* Time to first certified contribution, reduction in repeated 'basic questions' in Slack or tickets.

### Governance: turning rules into trust

Governance is where intent often collapses into bureaucracy. The interventions here focus on making rules visible, lightweight and renewable, so trust becomes something operational rather than ceremonial.

#### *Lightweight certification with expiry*

- *When to use:* When duplication and glossary drift undermine trust.
- *What to change:* Certification workflows that take hours, not weeks. Assets expire unless recertified, ensuring trust is always current.
- *How to measure:* Recertification rates, drop in duplicated metrics, confidence survey scores.

#### *Single glossary per concept with local variants*

- *When to use:* When three teams hold competing definitions of 'active user' or 'net revenue.'

- *What to change:* One canonical definition per concept, with clearly flagged local variants where context requires.
- *How to measure:* Reduction in glossary duplication, adoption of canonical terms in reporting.

#### *Data contracts on critical interfaces*

- *When to use:* When schema changes repeatedly break pipelines or dashboards.
- *What to change:* Define schema stability, freshness targets and notification protocols for changes. Contracts move handshake agreements into explicit commitments.
- *How to measure:* Number of contract breaches, adherence to SLAs, time from breach to resolution.

### Technology: embedding observability and trust

Technology interventions focus less on buying new tools and more on making existing platforms visible, traceable and usable. The goal is not raw power, but resilience and clarity at the points of highest friction.

#### *End-to-end lineage*

- *When to use:* When engineers firefight in the dark and analysts cannot explain KPI derivations.
- *What to change:* Deploy automated lineage across transformation, orchestration, storage and BI.
- *How to measure:* Reduction in mean time to root cause, increase in lineage views accessed per week.

#### *Trust indicators where people search*

- *When to use:* When adoption stalls because users cannot tell which dataset or dashboard is trustworthy.
- *What to change:* Embed certification badges, steward names and SLA commitments in catalog search, dashboards and query tools.
- *How to measure:* Share of queries run against certified assets, reduction in duplicated dashboards.

### *Usage telemetry instrumented*

- *When to use:* When no one knows if catalogs or governance workflows are being used.
- *What to change:* Instrument searches, clicks and asset views. Use telemetry to see where adoption is strong and where friction persists.
- *How to measure:* Active user counts, adoption curves by domain, search-to-click success rates.

## Enablement: closing the loop

Enablement is where interventions become sticky. Without reinforcement, even the best design fades into disuse. These moves ensure that changes embed into daily practice and keep improving over time.

### *In-tool help*

- *When to use:* When Slack and ticket queues are clogged with the same repeated questions.
- *What to change:* Provide glossary links, examples and playbooks directly inside the tools analysts and engineers already use.
- *How to measure:* Drop in repeated support requests, survey feedback on ease of finding answers.

### *Monthly adoption reviews*

- *When to use:* When usage varies across domains and success stories are not shared.
- *What to change:* Convene domain champions monthly to review telemetry, highlight what worked and refine workflows.
- *How to measure:* Growth in cross-domain adoption, reduction in variance between high- and low-adoption teams.

### *Narrative release notes for certified assets*

- *When to use:* When certification is invisible and new assets fail to gain traction.
- *What to change:* Publish short narrative updates, what was certified, who owns it and how to use it, not just technical logs.
- *How to measure:* Engagement with release notes, usage increase for newly certified assets.

**Model in practice: three quick wins**

When one high-growth organisation began applying this catalog, three interventions created visible momentum in under a quarter.

1. *Named ownership on executive KPIs:* Every critical dashboard gained a named steward. Within weeks, incident resolution time dropped by a quarter because people knew exactly who to contact.
2. *Certification with expiry:* Lightweight expiry flushed out dozens of stale glossary entries. Confidence rose quickly because people knew that a 'certified' badge meant something current.
3. *Trust indicators in BI tools:* Badges and steward names surfaced directly in dashboards. Analysts naturally chose certified assets because they were easier to find. Within three months, repeated metric questions in Slack had halved.

## Execution playbook: 0–30–60–90 days

Many data transformations lose momentum because they lack rhythm. Leaders announce ambitious goals, but day-to-day action quickly fragments. The 0–30–60–90 playbook provides a clock you can run, a way to pace activity, build evidence and sequence adoption. It does not replace strategy; it operationalises it into phases that build confidence through visible outcomes.

Each phase lasts roughly a month and is designed to build on the previous one. The early emphasis is on listening and diagnosis. The middle phase moves into proving and designing. The final phase is about embedding, scaling and making adoption measurable.

### 0–30 days: diagnose and align

*Core activities*

- Conduct structured interviews and shadowing across five to seven pivotal personas.
- Score the diagnostic rubric by persona, capture one-sentence 'why' notes for each score.
- Build a friction map across People, Governance, Technology and Enablement.
- Identify three to five potential quick wins that reduce pain without requiring major investment.

*Artefacts produced*

- Stakeholder map and interview notes
- Persona-based rubric scores and heatmap baseline
- Friction map with evidence quotes and telemetry references
- Quick-win backlog with impact vs effort matrix.

*Decision gates*

- Agreement from sponsors on the top two to three friction areas to prioritise
- Validation of diagnostic baseline by domain leads.

*Risks and mitigations*

| Risk | Mitigation |
|---|---|
| Pressure to act fast undermines diagnosis. | Publish a visible discovery plan and update weekly to show progress. |
| Stakeholders withhold candid feedback. | Use anonymous surveys alongside interviews to cross-check. |

## 31–60 days: design and prove

*Core activities*

- Launch pilots in two or three domains focused on the highest-friction areas.
- Agree on lightweight certification path with expiry for high-value assets.
- Close Platform Fit gaps for priority workloads, for example end-to-end lineage and trust indicators.
- Surface trust indicators in catalog and BI tools where users already search.

*Artefacts produced*

- Pilot charters with objectives, measures and owners
- Draft certification workflow and expiry schedule
- Platform Fit gap analysis with mitigation roadmap
- Prototype dashboards showing trust indicators such as badges, steward names and SLA annotations.

*Decision gates*

- Go or no-go decision on certifying the first batch of assets
- Agreement on Platform Fit investments needed to expand pilots.

*Risks and mitigations*

| Risk | Mitigation |
|---|---|
| Pilots stall due to lack of domain engagement. | Secure domain champion commitment before launch. |
| Certification becomes over-engineered. | Start with minimum viable criteria and iterate with adoption feedback. |

## 61–90 days: embed and scale

*Core activities*

- Nominate trust champions across all key domains.
- Roll out Data Academy onboarding track with role-based paths.
- Instrument adoption telemetry such as catalog searches, certified asset use and lineage views.
- Run first monthly adoption review with domain champions.

*Artefacts produced*

- Trust champion roster with responsibilities
- Data Academy materials and onboarding plan
- Telemetry dashboards tracking usage, adoption and certification throughput
- Adoption review notes with shared quick wins and blockers.

*Decision gates*

- Formal adoption of champions by domain leads.
- Agreement to publish telemetry dashboards organisation-wide.
- First quarterly review comparing baseline versus post-pilot adoption.

*Risks and mitigations*

| Risk | Mitigation |
|---|---|
| Champions treated as extra admin duty. | Recognise champions publicly and align responsibilities to business OKRs. |
| Adoption telemetry is collected but unused. | Review metrics monthly and tie insights to backlog prioritisation. |

**Model in practice: milestones**

In one large-scale metadata initiative, the 0–30–60–90 rhythm created clarity and momentum. Four milestones stood out:

- *Day 30:* Friction map revealed that glossary duplication and lineage gaps were the biggest pain points, validated by both analysts and engineers.
- *Day 45:* First pilot certified 12 high-value KPIs using lightweight expiry rules. Adoption feedback was positive because the process was fast.
- *Day 70:* Trust indicators appeared in BI dashboards. Analysts began defaulting to certified assets because they were visibly easier to find.
- *Day 90:* Monthly adoption review launched with champions from five domains. For the first time, telemetry made adoption visible and incident resolution times dropped by nearly 20%.

## Measuring what matters

Many data leaders fall into the trap of celebrating delivery: the number of pipelines created, the number of glossary terms documented or the percentage of sources connected. These are easy to count, but they are vanity metrics. They measure activity, not impact. They show effort expended, not whether the system has become more usable, trusted or enabling.

The Enabling Data Model asks us to measure what really matters: whether friction is reducing, whether adoption is spreading and whether trust is becoming embedded in daily work. These are not side questions. They are the only meaningful signals of progress. If people still hesitate to trust a number, if onboarding still takes weeks or if incidents still surprise executives, then no amount of delivery volume can be called success.

### From delivery to adoption

The shift is simple but profound: move from counting what has been built to tracking how people use it. Adoption metrics are behavioural, cultural and relational. They tell you if data products are enabling decisions, if governance is helping rather than hindering and if engineers and analysts are spending less time firefighting and more time delivering value.

Adoption metrics do three things:

1. *They show whether new behaviours are sticking.* If onboarding time is falling quarter by quarter, it means new joiners are benefiting from structural clarity, not just individual heroics.
2. *They highlight where to focus.* If certification throughput is rising but recertification rates are lagging, you know trust is not being maintained.

3 *They build credibility.* Executives are far more persuaded by evidence that productivity is improving and incidents are falling than by a graph showing pipeline counts.

## Compact KPI set

A lean but powerful set of indicators can capture these dynamics. Each one is tied to behaviour rather than output.

- *Onboarding time saved per analyst per week:* Signals how quickly new joiners move from searching to delivering. If this number drops, it proves that documentation, catalogs and onboarding tracks are working. Indicative range: Two to four hours saved per week within the first quarter.
- *Reduction in repeated metric questions:* Monitored via chat and ticket volumes. Fewer repeated questions show that certified assets and lineage are trusted.
  Indicative range: 30–50% reduction within three to six months.
- *Active data catalog users and repeat usage ratio:* Tracks adoption depth. One-off logins mean little; repeat usage means integration into daily work. Indicative range: 90–140% growth in active users over six months, with majority repeat visits.
- *Certification throughput and recertification rate:* Initial certification shows momentum. Recertification shows discipline. Both are needed to sustain trust.
  Indicative range: 1.8–2.3 times increase in certified assets within nine months, with recertification cycles established.
- *Time to detect and time to resolve lineage-related incidents:* When observability works, breakages are discovered by systems, not end users. Faster resolution shows that ownership and contracts are clear.
  Indicative range: 15–30% faster incident resolution after lineage instrumentation.
- *Share of executive KPIs backed by certified definitions:* Perhaps the most powerful cultural signal. If leadership dashboards rely on certified definitions, it sends a message throughout the organisation that trust is non-negotiable.
  Indicative range: Shift from minority coverage to majority coverage within two to three quarters.

## Baseline first

Every organisation begins from a different point. A 30% reduction in repeated questions may be revolutionary in one company and negligible in another. This is why baselining is critical. Capture the 'before' picture with:

- telemetry from catalog searches, tickets and usage logs
- surveys asking analysts, engineers and business users how much time they lose to searching or reconciling
- artefact reviews of glossary freshness, lineage coverage and ownership clarity.

Without baselines, you cannot know if adoption is improving or just being perceived as such.

## Interpreting early signals

Adoption metrics are rarely smooth. In the first months you may see unusual spikes – for example, a rise in catalog searches that actually reflects people exploring rather than reusing. This is normal. The point is to interpret the patterns. Look for:

- *Trend direction, not single points.* Are repeated questions falling quarter on quarter, even if the first dip is small?
- *Cross-validation.* Do telemetry, survey feedback and interviews tell the same story?
- *Behavioural change.* Are people defaulting to certified assets, and are shadow glossaries disappearing?

**Model in practice: early signal pack**

In one large-scale metadata initiative, the team published a one-page 'early signal pack' after the first quarter. It included three adoption metrics:

| Metric | Baseline | Q1 result | Movement |
|---|---|---|---|
| Onboarding time per analyst (hours per week) | 6 | 3.5 | ↓ 42% |
| Repeated metric questions (tickets per month) | 240 | 155 | ↓ 35% |
| Active data catalog users | 220 | 360 | ↓ 64% |

The numbers were modest in absolute terms, but they changed the narrative. Executives saw that the initiative was not about another tool but about measurable behavioural improvements. Practitioners saw that their effort was paying off. Most importantly, the conversation shifted: success was now defined by adoption and trust, not by delivery volume.

# Appendix 2: Model in practice: metadata as a product

When a global digital operator with multi-market operations began to take stock of its data landscape, it faced an unsettling paradox. The organisation was not short of metadata. In fact, it had invested heavily in tools that promised lineage, cataloguing and governance. But none of it made a difference to the people who mattered most. Analysts spent their mornings in Slack threads chasing definitions. Engineers carried lineage in their heads, often realising dependencies only when something broke. Business leaders found themselves in meetings where two teams presented different numbers for the same KPI and neither could say which was right.

The instinct in many organisations would have been to buy a new tool. After all, several catalogs now promised AI-powered discovery, automated lineage and glossy dashboards. But there was a dawning realisation: this was not a tooling gap. It was a capability gap. The real challenge was not to capture metadata but to make it usable, trusted and embedded in everyday work.

## Diagnose: surfacing the friction

The programme began not with procurement, but with listening. Structured interviews were run across multiple domains, combined with shadowing sessions where analysts and engineers were observed at work. The findings were sobering. Analysts admitted that glossary entries were outdated and contradictory. Engineers confessed that lineage was reconstructed manually from code and memory. Product managers shared that they often delayed decisions because they were unsure which numbers to trust.

Telemetry and artefacts confirmed the picture. Only one in four glossary entries had been updated in the past year. Catalog usage was negligible. Tickets relating to 'metric clarification' accounted for a disproportionate share of support volume. Perhaps most telling, multiple versions of 'active customer' existed across markets; each was considered canonical by its owner, but none aligned.

Through the lens of the Enabling Data Model, the diagnosis came into focus. The People pillar showed dependency on a handful of experts. Governance revealed duplication and drift. Technology was fragmented, with lineage broken across tools. Enablement was absent, with no feedback loops or adoption tracking. What had looked like disconnected frustrations became a coherent map of systemic friction.

### Design: from features to capabilities

Armed with this diagnosis, the team reframed the problem. Instead of asking 'Which catalog has the most features?' the question became 'What capabilities would make metadata usable and trusted?' This was a pivotal shift.

Success was defined as three outcomes: reducing rework, accelerating onboarding and embedding trust into daily workflows. From these, design principles were drawn:

- Contribution had to be federated so that domains could certify their own assets.
- Lineage had to be end-to-end, spanning transformation, orchestration, storage and BI.
- Trust indicators had to be surfaced where people searched, not buried in a separate tool.
- Metadata had to be observable, with telemetry showing what was used and by whom.

A Platform Fit Canvas was used to evaluate options. Vendors were not scored by raw feature count but by workflow alignment, latency fit and persona needs. Analysts, engineers and business leads were each asked to test prototypes and give feedback. The outcome was not a choice of 'the best tool' but a design that aligned with capabilities the organisation actually needed.

### Deliver: pilots, Governance and Enablement

The next phase moved into delivery, but carefully. Pilots were launched in a handful of domains, chosen for their mix of urgency and influence. Each pilot had clear objectives: shorten onboarding, certify high-value assets, close lineage gaps and embed trust directly in the search experience.

Governance was federated rather than centralised. Each domain nominated a 'trust champion', a practitioner with the credibility to own certification workflows and glossary alignment. Their role was not to fill in documentation but to make trust operational on the ground. A lean central enablement team supported them, providing training, templates and telemetry.

Enablement glued the system together. A 'Data Academy' was created, with role-based onboarding tracks. In-tool guidance appeared in BI dashboards and transformation platforms. Telemetry dashboards tracked catalog searches, asset certifications and adoption velocity. Monthly adoption reviews gave champions the space to share blockers and successes.

The difference was visible within weeks. New joiners saved hours each week during onboarding. Chat volumes for repeated metric questions fell. Catalog usage grew steadily, not because people were told to use it, but because it made their lives easier.

## Scale: from data catalog to contracts

As adoption spread, a new realisation emerged. Certification gave confidence in what had been trusted yesterday – but what about tomorrow? Trust needed to be not only retrospective but predictive.

The programme began to embed contracts into the metadata layer. Certified tables now carried schema stability expectations. Service levels and freshness commitments were made visible in search results. Producer responsibilities were aligned with alerting and quality scores. Metadata became prescriptive as well as descriptive.

Looking further, the roadmap extended this principle into three horizons:

- *AI-augmented metadata:* Large language models to auto-generate summaries, recommend stewards and flag undocumented but high-usage assets.
- *Predictive trust scoring:* Usage patterns, incident history and documentation completeness combined to highlight risky assets before they failed.
- *Metadata as a service:* Catalog metadata powering downstream workflows, from auto-tagging in quality monitors to contextual prompts in BI and checks in CI/CD pipelines.

## Lessons learned

The most important lesson was cultural. Metadata was never about cataloguing for its own sake. It was about creating scaffolding that made trust the default. Analysts stopped hesitating before using a number. Engineers began to see documentation not as overhead but as interface design. Business leaders anchored their decisions in certified assets.

Every step of the journey tied back to the toolkit. Diagnosis revealed friction across the four pillars. Design reframed features as capabilities. Delivery embedded Governance and Enablement into daily work. Scaling introduced contracts and predictive trust. The playbook was not theoretical; it was lived.

What began as an attempt to fix a failing catalog ended as a systemic shift. Metadata was transformed from a static artefact into a product, from documentation into culture, from friction into flow.

## Templates and artefacts

One of the most consistent requests we hear from data leaders and practitioners alike is for concrete tools they can take into the room. Principles and frameworks are valuable, but when the workshop begins or the sponsor asks 'what next', you need something tangible to work with. This section provides exactly that: a set of templates and artefacts we have used in practice to surface friction, align teams and measure adoption.

These are not exhaustive, and they are not the only way to approach diagnostics or design. Think of them instead as scaffolding. They provide enough structure to get started, to shape a conversation or to test an idea. From there, you can adapt them to your culture, your maturity and your needs. Some readers may use them directly; others may combine them with existing tools. Both approaches are valid.

What matters is that you do not leave these ideas at the level of abstraction. Put them to work. A rubric filled in with real scores, a persona card printed on the wall or a Platform Fit Canvas scribbled on in a workshop will always teach you more than a diagram on a slide.

### Included tools

- *Rubric scoring sheet by persona.* Score each pillar and dimension, with a one-sentence 'why' per score.
- *Friction taxonomy worksheet.* Map observed frictions to pillars, dimensions, consequences and severity.
- *Persona card template.* Capture goals, top frictions, rubric dimensions and definition-of-done signals.
- *Platform Fit Canvas.* Test alignment between workloads, personas, capability layers and ideal experience.
- *Certification workflow and expiry checklist.* Define lightweight criteria, expiry dates and recertification triggers.

- *Trust indicator specification.* Decide which trust signals (badges, steward names, SLAs) appear in search and dashboards.
- *Adoption dashboard starter metrics.* Use SQL hints for tracking searches, repeat usage, certified asset queries and incident resolution.
- *Data contract negotiation template.* Capture asset owner, consumer teams, schema stability, freshness SLAs, escalation paths and change protocols.

Use these artefacts as a *field kit*. They work best when combined: friction mapped with personas, scored with rubrics, linked to Platform Fit and monitored with adoption metrics.

## Pitfalls and anti-patterns

Every transformation effort carries risk, not only of failure but of misdirection. Data initiatives, in particular, are vulnerable to what we might call 'false progress'. Dashboards fill up with activity metrics. New tools are purchased and proudly launched. Glossaries and lineage diagrams appear in central repositories. Yet, beneath the surface, little changes in how people actually work.

This section names the most common traps we have seen across organisations and offers simple alternatives. They are not theoretical. These are patterns that repeatedly undermine trust and adoption when left unchecked. By surfacing them here, our goal is to help you recognise the early warning signs in your own programmes and to course-correct before momentum is lost.

Think of this page as a short diagnostic in itself. As you read, ask yourself: 'Do any of these descriptions sound uncomfortably familiar?' If so, do not

**Table A1.8** *Common pitfalls*

| Pitfall | Trap | Do instead |
|---|---|---|
| Tool swap disguised as transformation | Buying a new catalog or platform and calling it change | Define success as reduced friction and increased trust. Choose tools after diagnosing capabilities. |
| Centralised governance that chokes contribution | Requiring every change to pass through a central team | Federate stewardship to domains, with lightweight standards and expiry rules. |
| Documentation theatre with no usage telemetry | Producing glossaries and lineage views that nobody uses | Instrument usage. Track adoption and retire artefacts that add no value. |
| Feature checklist procurement | Selecting vendors based on the longest feature list | Use the Platform Fit Canvas to evaluate alignment with workflows, personas and latency needs. |
| KPIs that measure volume, not behaviour | Reporting on pipelines built or glossary terms created | Measure adoption behaviours such as onboarding time saved, reduction in repeated questions and certified asset usage. |

despair. These pitfalls are common precisely because they are easy mistakes to make. The good news is that each one has a practical countermeasure, a way to redirect energy towards behaviours that build real capability.

## FAQs for sponsors and teams

No matter how carefully you prepare, certain questions will always surface when you present the Enabling Data Model to sponsors or teams. These are not trivial queries; they are the pressure points where theory meets organisational reality. Why not centralise governance? How many champions are enough? What if we cannot document everything at once?

The answers offered here are concise by design. They are meant to give you a clear, confident starting point when these questions arise. Each response fits into a single paragraph, simple enough to communicate in a meeting or presentation, but grounded enough to avoid sounding like platitudes.

Use this section as a ready reference, a way to pre-empt doubts and provide clarity. It can also serve as a conversation starter. If sponsors or teams push back, that is not failure, it is engagement. The goal is not to silence questions, but to equip you with responses that keep the dialogue focused on principles, outcomes and trade-offs.

- *Why federate stewardship rather than centralise?*
  Trust must live where data is produced and consumed. Central teams cannot keep up with domain-specific changes. Federation creates ownership at the edges while maintaining shared standards.
- *How many champions per domain is enough?*
  One per critical domain is a minimum. Larger or more complex domains may need two. The rule of thumb is coverage: every major dataset or KPI should have a visible steward.
- *How do we avoid catalog bloat?*
  Certify what matters. Start with high-value assets and apply expiry rules. A smaller catalog that people trust is more valuable than a comprehensive one nobody uses.
- *What if we lack lineage for legacy assets?*
  Focus on high-impact assets first. Automate where possible, but do not wait for completeness. Treat gaps as signals for modernisation, not excuses for delay.
- *When are contracts overkill?*
  Use contracts when assets cross domains and carry material risk, such as executive reporting or operational systems. Avoid them for exploratory or low-stakes datasets.

# References


Accenture (2020) *The Human Impact of Data Literacy: How Data Literacy Fuels Business Value and Innovation*, https://www.accenture.com/content/dam/accenture/final/a-com-migration/r3-3/pdf/pdf-118/accenture-the-human-impact-data-literacy.pdf

Alation (2023) *Understanding Data Governance Models: Centralised, Decentralised, Federated*, https://www.alation.com/blog/understand-data-governance-models-centralized-decentralized-federated/

Amazon Web Services (2025) *Capital One on AWS*, https://aws.amazon.com/solutions/case-studies/innovators/capital-one/

Angelov, B. (2023) *Elements of Data Strategy: A Framework for Data and AI-Driven Transformation*, Leanpub.

Angelov, B. (2024) 2 Essential Strategies for CDOs to Balance Visible and Invisible Data Work under Pressure, *CDO Magazine*, 16 July, https://www.cdomagazine.tech/opinion-analysis/2-essential-strategies-for-cdos-to-balance-visible-and-invisible-data-work-under-pressure

Araja, D., Berkis, U. and Murovska, M. (2022) *COVID-19 Pandemic-Revealed Consistencies and Inconsistencies in Healthcare: A Medical and Organizational View*, National Library of Medicine, 13 May, https://pmc.ncbi.nlm.nih.gov/articles/PMC9223168/

Argyris, C. (1991) Teaching smart people how to learn, *Harvard Business Review*, May–June.

Atlan (2022) *Federated Data Governance Explained*, https://atlan.com/know/data-governance/federated-data-governance/

Atwal, H. (2019) *Practical DataOps: Delivering Agile Data Science at Scale*, Apress (Springer).

Basel Committee on Banking Supervision (2018) *Progress in adopting the Principles for effective risk data aggregation and risk reporting*, Bank for International Settlements, 21 June, https://www.bis.org/bcbs/publ/d443.htm

Basiri, A., Behnam, N., Hochstein, L., Kosewski, L., Rosenthal, C. and Turcu, C. (2016) Chaos Engineering, *IEEE Software*, **33** (3), 35–41.

Beck, K. et al. (2001) *Manifesto for Agile Software Development*, http://agilemanifesto.org/

Brandolini, A. (2019) *Introducing EventStorming: An Act of Deliberate Collective Learning*, Leanpub.

Brooks, F. P. (1995) *The Mythical Man-month: Essays on Software Engineering*, Addison-Wesley.

Bryar, C. and Carr, B. (2021) *Working Backwards: Insights, Stories, and Secrets from Inside Amazon*, St. Martin's Press.

Burns, B., Grant, B., Oppenheimer, D., Brewer, E. and Wilkes, J. (2016) Borg, Omega, and Kubernetes, *Communications of the ACM*, **59** (5), 50–7.

Carruthers, C. and Jackson, P. (2018) *Data Driven: Creating a Data Culture*, Facet Publishing.

Carucci, R. (2025) The Emotional Strength You Need to Lead through Change, *Harvard Business Review*, 17 September, https://hbr.org/2025/09/the-resilience-you-need-to-lead-through-change

Christian, B. (2017) To Increase Data Skills, Airbnb Has Started its Own University, *Wired*, 7 December, https://www.wired.com/story/airbnb-in-house-data-university-employee-skills

Chui, M., Yee, L., Hall, B. and Singla, A. (2023) *The State of AI in 2023: Generative AI's Breakout Year*, McKinsey & Company, https://www.mckinsey.com/capabilities/quantumblack/our-insights/the-state-of-ai-in-2023-generative-ais-breakout-year

Conway, K., Saleme, A. and Tyrman, K. (2023) *The FinOps Way: How to Avoid the Pitfalls to Realizing Cloud's Value*, McKinsey & Company, 18 January, https://www.mckinsey.com/capabilities/people-and-organisational-performance/our-insights/the-finops-way-how-to-avoid-the-pitfalls-to-realizing-clouds-value

Conway, M. E. (1968) How Do Committees Invent?, *Datamation*, **14** (4), 28–31.

Creasey, T. (2021) Best Practices in Change Management, *Prosci*, 22 November, https://www.prosci.com/blog/change-management-best-practices

Cusumano, M. A. and Yoffie, D. B. (1999) *Software Industrialization: Lessons from History*, MIT Sloan School of Management.

DAMA International (2017) *The DAMA Guide to the Data Management Body of Knowledge (DAMA-DMBOK)*, Technics Publications.

Databricks (2023) *What Is Data Governance? A Comprehensive Guide*, https://www.databricks.com/discover/data-governance

DataIQ (2025) *2025 AI and Data Leadership: Executive Benchmark Survey*, https://www.dataiq.global/articles/2025-ai-and-data-leadership/

Davenport, T. H. and Miller, S. M. (2022) *Working with AI: Real Stories of Human-Machine Collaboration*, MIT Press.

Davenport, T. H. and Prusak, L. (1998) *Working Knowledge: How Organizations Manage What They Know*, Harvard Business School Press.

Davenport, T. H. and Redman, T. C. (2022) How AI Is Improving Data Management, *MIT Sloan Management Review*, 22 December, https://sloanreview.mit.edu/article/how-ai-is-improving-data-management/

Davenport, T. H. and Westerman, G. (2018) Why So Many High-profile Digital Transformations Fail, *Harvard Business Review*, 9 March, https://hbr.org/2018/03/why-so-many-high-profile-digital-transformations-fail

Dehghani, Z. (2019) *How to Move Beyond a Monolithic Data Lake to a Distributed Data Mesh*, https://martinfowler.com/articles/data-monolith-to-mesh.html

Dehghani, Z. (2022) *Data Mesh: Delivering Data-driven Value at Scale*, O'Reilly Media.

Deloitte Insights (2024) *Tech Leaders' Influence in the C-suite Is Growing, New Deloitte Research Suggests*, https://www.deloitte.com/us/en/insights/deloitte-insights-magazine/issue-33/tech-leaders-influence-business-strategy.html

Díaz, A., Rowshankish, K. and Saleh, T. (2018) Why Data Culture Matters, *QuantumBlack AI by McKinsey*, 6 September, https://www.mckinsey.com/capabilities/people-and-organizational-performance/our-insights/why-data-culture-matters

Doerr, J. (2018) *Measure What Matters: OKRs, the Simple Idea that Drives 10x Growth*, Portfolio.

Eastwood, B. (2022) Chief Data Officers Don't Stay in Their Roles Long. Here's Why, *MIT Sloan Management Review*, 1 September, https://mitsloan.mit.edu/ideas-made-to-matter/chief-data-officers-dont-stay-their-roles-long-heres-why

Economist (2025) *What if AI Made the World's Economic Growth Explode?* 24 July, https://www.economist.com/briefing/2025/07/24/what-if-ai-made-the-worlds-economic-growth-explode

Edmondson, A. C. (2012) *Teaming: How Organizations Learn, Innovate, and Compete in the Knowledge Economy*, Jossey-Bass.

Ellens, T. (2024) Five Common Challenges when Building Data Mesh, *Valcon*, https://valcon.com/en/insights/five-common-challenges-when-building-data-mesh/

Enlighten Services (2023) *Metric Overload: When Too Much Data Becomes a Problem*, https://www.enlighten.services/p/metric-overload

Evans, E. (2003) *Domain-driven Design: Tackling Complexity in the Heart of Software*, Addison-Wesley Professional.

Ewenstein, B., Smith, W. and Sologar, A. (2015) *Changing Change Management*, McKinsey & Company, 9 July, https://www.mckinsey.com/featured-insights/leadership/changing-change-management

Feng, J., Coffman, E. and Grewal, E. (2017) How Airbnb Democratizes Data Science with Data University, *The Airbnb Tech Blog*, 24 May, https://medium.com/airbnb-engineering/how-airbnb-democratizes-data-science-with-data-university-3eccc71e073a

Flexera (2025) *New Flexera Report Finds that 84% of Organizations Struggle to Manage Cloud Spend*, 19 March, https://www.flexera.com/about-us/press-center/new-flexera-report-finds-84-percent-of-organizations-struggle-to-manage-cloud-spend

Forrester (2023) *Data Governance Unlocks the Impact of Analytics*, Forrester Blogs, 2 November, https://www.forrester.com/blogs/data-governance-unlocks-the-impact-of-analytics-data-strategy-insights-2023/

Franke, M. R. et al. (2023) *Any Company Can Become a Resilient Data Champion*, Boston Consulting Group, 26 April, https://www.bcg.com/publications/2023/company-data-champions-driving-resilience

Gartner (2018) *Hype Cycle for Emerging Technologies*, Gartner.

Gartner (2023) *Gartner Survey Reveals Less than Half of Data and Analytics Teams Effectively Provide Value to the Organization*, Gartner.

Gartner (2025) *Gartner Survey Finds One-third of CDAOs Cite Measuring Data, Analytics and AI Impact as Top Challenge*, 20 February, https://www.gartner.com/en/newsroom/press-releases/2025-02-20-gartner-survey-finds-one-third-of-cdaos-cite-measuring-data-analytics-and-ai-impact-as-top-challenge

Gavish, L. (2023) *What is a Data Mesh – and How Not to Mesh it Up*, https://www.montecarlodata.com/blog-what-is-a-data-mesh-and-how-not-to-mesh-it-up/

Gioia, A. (2024) *Managing Data as a Product: Design and Build Data-product-centered Socio-technical Architectures*, Packt Publishing.

Grande, D., Machado, J., Petzold, B. and Roth, M. (2020) *Reducing Data Costs without Jeopardizing Growth*, McKinsey & Company, 31 July, https://www.mckinsey.com/capabilities/mckinsey-digital/our-insights/reducing-data-costs-without-jeopardizing-growth

Greenhalgh, T. et al. (2010) Adoption and Non-adoption of a Shared Electronic Summary Record in England: A Mixed-method Case Study, *BMJ* 2020;340:c3111

Grover, M. (2019) *Amundsen–Lyft's Data Discovery and Metadata Engine*, Lyft Engineering, 2 April, https://eng.lyft.com/amundsen-lyfts-data-discovery-metadata-engine-62d27254fbb9

Hanf, M. (2021) *Getting Ready for StratOps*, Taival, 13 April, https://www.taival.com/getting-ready-for-stratops/

Heaven, W. D. (2020) AI Could Help with the Next Pandemic – but Not with this One, MIT *Technology Review*, 12 March, https://www.technologyreview.com/2020/03/12/905352/ai-could-help-with-the-next-pandemicbut-not-with-this-one/

Heinemeier Hansson, D. (2025) Opening Keynote, Rails World 2025, 4 September, https://www.rubyevents.org/talks/opening-keynote-rails-world-2025

HelloFresh Group (2021) *10 years HelloFresh: From Start-up to Scale-up*, HelloFresh Group, 26 November, https://www.hellofreshgroup.com/en/newsroom/stories/10-years-hellofresh-from-start-up-to-scale-up/

HelloFresh Group (2024) *ESG: Our commitment*, https://www.hellofreshgroup.com/en/esg/

Henschen, D. (2012) P&G's CIO Details Business-savvy Predictive Decision Cockpit, *Information Week*, 11 September, https://www.informationweek.com/data-management/p-g-s-cio-details-business-savvy-predictive-decision-cockpit

Holling, C. S. (1973) Resilience and Stability of Ecological Systems, *Annual Review of Ecology and Systematics*, **4**, 1–23.

Holmgren, A., Hendrix, N. and Maisel, N. (2024) Electronic Health Record Usability, Satisfaction, and Burnout among Family Physicians, *JAMA Network Open*, **7** (8), doi:10.1001/jamanetworkopen.2024.26956

Kesari, G. (2025) Building a Data-Driven Culture: Four Key Elements, *MIT Sloan Management Review*, 23 January, https://sloanreview.mit.edu/article/building-a-data-driven-culture-four-key-elements/

Kiechel, W. (2010) *The Lords of Strategy*, Harvard Business Press.

Kiron, D., Schrage, M., Candelon, F., Khodabandeh, S. and Chu, M. (2023) Strategic Alignment with AI and Smart KPIs, *MIT Sloan Management Review*, 5 September, https://sloanreview.mit.edu/article/strategic-alignment-with-ai-and-smart-kpis

Kiron, D., Shockley, R., Kruschwitz, N., Finch, G. and Haydock, D. M. (2011) Analytics: The Widening Divide, *MIT Sloan Management Review*, 7 November, https://sloanreview.mit.edu/projects/analytics-the-widening-divide/

Kniberg, H. and Ivarsson, A. (2012) Scaling Agile @ Spotify with Tribes, Squads, Chapters and Guilds, *Crisp*, October, https://blog.crisp.se/wp-content/uploads/2012/11/SpotifyScaling.pdf

Kotter, J. P. (2012) *Leading Change*, Harvard Business School Press.

Kronsbein, T. and Müller, R. M. (2019) 'Data Thinking: A Canvas for Data-Driven Ideation Workshops', Proceedings of the 52nd Hawaii International Conference on System Sciences (HICSS), https://aisel.aisnet.org/hicss-52/cl/visual_tools/4/

Laney, D. B. (2018) *Infonomics: How to Monetize, Manage, and Measure Information as an Asset for Competitive Advantage*, Bibliomotion.

Leffingwell, D. (2021) *SAFe 5.0 Reference Guide: Scaled Agile Framework for Lean Enterprises*, Addison-Wesley.

LogRocket (2024) *Metrics Overload: When Too Much Data Becomes a Problem*, 26 June, https://blog.logrocket.com/product-management/metrics-overload-when-too-much-data-becomes-problem/

Loufek, B., Vidal, D., McClintock, D. S., Lifson, M., Williamson, E., Overgaard, S., McNaughton, K., Lipford, M. C. and Pardi, D. S. (2024) Embedding Internal Accountability into Health Care Institutions for Safe, Effective, and Ethical

Implementation of Artificial Intelligence into Medical Practice: A Mayo Clinic Case Study, *Mayo Clinic Proceedings: Digital Health*, **2** (4), 574–83, doi:10.1016/j.mcpdig.2024.08.008

Marr, B. (2017) *Data Strategy: How to Profit from a World of Big Data, Analytics and the Internet of Thing*, Kogan Page Publishers.

Martin, J. (2019) *Electronic Health Records*, MHRA Inspectorate, 23 July, https://mhrainspectorate.blog.gov.uk/2019/07/23/electronic-health-records/

McAfee, A. and Brynjolfsson, E. (2008) Investing in the IT that Makes a Competitive Difference, *Harvard Business Review*, July–August, https://hbr.org/2008/07/investing-in-the-it-that-makes-a-competitive-difference.

McKinsey & Company (2018) *Unlocking Success in Digital Transformations*, 29 October, https://www.mckinsey.com/capabilities/people-and-organizational-performance/our-insights/unlocking-success-in-digital-transformations

McKinsey & Company (2019a) *Catch Them if You Can: How Leaders in Data and Analytics Have Pulled Ahead*, 19 September, https://www.mckinsey.com/capabilities/quantumblack/our-insights/catch-them-if-you-can-how-leaders-in-data-and-analytics-have-pulled-ahead

McKinsey & Company (2019b) *Digital Transformation: Improving the Odds of Success*, 22 October, https://www.mckinsey.com/capabilities/mckinsey-digital/our-insights/digital-transformation-improving-the-odds-of-success

McKinsey & Company (2020a) *How to Build a Data Architecture to Drive Innovation – Today and Tomorrow*, 3 June, https://www.mckinsey.com/capabilities/mckinsey-digital/our-insights/how-to-build-a-data-architecture-to-drive-innovation-today-and-tomorrow

McKinsey & Company (2020b) *Designing Data Governance that Delivers Value*, 26 June, https://www.mckinsey.com/capabilities/mckinsey-digital/our-insights/designing-data-governance-that-delivers-value

McKinsey & Company (2021) *The Impact of Agility: How to Shape Your Organization to Compete*, 25 May, https://www.mckinsey.com/capabilities/people-and-organizational-performance/our-insights/the-impact-of-agility-how-to-shape-your-organization-to-compete

McKinsey & Company (2022a) *The Data-driven Enterprise of 2025*, 28 January, https://www.mckinsey.com/capabilities/quantumblack/our-insights/the-data-driven-enterprise-of-2025

McKinsey & Company (2022b) *How to Unlock the Full Value of Data? Manage it Like a Product*, 14 June, https://www.mckinsey.com/capabilities/quantumblack/our-insights/how-to-unlock-the-full-value-of-data-manage-it-like-a-product

McKinsey & Company (2022c) *New-business Building in 2022: Driving Growth in Volatile Times*, 14 November, https://www.mckinsey.com/capabilities/mckinsey-digital/our-insights/new-business-building-in-2022-driving-growth-in-volatile-times

McKinsey & Company (2022d) *Accelerating Data and Analytics Maturity in the US Public Sector*, 21 November, https://www.mckinsey.com/industries/public-sector/our-insights/accelerating-data-and-analytics-maturity-in-the-us-public-sector

McKinsey & Company (2023) *The State of AI in 2023: Generative AI's Breakout Year*, 1 August, https://www.mckinsey.com/capabilities/quantumblack/our-insights/the-state-of-ai-in-2023-generative-ais-breakout-year

McKinsey & Company (2024) *Rewired and Running Ahead: Digital and AI leaders Are Leaving the Rest Behind*, 12 January, https://www.mckinsey.com/capabilities/mckinsey-digital/our-insights/rewired-and-running-ahead-digital-and-ai-leaders-are-leaving-the-rest-behind

McKinsey & Company (2025) *A New Operating Model for a New World*, 18 June, https://www.mckinsey.com/capabilities/people-and-organizational-performance/our-insights/a-new-operating-model-for-a-new-world

Morgenshtern, O., Rosenstein, R. and Allen, P. L. (2022) The Quest for a Killer KPI: How Radically Simplifying Performance Metrics Helped One Company Align Employee Behaviour with Organisational Goals, *MIT Sloan Management Review*, 8 March, https://sloanreview.mit.edu/article/the-quest-for-a-killer-kpi/

National Audit Office (2019) *Digital Transformation in the NHS*, https://www.nao.org.uk/reports/the-use-of-digital-technology-in-the-nhs/

Ohno, T. (1988) *Toyota Production System: Beyond Large-Scale Production*, Productivity Press.

O'Keefe, K. and O'Brien, D. (2023) *Data Ethics: Practical Strategies for Implementing Ethical Information Management and Governance*, Kogan Page.

Ostrom, E. (1990) *Governing the Commons: The Evolution of Institutions for Collective Action*, Cambridge University Press.

Perucci, F. and Swanson, E. (2024) *Building Trust and Facilitating Use of Data*, Open Data Watch, 15 March, https://opendatawatch.com/publications/building-trust-and-facilitating-use-of-data/

Porter, M. E. (1985) *Competitive Advantage: Creating and Sustaining Superior Performance*, Free Press.

Prudential Regulation Authority (PRA) (2021) *Outsourcing and Third-party Risk Management (Supervisory Statement SS2/21)*, 29 March, https://www.bankofengland.co.uk/prudential-regulation/publication/2021/march/outsourcing-and-third-party-risk-management-ss

Ransbotham, S., Kiron, D., Gerbert, P. and Reeves, M. (2020) Expanding AI's Impact With Organizational Learning, *MIT Sloan Management Review & Boston Consulting Group*, https://sloanreview.mit.edu/projects/expanding-ais-impact-with-organizational-learning/

Redman, T. C. (2018) 5 Ways Your Data Strategy Can Fail, *Harvard Business Review*, 11 October, https://hbr.org/2018/10/5-ways-your-data-strategy-can-fail

Redman, T. C. (2023) *People and Data: Uniting to Transform Your Business*, Kogan Page.

Reeves, M. and Whitaker, K. (2020) A Guide to Building a More Resilient Business, *Harvard Business Review*, 2 July, https://hbr.org/2020/07/a-guide-to-building-a-more-resilient-business

Renieris, E. M., Kiron, D., Mills, S. and Kleppe, A. (2025) AI Explainability: How to Avoid Rubber-Stamping Recommendations, *MIT Sloan Management Review*, 12 June, https://sloanreview.mit.edu/article/ai-explainability-how-to-avoid-rubber-stamping-recommendations/

Reuters (2020) *HelloFresh raises 2020 outlook on lockdown hunger for meal kits*, 4 May, https://www.reuters.com/article/world/hellofresh-raises-2020-outlook-on-lockdown-hunger-for-meal-kits-idUSKBN22H0DO

Rigby, D. K., Sutherland, J. and Takeuchi, H. (2016) Embracing agile, *Harvard Business Review*, May, https://hbr.org/2016/05/embracing-agile

Roberts, A. and Eisert, M. (2024) What Are the Hidden Costs of Maintaining Legacy Systems? *RecordPoint*, 28 August, https://www.recordpoint.com/blog/maintaining-legacy-systems-costs

Rogers, D. L. (2016) *The Digital Transformation Playbook: Rethink Your Business for the Digital Age*, Columbia Business School Publishing.

Rollin, H. (2023) *When Not to Use Data Mesh*, https://medium.com/@hannes.rollin/when-not-to-use-data-mesh-7767feca8a9a

Rossi, P. (2021) *Shopify's Unique Data Science Hierarchy of Needs*, 21 December, https://shopify.engineering/shopify-unique-data-science-hierarchy-of-needs

Sambasivan, N., Kapania, S., Highfill, H., Akrong, D., Paritosh, P. and Aroyo, L. (2021) Everyone Wants to Do the Model Work. No One Wants to Do the Data Work: Cascades in High-Stakes Data, *Google Research*, https://research.google/pubs/everyone-wants-to-do-the-model-work-not-the-data-work-data-cascades-in-high-stakes-ai/

Sawaya, A., Wang, K. W., Bu, L. and Chang, M. (2025) *Beyond the Hype: Unlocking Value from the AI Revolution*, McKinsey & Company, 8 September, https://www.mckinsey.com/capabilities/mckinsey-digital/our-insights/beyond-the-hype-unlocking-value-from-the-ai-revolution

Schein, E. H. (2010) *Organizational Culture and Leadership (4th edn)*, Jossey-Bass.

Schein, E. H. (2013) *Humble Inquiry: The Gentle Art of Asking Instead of Telling*, Berrett-Koehler.

Sculley, D. et al. (2015) Hidden Technical Debt in Machine Learning Systems, *Advances in Neural Information Processing Systems*, **28**.

Senge, P. M. (2006) *The Fifth Discipline: The Art and Practice of the Learning Organization*, Doubleday.

Skelton, M. and Pais, M. (2019) *Team Topologies: Organizing Business and Technology Teams for Fast Flow*, IT Revolution Press.

Speake, J. and Simpson, J. (2015) *The Oxford Dictionary of Proverbs,* Oxford University Press.

Spotify Engineering (2020) Spotify's New Experimentation Platform: Part 1, *Spotify Engineering Blog,* https://engineering.atspotify.com/2020/10/spotifys-new-experimentation-platform-part-1

Strengholt, P. (2024) Data Mesh: Topologies and Domain Granularity, *Medium,* 24 May, https://medium.com/data-science/data-mesh-topologies-and-domain-granularity-65290a4ebb90

Tableau (2025) *What Is Augmented Analytics?* https://www.tableau.com/analytics/what-is-augmented-analytics

Taleb, N. N. (2012) *Antifragile: Things that Gain from Disorder,* Random House.

TDAN (2021) Decentralised, Centralised, and Federated Data Governance, *The Data Administration Newsletter,* https://tdan.com/decentralized-centralized-federated-data-governance/30687

Thaler, R. H. and Sunstein, C. R. (2008) *Nudge: Improving Decisions about Health, Wealth, and Happiness,* Yale University Press.

Thoughtworks (2022) *Data Mesh in Practice: Organizational Operating Model (Part II),* 19 May, https://www.thoughtworks.com/insights/articles/data-mesh-in-practice-organizational-operating-model

Tufte, E. R. (2001) *The Visual Display of Quantitative Information,* Graphics Press.

Uber (2017) *Meet Michelangelo: Uber's Machine Learning Platform,* https://www.uber.com/blog/michelangelo-machine-learning-platform

US Department of Health and Human Services (HHS) (2020) Healthcare Data Breach Statistics, *HIPAA Journal,* https://www.hipaajournal.com/healthcare-data-breach-statistics/

Valinsky, J. (2020) Booking.com Aims to Lay Off 25% of its Workforce, *CNN Business,* 4 August, https://edition.cnn.com/2020/08/04/business/booking-layoffs-coronavirus

Van Belle, S. and Mayhew, S. H. (2016) Public accountability needs to be enforced: a case study of the governance arrangements and accountability practices in a rural health district in Ghana, *BMC Health Services Research,* 16, 568, https://doi.org/10.1186/s12913-016-1836-1

Van Beusekom, M. (2024) *Study: Confusing Government COVID Reporting Requirements Led to Disparities in Hospital Data Sharing,* Center for Infectious Disease Research and Policy, 11 January, https://www.cidrap.umn.edu/covid-19/study-confusing-government-covid-reporting-requirements-led-disparities-hospital-data

Vera, D., Samba, C., Kong, D. T. and Maldonado, T. (2020) Resilience as Thriving: The Role of Positive Leadership Practices, *Organizational Dynamics,* **50** (2), 100784.

Wade, M. (2019) *The Five Stages of the Chief Digital Officer and Why They Often Fail,* IMD Business School, https://www.imd.org/research-knowledge/digital/articles/the-five-stages-of-the-chief-digital-officer-and-why-they-often-fail

Wang, R. Y. (1998) Manage Your Information as a Product, *MIT Sloan Management Review*, 15 July, https://sloanreview.mit.edu/article/manage-your-information-as-a-product/

Watkins, M. D. (2003) *The First 90 Days: Proven Strategies for Getting up to Speed Faster and Smarter*, Harvard Business Press.

Wavestone (2024) *2024 Data and AI Leadership Executive Survey: Executive Summary of Findings*, Wavestone, 9 January, https://www.wavestone.com/en/news/2024-data-and-ai-leadership-executive-survey-41/

Weill, P. and Woerner, S. L. (2018) *What's Your Digital Business Model? Six Questions to Help You Build the Next-generation Enterprise*, Harvard Business Review Press.

Williams, C., Brumbaugh, E., Feng, J., Bodley, J. and Thomas, M. (2017) Democratizing Data at Airbnb, *The Airbnb Tech Blog*, 12 May, https://medium.com/airbnb-engineering/democratizing-data-at-airbnb-852d76c51770

Zylo (2024) *2024 SaaS Management Index Reveals an Average of $18m in Wasted SaaS Spend*, 27 February, https://zylo.com/news/2024-saas-management-index/

# Index

agile methodology 53, 75–6, 96, 117, 136, 142
AI *see* artificial intelligence
Airbnb 82, 98, 119, 126, 128, 131–2
Alibaba 11
Amazon 2, 10, 94–5, 97
  Web Services (AWS) 38, 93, 130, 132
  *see also* Building Backwards method
analytics
  advanced xxv, 6, 13–14, 104–5
  descriptive 103, 131, 167
  predictive 9, 103–5, 167–8
  *see also* artificial intelligence (AI); business intelligence (BI); machine learning (ML)
Antifragile (Taleb) 7–8, 60–1, 78, 83
  *see also* Taleb, Nassim Nicholas; via negativa
anti-patterns 10, 169
API *see* application programming interface
application programming interface (API) 9, 42, 68, 91
artificial intelligence (AI) xix–xxii, xxvi
  generative 5, 17–18, 21, 95, 102
  narrow 18
  promise of xxv, 6, 14, 54–5, 71
  *see also* machine learning (ML)
Atlan 42, 44, 59, 100
AWS *see* Amazon Web Services

Basel Committee on Banking Supervision 101, 103
Basiri, Ali 61, 77, 83
BI *see* business intelligence
BigQuery 4
Booking.com 27–9, 33
Brandolini, Alberto 6
Building Backwards method 95
  *see also* Amazon
bureaucracy 48, 118, 121, 152, 155
burnout 69, 124
business intelligence (BI)
  generative (genBI) 5, 17–18, 20–1, 95, 102

California Consumer Privacy Act (CCPA) 101, 121
Capital One 79–80, 130, 132
cargo cult 5, 11–12, 96–7, 108, 113
Carruthers, Caroline 108–10, 112, 115, 118
case studies
  building backwards at an enterprise xxvii, 94–6
  data mesh 5
  generative business intelligence 17
catalog, data 17, 22–3, 42, 48, 50–1, 84, 128, 135, 167
CCPA *see* California Consumer Privacy Act
CEO *see* chief executive officer

change management 116, 120
Chaos Monkey 61, 77, 83
*see also* Netflix
chief data officer (CDO) 17, 67, 71, 92
chief executive officer (CEO) 27, 30, 33, 66–8, 79
chief technical officer (CTO) 3, 29, 65
CI/CD *see* continuous integration and deployment
Cloudera 32, 36, 46
complexity
merchants of xxvi, 2–3, 6, 78, 133
compliance
as culture, versus curiosity 67–8, 118–19
embedded in enablement 126, 129–30, 152
regulatory 101, 103–4, 121, 124
*see also* ethics; privacy; security
continuous integration and deployment (CI/CD) 2–3, 167
Conway principle 3, 28, 78, 80
cross-functional teams 42, 117, 131, 142
CTO *see* chief technical officer

DAMA International 56–7, 60, 102–3, 108, 115, 119
*see also* data governance; Data Management Body of Knowledge (DMBOK)
data
as a liability xxvi, 79, 101–2
as a product 50, 52, 122, 136, 165
contracts 39, 41–2, 47–8, 120, 147, 169
democratisation of 4, 82
hierarchy of needs 6
lineage 37, 41, 43, 45, 121, 130, 154, 162
mesh 5–6, 32–3, 37, 42, 44, 46, 52, 59–60, 117, 123
monetisation xxi, xxvi, 2
producers 5, 40–2, 112, 117, 120, 147
products xxi, 41, 51–2, 63, 72, 94, 120
quality xix–xxii, 13–14, 41, 43, 48, 99–100, 103–5
stewardship 60, 99–102, 116–17, 153–4, 170
strategy xxvi–xxvii, 11, 27, 32, 41, 108–9, 123
Databricks 5, 23–4, 60, 62
data governance 2, 35, 41–2, 100, 120, 131–2
*see also* DAMA International; Data Management Body of Knowledge (DMBOK)
DataIQ 67
Data Management Body of Knowledge (DMBOK) 56, 102–3
Data Manifesto xxvi, 12, 73, 75, 77, 152
data modelling 102, 104
data science xix–xx, xxii, 4, 9–10, 76, 82, 84, 98, 146
data warehouse 37, 122
Davenport, Thomas H. xxi, 53, 61, 78, 85–6, 97, 108–9, 113, 119, 123, 153
dbt 4
*see also* modern data stack (MDS)
Dehghani, Zhamak 5, 32, 37, 44, 46, 49, 52, 59, 96, 119, 123
*see also* data, mesh
diagnostic rubric 141–2, 158
digital transformation 11, 77, 105
Docker 9
Domain Driven Design 6
dotcom bubble 7
dunnhumby 29, 33

EHR *see* electronic health records
electronic health records (EHR) 103, 124
Enabling Data Model
Enablement pillar 125–7
Governance pillar 118–19, 121
People pillar 115–18, 166
Technology pillar 122, 124
ethics xxi
*see also* compliance; privacy; security
ETL *see* extract, transform, load

Evans, Eric 6
  *see also* Domain Driven Design
Event Storming 6
experimentation 59, 79–80, 105, 126
extract, transform, load (ETL) 4, 32–3

Facebook 56, 83
first principles xxvi, 1–2, 6, 68, 76
Flywheel of Insight 110–11, 114, 116, 126, 132
forecasting 48, 53, 85, 89, 105, 124

Gavish, Avi 32, 39, 41, 45, 48
GDPR *see* General Data Protection Regulation
genBI *see* generative business intelligence
General Data Protection Regulation (GDPR) 41, 101, 121
Google xix, 4, 11–12, 56, 83–4, 87, 105
Greenhalgh, Trisha 77, 98, 103
Groundhog Day (film) 1, 6, 133

Hadoop 4, 46
Hanf, Matthias xxvii
Hannemeier-Hanson, David (DHH) 2, 5
Health Insurance Portability and Accountability Act (HIPAA) 101
HelloFresh
  Data University 98, 119, 126, 128, 131–2
HIPAA *see* Health Insurance Portability and Accountability Act
Holling, C. S. 61, 80, 86

iceberg analogy 6, 30, 32–3, 107, 109, 127, 132–4
Impala 36, 46–7
industrialisation xxi, 52–4
infonomics xxi
  *see also* Laney, Doug
IT department 5

Jackson, Peter 108–10, 112, 115, 118
JP Morgan 91, 126, 129

key performance indicators (KPIs) 33, 44, 84, 88, 148, 155–6, 162, 165, 170
  *see also* objectives and key results (OKRs)
Kiechel, Walter 2
Kiron, David 84–6, 105
Kozyrkov, Cassie 12
KPI *see* key performance indicators

Laney, Doug xxi, xxvi
  *see also* infonomics
leadership
  as design, not control 63, 70, 72–3
  data 66–9, 71, 78
  sponsorship and commitment 108–9, 116, 162
lean management 8
  *see also* waste
Looker 4

machine learning (ML)
  operations (MLOps) xxvi–xxvii, 3, 10
  *see also* artificial intelligence (AI); data science
MAD landscape 2
matrix organisation 12
  *see also* Spotify model
MDS *see* modern data stack
mental models 107, 137
Metabase 4
metadata
  as a product 50, 52, 122, 136, 165
Michelangelo platform 82, 84
  *see also* Uber
Microsoft 20, 76, 85, 117
Miller, Steven xxi, 78, 85–6, 97, 108–9, 113, 123
MIT Sloan Management Review 57, 86, 88, 98, 105

ML *see* machine learning
MLOps *see* machine learning operations
modern data stack (MDS) 3–4, 6, 29

National Health Service (NHS) 77, 85, 90, 98, 126, 131
Netflix 61, 77, 83, 97, 126, 128
*see also* Chaos Monkey
NHS *see* National Health Service
North Star 6, 17, 27, 37, 87

objectives and key results (OKRs) 35–6, 87, 117, 142, 146, 148, 160
*see also* key performance indicators (KPIs)
O'Brien, Katherine xxi
observability 37, 41, 47–8, 105, 121, 123, 130, 140, 156, 162
O'Keefe, Katherine xxi
OKR *see* objectives and key results
OpenAI 21
open source 10

personas 56, 128–9, 145, 149–50, 158, 168–9
pharma industry 6, 10, 92
PHP 2
pilotitis 3, 89–91
pilots, data 3, 89–91, 133, 159–61, 166
Platform Fit Canvas 114–15, 129, 149–50, 166, 168–9
PoC *see* proof of concept
Postgres 4
pricing 4, 79–80, 82, 84
privacy xxi, 49, 101, 121, 123, 142–3
*see also* compliance; ethics; security
Procter & Gamble 91, 116, 130
product manager 51
product owner 95, 128, 145–6
product thinking xxvi, 50–1, 96
proof of concept (PoC) 3, 9, 22, 26, 56

quarterly alliance review (QAR) 40, 44–6
quarterly business review (QBR) 50
quarterly data review (QDR) 40, 42

Redman, Thomas C. xix–xxi, 72–3, 100, 102–3, 105, 110, 113, 116, 119–20, 125, 133
regulation 41, 67, 124
resilience 28, 60–2, 70–3, 78, 86, 110
return on investment (ROI) 53, 68
roadmap, data 26, 32, 78, 95, 143, 159, 167
ROI *see* return on investment
root cause analysis 2, 6, 36, 77, 125, 143, 156
Ruby on Rails 2

SaaS *see* software as a service
Sambasivan, Nithya xx
security xxi, 59, 81, 121, 123, 143
*see also* compliance; ethics; privacy
self-service 20, 54–6, 58, 116, 121–2
service level agreement (SLA) 150–1, 154, 156, 159
service level objective (SLO) 41, 43, 143
silos xxi, xxiii, 32, 59–60, 98, 110, 115, 117, 123
SLA *see* service level agreement
SLO *see* service level objective
Snowflake 5, 23–4, 79, 149
software as a service (SaaS) 2, 81, 123
Spotify 12, 80, 96–7, 126, 129
Spotify model 97
*see also* matrix organisation
SQL *see* structured query language
strategic operations (StratOps) xxvi, 10, 112
StratOps *see* strategic operations
Strengholt, Piethein 5
structured query language (SQL) 4, 19–22, 56

Tableau 20, 46, 56–7
Taleb, Nassim Nicholas 7–8, 60–1, 78, 83
*see also* Antifragile; via negativa
Thoughtworks 5, 42, 52, 60
Tolstoy, Leo xxiv
transformation xxi–xxiii
digital 11, 77, 105

Uber 82, 84
*see also* Michelangelo platform

via negativa xxv, 7–8
*see also* Antifragile (Taleb); Taleb, Nassim Nicholas; waste

waste xxv, 7, 15, 109, 123
*see also* lean management; via negativa
Wavestone 69, 123